Betting Thoroughbreds

*A Professional's Guide for
the Horseplayer*

Betting Thoroughbreds

A Professional's Guide for the Horseplayer

Steven Davidowitz

E. P. Dutton / New York

Library of Congress Cataloging in Publication Data

Davidowitz, Steven.
Betting thoroughbreds.

Bibliography: p.
1. Horse race betting.   I. Title.
SF331.D36 1977   798'.401   76–30458

ISBN: 0–525–06632–2

Published simultaneously in Canada by
Clarke, Irwin & Company Limited,
Toronto and Vancouver

10 9 8 7 6 5 4 3 2 1
First Edition

Designed by The Etheredges

Acknowledgments

The charts appearing on pages 2, 3, 4, 18, 20, 21, 22, 23, 24, 32, 33, 34, 35, 37, 38, 39, 40, 41, 42, 44, 57, 60, 61, 65, 66, 71, 74, 75, 76, 77, 78, 79, 80, 85, 86, 87, 89, 97, 98, 99, 100, 101, 102, 103, 107, 115, 117, 118, 119, 120, 122, 123, 124, 126, 127, 130, 131, 132, 133, 135, 136, 137, 138, 139, 140, 141, 144, 150, 168, 175, 176, 181, 182, 183, 185, 186, 190, 194, 195, 196, 197 of this book are reprinted by special arrangement with Triangle Publications, Inc. (DAILY RACING FORM). Copyright © 1962, 1963, 1968, 1969, 1972, 1973, 1974, 1975, 1976 by Triangle Publications, Inc. Reprinted with permission of the copyright owner.

And special thanks to *Turf and Sport Digest* for the use of its Racing Library in the preparation of this book.

To my father,
my mother,
my wife,
and my son

Contents

Foreword

by Andrew Beyer

One of the luckiest moments in my life as a horseplayer occurred in 1971 when, by sheer chance, I sat next to Steve Davidowitz on a bench at Saratoga Racetrack. At the time I viewed racing the way many readers of this book probably do now. I desperately wanted to be a successful handicapper. But I wasn't convinced that this was possible, and I had no idea how to achieve my goal.

After striking up a conversation with Steve, I associated with him throughout that Saratoga season and got the opportunity to watch a consummate professional in operation. I was impressed not only by his success at the betting windows but also by his unique understanding of the nature of the game.

One aspect of Steve's approach to racing struck me as original and helped show me the way to win at the track. Steve was not a dogmatist. Most handicappers, even the good ones, define themselves by the primary methods they use. There are speed handicappers—pace handicappers—class handicappers—angle handicappers—and so on.

Steve perceived that there is a time and place for all these approaches. He swore by none and discarded none. The key to winning at the track was not to find one all-powerful secret, but to learn the right tools to use at the right time.

Most handicapping books purport to offer their readers all-encompassing formulas that will work anywhere. But, in practice, the horseplayer at Aqueduct and the horseplayer at Cahokia Downs are playing very different games. *Betting Thoroughbreds* recognizes their different needs and helps them both.

Steve's chapter on class at minor tracks explains an approach to the game which, as far as I know, has never appeared in a book before. Steve explains that the $1,500 claiming ranks at a cheap track may in fact include a half dozen different class stratifications. A handicapper who appreciates those differences will be able to find outstanding bets that elude almost everyone who reads the *Daily Racing Form*. For the bettor at any minor racetrack, that chapter alone is worth the price of the book.

For the handicapper who follows major-league racing, Steve's perceptions about the bias of the racing surface and his analysis of the way good trainers handle their horses are both invaluable. Those were the first things he taught me that summer at Saratoga. We examined a set of past performances and Steve said, "Let's train this horse." He then reviewed the horse's record race by race, considered what the trainer was trying to do with the animal, and determined whether the horseman was succeeding. By the time we came to the most recent race we had a very good idea of what the horse was likely to do that day, as well as insight into the trainer's methodology and competence.

This is a far cry from the approach of the dogmatists who distill the art of handicapping into neat, inflexible rules. But it is the only intelligent, realistic way to tackle the game. Steve's guidance pointed me in the right directions and ultimately enabled me to become a winning horseplayer and to beat him into print as the author of a handicapping book.

A book that examines all the complexities of handicapping may not sell in Peoria. Casual racetrack gamblers generally want systems and rules that will enable them to get rich quick without expending much effort. *Betting Thoroughbreds* offers no such simplistic strategies. But Steve's teachings will be a revelation for the handicappers who, like me in 1971, truly want to learn how to beat the game.

Introduction

For some horseplayers, the romance of the track is linked only to the number of trips made to the cashier's window. For others, it is the spectacle of a Secretariat or a Saratoga or the chance to root away the frustrations of daily living in 1:11⅖.

But for numerous racing fans—the ones for whom this book is written—Thoroughbred horseracing is all of the above and one of the most intellectually challenging pastimes man has ever invented. Through the art/science of handicapping and the wagering instrument, the fan in the stands is as much a participant as the horse itself. Armed with a copy of the *Daily Racing Form,* the horseplayer becomes a detective, and there are many mysteries to be solved.

How important are speed-pace-class-distance-track condition-weight-jockey-and-trainer? What role do they play in determining the outcome of a race? Are there patterns of predictability? Is the game based on logic or ruled by chance? What about drugs and year-round racing? And, at rock bottom, is it possible to play the game well enough to overcome the stiff 20 percent betting tax and still show a profit for the effort?

Virtually every serious or semi-serious fan has endured periods of frustration and self-doubt while trying to find workable answers to these and other racetrack riddles. The path is littered with thousands of torn-up pari-mutuel tickets. The clues are complex, sometimes contradictory. The secrets of the game are subtle and elusive. And there is just so much bad advice floating around.

Dozens of ads promise to make the racing game easy pickings but in every instance fall way short of the mark. Indeed, the racetrack experience is such that there are no absolute truths to memorize, no ironclad list of dos or don'ts, no simplistic three-rule systems that do your thinking for you.

It may sound like good advice to avoid playing a filly against colts, or to demand a recent race from a potential contender; but it has been my experience that the people who give such advice, and sell it too, have rarely had a winning season in their lives.

Along every step of the handicapping process the player must learn to make well-thought-out judgments: to separate contenders, to eliminate also-rans, to detect relevant information hidden in the hieroglyphics of the *Daily Racing Form*'s past performance records, and to glean valid insights from the fast-paced action on the track.

To acquire that kind of reality-based insight, most successful horseplayers have had to discard the majority of popular handicapping notions, substituting in their place more flexible concepts gained through practical experience, intensive private research, and conversations with the best players in the game.

I would love to assure you that reading this book will automatically make you a winner. But I can't. The truth is you may not have the competitiveness, the patience, or the inclination to follow the steps necessary to improve your game sufficiently.

It is my belief, however, that thousands, perhaps even tens of thousands, of racing fans could win at the races but are presently unable to do so because they do not know what skills are important, what sources of information are reliable, and what tools are most useful for the task. Thousands more, maybe millions, gain considerable pleasure in their initial outings to the track but for lack of good teachers and other aids find the experience too expensive to pursue. And there are others, too many in fact, who continue to play the game without knowing some of the strategies that could reduce the cost considerably.

The purpose of this book is to lend a hand and fill the void. It is a sourcebook, not about Thoroughbred horseracing per se, but about ideas, concepts, tools, and suggestions taken from seventeen years of personal and professional racetrack experience. It is designed so that any player, regardless of past history or present skill, can gain sufficient insights to build a solid plan of attack. Good luck, and I hope it helps your game.

Betting Thoroughbreds

A Professional's Guide for
the Horseplayer

1.
Through the Looking Glasses

Secretariat ✗					Ch. c (1970), by Bold Ruler—Somethingroyal, by Princequillo.					
					Breeder, Meadow Stud, Inc. (Va.).	1973	12	9	2	1	$860,404
Owner, Meadow Stable. Trainer, L. Laurin.						1972	9	7	1	0	$456,404
Oct28-73⁸WO	mc 1⅜ 2:41⅘fm	1-5 ▲117	2⅛	15	1¹²16½	MapleE¹²	WfaS 96	Secretariat117	BigSpruce	GoldenDon 12
Oct 8-73⁷Bel	⊤ 1½ 2:24⅘fm	1-2 ▲121	11½	11½	13	15	T'c'teR³	WfaS 103	Secretariat 121	Tentam	Big Spruce 7
Sep29-73⁷Bel	1½ 2:25⅘sy	1-3 ▲119	2¹½	1ʰ	2¹½	24½	Turc'teR⁵	WfaS 86	ProveOut126	Secretariat	CougarII. 5
Sep15-73⁷Bel	1 1-8 1:45⅖ft	2-5e▲124	5⁴	3½	12	13½	T'rc'teR⁷	InvH 104	Secretariat124	RivaRidge	Cougar II. 7
Aug 4-73⁷Sar	1 1-8 1:49½ft	1-10 ▲119	4⁴	2½	2ʰ	2¹	Turc'teR³	AlwS 94	Onion 119	Secretariat	Rule by Reason 5
Jun30-73⁸AP	1 1-8 1:47	ft 1-20 ▲126	13	12½	16	19	Turc'tteR⁴	InvA 99	Secretariat 126	MyGallant	OurNative 4
Jun 9-73⁸Bel	1 1-2 2:24	ft 1-10 ▲126	1ʰ	120	128	131	Tur'teR¹	ScwS 113	Secretariat126	Twice aPr'ce	MyGal'nt 5
May19-73⁸Pim	1⁷⁄₁₆ 1:54⅖ft	1-3 ▲126	45½	12½	12½	12½	Turc'teR³	ScwS 98	Secretariat 126	Sham	Our Native 6
May 19—Daily Racing Form Time, 1:53⅖.										
May 5-73⁹CD	1 1-4 1:59⅖ft	3-2e▲126	11⁸³	2½	1½	12½	T'tteR¹⁰	ScwS 103	Secretariat 126	Sham	Our Native 13
Apr21-73⁷Aqu	1 1-8 1:49⅘ft	1-3e▲126	75½	55½	45½	34	T'rc'teR⁶	ScwS 83	Angle Light 126	Sham	Secretariat 8
Apr 7-73⁷Aqu	1 1:33⅖ft	1-10 ▲126	3¹	12	1½	13	T'rc'teR³	AlwS 100	Secret'riat126	Ch'mp'gneCh'rlie Flush 6
Mar17-73⁷Aqu	7 f 1:23½sy	1-5 ▲126	5⁶	5³	1ʰ	14½	Tur'tteR⁴	AlwS 85	Sec'tar't12b	Ch'pagneCh'lie Impec'n's 6
Nov18-72⁸GS	1⁷⁄₁₆ 1:44⅖ft	⊤-10e▲122	6⁹½	33	11½	13½	Tur'teR⁶	ScwS 83	Secretariat122	AngleLight StepNicely 6
Oct28-72⁷Lrl	1⁷⁄₁₆ 1:42⅘sv	1-10e▲122	6¹⁴	5³	15	18	T'rc'teR⁵	ScwS 99	Secretar't122	St'p t'eM'sic AngleL'ht 6
Oct14-72⁷Bel	1 1:35	ft 2-3e▲122	11¹³	53½	1½	12†	Tur'teR⁴	ScwS 97	Secr'tar't122	St'p theM'sic St'pNic'ly 12
†Disqualified and placed second.										
Sep16-72⁷Bel	6½ f 1:16⅖ft	1-5 ▲122	65½	53½	12	11¾	Turc'teR⁴	ScwS 98	S'cr't'r't122	St'p t'eMusic Sw'tC'rier 7
Aug26-72⁷Sar	6½ f 1:16½ft	1-3 ▲121	96½	1ʰ	14	15	Turc'teR⁸	SpwS 97	Secretariat121	Fl't toGl'y St'p theM'c 9
Aug16-72⁷Sar	6 f 1:10	ft 3-2 121	·5⁴	42	1½	13	Turc'teR²	SpwS 96	Secr'riat121	L'da'sCh'f N'thst'rD'c'r 5
Jly 31-72⁴Sar	6 f 1:10⅘ft	2-5 ▲118	7³¾	3½	1ʰ	11½	TurcotteR⁴	Alw 92	Secretariat 118	Russ Miron Joe Iz 7
Jly 15-72⁴Aqu	6 f 1:10⅗ft	6-5 ▲113*	66½	43	1½	16	Felic'noP⁸	Mdn 90	Secret'riat113	M'sterAch'v'r BetOn It 11
Jly 4-72²Aqu	5½ f 1:05	ft 3 ▲113*10⁷	108¾	75½	41½	Felic'noP²	Mdn 87	Herbull 118	MasterAch'v'r Fl't 'nR'y'l 12
Oct 5 Bel tc 5f fm :56⅘h			Sept 25 Bel tc 1m yl 1:38h					Sept 21 Bel tc 4f sf :48⅗b		

Thanks to television's coverage of the 1973 Triple Crown races, almost every person with the vaguest interest in horse-racing knows that the horse whose lifetime record is shown above was one of a kind, a champion of his age, if not, in fact, one of the greatest racehorses ever to appear on this planet.

As a two-year-old, before the TV cameras discovered him, Secretariat was just as spectacular to watch, officially winning eight races in ten starts, including a defeat only the stewards could hang on him in the Champagne Stakes. But it is his other defeat I want to tell you about. His first lifetime start.

Secretariat	113	Ch. c (1970), by Bold Ruler—Somethingroyal, by Princequillo.					
		Breeder, Meadow Stud, Inc. (Va.).	1972	0	M	0	0	(——)
Owner, Meadow Stable. Trainer, L. Laurin.							
June 29 Bel 3f ft :35h		June 24 Bel 6f sly 1:12⅘h		June 15 Bel 5f ft 1:00⅓hg			

One, two, three strides out of the starting gate with inexperienced Paul Feliciano barely able to stay in the saddle, Secretariat was welcomed to the sport of kings with a bang. Make that two bangs. One from the left and one from the right.

"Forget *that* horse," I said to console myself and made a mental note to see him a bit later in the race. Ten lengths to the front, a pack of expensively bred two-year-old maidens were trying to win the first race of their careers. It was time to see how the race was taking shape.

I love two-year-old racing. I'm fascinated by its freshness and its promise, and I've gained valuable insights about speed, class, distance potential, and trainers through watching these young horses progress from race to race. Besides, the better ones run fast, very formfully, and provide some of the best bets in all of racing.

When the great filly Ruffian, for example, made her debut in 1974, I was absolutely astonished to get a $10.40 payoff. Her trainer, Frank Whiteley Jr., is one of the deadliest trainers of first-time starters in the history of racing— a man who wins upward of 40 percent of all such attempts, a man who trains horses like they are put together with Swiss-clockwork efficiency.

Not only did Ruffian score by fifteen lengths in track record time, but she was the third straight first-time starter Whiteley put over in three early season attempts. It also turned out to be a typical Ruffian performance.

THIRD RACE
Belmont
MAY 22, 1974

5 ½ FURLONGS. (1.03) MAIDEN SPECIAL WEIGHTS. Purse $9,000. Fillies, 2–year–olds, weights, 116 lbs.

Value of race $9,000, value to winner $5,400, second $1,980, third $1,080, fourth $540. Mutuel pool $144,330, OTB pool $47,785. Track Exacta Pool $182,574. OTB Exacta Pool $83,829.

Last Raced	Horse	Eqt.A.Wt PP St	¼	½	Str	Fin	Jockey	Odds $1
	Ruffian	2 116 9 8	1³	1⁵	1⁸	1¹⁵	Vasquez J	4.20
	Suzest	2 113 3 3	3hd	2⁴	2⁵	2⁵	Wallis T³	1.50
	Garden Quad	2 116 10 9	5²	4½	4³	3½	Baltazar C	26.20
	Fierce Ruler	2 116 7 5	6½	5¹	3¹	4³½	Rivera M A	20.80
	Flower-Basket	2 116 8 6	8³	7½	5½	5½	Turcotte R	45.30
	Curlique	b 2 116 5 7	7½	8⁴	6³	6nk	Maple E	14.10
4May74 6CD12	Funny Cat	2 116 6 10	10	10	8½	7⁵	Hole M	32.70
14May74 4Bel3	Merrie Lassie	2 116 4 4	9⁶	9⁵	9⁴	8⁴½	Gustines H	13.90
	Precious Elaine	2 116 1 1	2hd	3¹	7½	9⁶½	Castaneda M	4.50
28Feb74 3GP2	Great Grandma Rose	2 116 2 2	4²	6¹½	10	10	Cordero A Jr	4.60

OFF AT 2:32 EDT. Start good, **Won ridden out.** Time, :22⅕, :45, :57, 1:03 Track fast.

Equals track record.

$2 Mutuel Prices:

9–(L)–RUFFIAN	10.40	4.60	3.80
3–(D)–SUZEST		3.20	3.00
10–(M)–GARDEN QUAD			7.00

$2 EXACTA 9–3 PAID $35.20.

dk b or br. f, by Reviewer—Shenanigans, by Native Dancer. Trainer Whiteley F Y Jr. Bred by Janney Jr Mrs & S S (Ky).

RUFFIAN, rushed to the front from the outside at the turn, quickly sprinted away to a good lead and continued to increase her advantage while being ridden out. SUZEST, prominent from the start, was no match for the winner while easily besting the others. GARDEN QUAD hustled along after breaking slowly, failed to seriously menace. FIERCE RULER had no excuse. FUNNY CAT was off slowly. PRECIOUS ELAINE had brief speed. GREAT GRANDMA ROSE was through early.

Owners— 1, Locust Hill Farm; 2, Olin J M; 3, Irving R; 4, LaCroix J W; 5, Reineman R L; 6, Calumet Farm; 7, Whitney C V; 8, T-Square Stable; 9, Brodsky A J; 10, Five Friends Farm.

Trainers— 1, Whiteley F Y Jr; 2, Stephens W C; 3, Johnson P G; 4, Toner J J; 5, Freeman W C; 6, Cornell R; 7, Poole G T; 8, Cincotta V J; 9, Conway J P; 10, Donato R A.

Scratched—Cross Words; Footsie (14May744Bel4); French Rule.

Throughout her two-year-old season Ruffian was never defeated, never threatened, never pushed to race any faster than she was willing to give on her own. But I'm not at all sure that pushing would have produced anything more than she was already willing to give.

Ruffian's striding action was very much like that of Valery Borzov, the Russian "doctor" of the sprint who won the gold medal in the 1972 100-meter dash at the Munich Olympics. Perfect rhythm. Maximum efficiency. Ruffian just came out of the gate running and never stopped, never missed a beat. Indeed, at six furlongs (three-quarters of a mile), I am convinced she could have beaten any horse that ever lived, including Secretariat, the fast-working son of Bold Ruler I had come to watch and bet in his debut, the colt we left in a tangle three steps out of the starting gate.

A few inches more to the left, a few more pounds of pressure, and we might never have heard about Secretariat. My notebooks are full of horses whose careers were terminated by less severe blows. But somehow this greenhorn kept his balance and settled slowly into stride far back of his field in the run down the backstretch.

On the turn I could see all the horses clearly at once, but the image I remember is that of the reddish brown colt going by three horses so fast it made me blink. Twice he changed gears to avoid further trouble. Twice more Feliciano choked him down to avoid running up on the heels of a tandem of horses that looked cloddish by comparison.

At the top of the stretch he moved again, into a higher gear, angling sharply to the inside, looking for room, shifting leads to gain better traction, losing precious time in the bargain. "A freak," I said to myself, but I had barely completed the thought when the red colt exploded in midstretch with a force that jiggled my binoculars right out of focus. He finished fourth, beaten by one and a half lengths. But it was the most electric exhibition of acceleration power I had seen since the mighty Kelso exploded seventy yards from the wire to gobble up Malicious in a stakes race eight years earlier.

It was only the beginning, only the tip of the iceberg; but being there, watching the race, knowing WHAT I was watching was a thrill—the kind of thrill that reaches the mind bringing awareness and awe.

Maybe your aim is to become a successful handicapper. Or perhaps you are reading this book just to improve your understanding of horseracing, putting it on a par with your comprehension of other hobbies and sports. In either case, the quickest, straightest line to the goal begins with the race itself and how to watch it. Unfortunately, all too many racing fans, it seems to me, do not know how to do that.

There are three simultaneous disciplines involved.

For one thing, you must see as much of the race as possible—the development of it, the flow of it, and the battle to the wire down the stretch. For another, your mind controls a switch for a focusing device like the zoom lens of a camera. You must train your mind to operate that switch—to zoom in and zoom out—the moment anything unusual hits the retina.

Combining these two disciplines into a smooth two-gear

transmission takes practice. You will have to learn when to switch away from the action in the front of the pack or away from the horse your money is riding on.

There are different ways to facilitate the learning process; but because the inclination of most horseplayers is to watch their bet, I suggest starting with that.

When the field hits the turn, when your grandstand vantage point makes it easy to see the entire field, without moving your binoculars, pull back on the zoom lens in your mind and see if you can spot the fastest-moving horses, the horses in trouble, the horses on the rail, the horses stuck on the outside.

Don't be concerned if you are not able to identify more than a couple of horses at once. Later you can use the videotape replays and result charts to put it all together.

In my judgment, the turn is the most important part of the race. It is the place where the majority of races are won and lost, the place where jockeys show their greatest skill and commit the most atrocious errors, the place where the fan can glean the most knowledge for the future.

Horses get into the most trouble on the turn. Centrifugal force pulls them naturally to the outside, and the ones that are weakly ridden, out of shape, or hurting are unable to hold their line as they turn the corner into the stretch.

Even more important, as I will describe in greater detail later, the action on the turn will reveal the true nature of the racetrack as the track itself influences race results.

There is no need for me to describe any further steps in the process of learning how to watch a race properly. If you master the turn, your ability to focus and shift focus to significant happenings will be firmly established. You will be able to use that skill anytime—at the start or in the stretch —at any stage of the race. After some practice you will even find yourself doing it automatically. Believe me, no other racetrack skill will ever be more useful.

The third discipline you need to master while watching races has nothing to do with the function of sight. And in all sincerity it is what the rest of this book is about. It is the discipline that all your racetrack judgments are based on— the discipline of enlightened insight.

Watching a race properly is only one of the ways you can acquire greater knowledge about particular horses. But to make maximum use of the skill, to put yourself in a position to recognize the unusual, important things that take place, you must first have some clear ideas about the limits of Thoroughbred performance, some understanding of the relative importance of track condition, trainers, class, and all the other pieces that make up the racetrack puzzle.

As I hinted in the introduction, most of the better players in the game have acquired that kind of knowledge only after many years of struggle. For some the effort was roughly equivalent to the pursuit of a college-level education. My own education was a case in point. And I mean that literally.

2.
A B.A. in Handicapping

The first race in my life took place at Aqueduct on April 18, 1960. I was an eighteen-year-old freshman at Rutgers University and I needed $100 to make it to Fort Lauderdale for spring recess. But I only had $42.

A few of my friends paid for the bus ticket, pushed me through the turnstiles, and armed me with a program and Jack's Little Green Card (a tout sheet). I bet $5 to show on Jack's best bet of the day—Happy Lion in the first race—but when I realized that wouldn't get me past the Delaware Memorial Bridge, I went back and bet a wheel in the daily double. Twice.

Of course, when Happy Lion sent me and my crazy friends barreling down the pike to a week of girl chasing in the Florida sun, I thought I had found the secret to a rich and easy life. Naturally, I became a devout believer in Jack's Little Green Card.

But the romance didn't last very long. Every time I skipped classes to go out to the track, Jack's Card would surely have three or four winners listed; but who could figure which of the three choices per race would turn out to be the right choice. It was my misfortune that the winner was rarely the top choice.

So I switched cards; bet the secret code selections of Ken Kling in the New York *Daily Mirror;* made a system founded on *Racing Form* consensus picks; bet repeaters; bet the top speed rating; followed the "horses to watch" list in *Turf and Sport Digest;* bought an assortment of systems and other gadgets at $5, $10, and $20 a pop; and then began to bet with a bookie.

At minus $1,200, it didn't take much of a handicapper to predict where I was headed; but the final straw was a last-place finish by my old friend Happy Lion. The irony of it all did not escape me.

My father, bless his heart, picked up the tab with the New Brunswick bookie and made me promise never to bet another horserace again. It was a promise I wasn't sure I wanted to keep, but I knew there wasn't much future in going out to the track just to lose. I was determined to find out if, in fact, it was possible to win.

For the next six months I stayed away from the track and bought, borrowed, and read everything I could find about the inner workings of the sport.

The history of it was fascinating enough: the stuff about Man O' War and Citation, Arcaro and Shoemaker. But I was appalled at the lack of good material in the field of handicapping. So much of it was so badly written, so illogical, so poorly documented that I became discouraged and abandoned the project. I was convinced that racing was nothing more than a game of roulette on horseback, a sucker's game of pure chance, and I might very well have held that view forever. An assignment my statistics professor handed out a few weeks later changed my mind. "Analyze the winning tendencies of post positions at Monmouth Park," he said. And the irony of *that* did not escape me either.

The task, simple enough, revealed very little useful information the first time through. But when I introduced track condition and distance into the equation, there were powerful indicators that suggested the need for more intensive research. My statistics professor—no fool, to be sure—probably took the hint and spent the rest of the summer buried in his *Racing Form*.

He wasn't the only one.

I looked up horses', trainers', and jockeys' records. I studied result charts and workouts diligently and kept a file on all the best horses and stakes races on the East Coast. I made endless comparisons and was not surprised when some patterns began to emerge, patterns that were never mentioned by the so-called experts who were publishing and selling their empty-headed systems and books to a starved racing public.

I discovered that each type of race had its own set of

key clues, its own major factors. I discovered that some trainers were consistently more successful than others and that most successful trainers were specialists who tended to repeat winning strategies. These strategies, I found, were frequently revealed in the past performance records of the horses they trained. By comparing these horses—comparing the dates between races, the workout lines, the distance and class manipulations—I began to gain some important insights into the conditioning process. The effort also cost me a failing grade in German 201, and I damn near flunked out of school. But it was worth it. I had begun to realize that there was a logic to the sport, and I suspected that I would be able to put all this time and effort to good use in the not-too-distant future. And I didn't have to wait very long to test out my thesis.

In late spring 1961 I spotted a horse named Nasomo in the past performance charts for Gulfstream Park. The half-mile workout from the starting gate attached to the bottom of his chart (.47bg) leaped off the page at me.

Nasomo hadn't shown such gate speed in any of his prior workouts, a deficiency he was content to carry over into his races. By habit he was a slow-breaking, Silky Sullivan-type whose late burst of speed had earned him absolutely nothing in eight tries. But my research into workout patterns had already convinced me that such a dramatic change in behavior on the training track invariably meant a vastly improved effort in competition. Barring bad racing luck—which is something that frequently plagues slow-breaking types—I was sure Nasomo would run the race of his life.

At 28–1 Nasomo turned in a spectacular performance, a nose defeat by the stakes prospect Jay Fox. Although that didn't score too many points with Nasomo's betting friends at the track, it was the first time I had ever felt confident about the performance of a horse before a race, the first time I began to think seriously about racing as a career.

Several weeks and several silent winning picks later, I broke my maiden on a horse called Flying Mercury. He was a retread sprinter that had once met top-class stock, but few people in the stands were able to appreciate his virtues (six outstanding workouts stretching back over a four-week period, all but one missing from the past performance records). Flying Mercury paid $78 to win, and I bought back my promise to my father with the proceeds of a $40 wager.

For the next two years I continued my studies into the mysteries of handicapping, keeping my losses to a minimum and my bets in perspective. But the Rutgers Dean of Men was not very pleased about my ragged classroom attendance, and he gave me a year off from school in September 1962, at the beginning of my senior year. In the true sense of the cliché, it turned out to be a blessing in disguise.

I visited racetracks in West Virginia, Louisiana, Ohio, Florida, New England, Michigan, Arkansas, Illinois, Maryland, California, New York, and New Jersey. Through those varied exposures and continued research, I detected two basic racetrack realities that seemed fundamental to handicapping. Yet I was sure that too few people in the stands were giving either of them the thought they deserved.

In the first place, I was surprised to learn that at many racetracks there was no way to measure the true class of horses by the claiming prices or race labels.

At most minor tracks, for example, a careful reading of result charts and race eligibility conditions suggested that there were five, six, or even seven separate class levels lumped into each claiming price. Moving up in company within a particular claiming price was frequently more difficult than ascending to the next claiming level.

At the major one-mile racetracks I frequently observed variations of this phenomenon in lower-level claiming events, maiden races, and nonclaiming (allowance) races. Very often these observations pointed out winners that were not otherwise discernible.

Secondly, because each racing surface—man-made and considerably different—had specific peculiarities, some race results were predetermined, or at least heavily influenced, by those characteristics.

In sprints at Monmouth Park, for example, post positions were of no consequence on fast-track racing days, but following any rain the track did not (and still does not) dry out evenly.

On days like that the rail was so deep and tiring that posts one, two, and three were at a terrible disadvantage. Stretch runners breaking from the outer post positions won everything. (At the Fair Grounds in New Orleans, where water can be found less than ten feet below the surface, the drainage system created precisely the opposite effect.)

Indeed, at every racetrack on my itinerary I noticed an influential track bias at work at one or more distances. And at some tracks a particular bias was so strong and so predictable that all handicapping questions had to be directed toward finding out which horse would be helped, hurt, or eliminated by the peculiarities of the running surface.

Of course, most handicappers seemed well aware of the difference between sloppy, fast, and other moisture-related track conditions, and a few even knew that Aqueduct in July favored speedy, front-running types while Belmont in September seemed to be deeper, slower, and kinder to stretch runners; but my observations about track bias suggested a stronger relationship between the track and actual horse performance. What I discovered was a relationship that sometimes eliminated the best horse in the race from contention, or else helped to promote an otherwise modestly qualified contender into a logical race winner.

By thinking first in these terms, before trying to compare the relative talents of the horses in a specific race, I found myself consistently able to recognize solid horses at every racetrack, horses that frequently went to post at generous odds. *It was also possible to interpret results and past performance lines more accurately when these horses ran back at a later date.*

With the first consistent profits of my handicapping career, I returned to Rutgers full of confidence.

On May 24, 1964, I finally did graduate from Rutgers, with a B.A. in psychology; but in truth it was only through the grace of my music professor, who raised my cumulative average to the passing level by changing a C to a B on the final day. Three weeks earlier the two of us accidentally met at Garden State Park, and he had a $280 reason to remember the event.

"I'm not doing this as a reward for your touting services," Professor Broome said while making the change of grade, "but I think you deserve some academic credit for your racing studies and this is the best I can do."

It was just enough.

3.
The Horseplayer's Bible

In the early morning hours at racetracks coast to coast, from January to December, thousands of horses of varying abilities are out on the training track. In the afternoons and evenings thousands more compete in races for fillies, colts, sprinters, routers, maidens, claimers, allowances, and stakes.

Some races are on the grass course, some on the dirt. Some tracks are fast; some are sloppy, muddy, or something in between. The possibilities are endless, the data voluminous. And at $1.25 per copy, most of it is all there in black and white.

Frankly, I'm not in the habit of endorsing the editorial policy of the *Daily Racing Form*. I think it could surely provide more pertinent investigative reporting and give sharper focus to issues affecting the plight of the player; but for hard racing news, statistics, and daily track poop, the *Daily Racing Form* is unequivocally the best publication of its kind in the world. Properly used, it is more valuable than the rest of racing literature put together. And they can quote me on that if they like.

Henrietta Sue			109	Ch. f (1973), by Royal Trio—Cavangal, by Cavan.										
				Breeder, Garrett & Carter (La.).					1976	6 1 0 1			$3,788	
Owner, T. Hickman.	Trainer, B. Flint.							$5.000	1975	9 M 3 0			$10.993	
16 Feb76 4FG	5½ f :22 :47 1:06²ft	7½	109	52½	55	52¾	33	SpiehlerG9	5000 83	SecondPolicy112	Dantlss Joe 12			
11 Feb76 1FG	6 f :22² :454 1:11 ft	6½	112	86½	8¹¹	78	4¹¹	SphielrG10	6500 79	AprilMoon120	JoustingRulah 12			
29 Jan76 7FG	1⁴0 :463 1:12 1:41²ft	37	112	10¹⁵	10¹⁸	10²⁸	9³⁹	SoirezW7	10000 47	LeCrack 119	ElChris 10			
17 Jan76 3FG	6 f :22² :464 1:123ft	5¼	109	54½	44½	45½	5¹²	SpiehlrG4	12000 70	Shannon's Goal 115	Cosgin 7			
11 Jan76 9FG	6 f :22¹ :464 1:131ft	13	109	31½	22½	3½	43	SpehlerG9	HcpS 76	ⒻItsYourProblem112	Tagita 12			
5 Jan76 4FG	6 f :22³ :482 1:14⁴gd	9-5	ᴬ¹¹15	21½	1½	13	16½	CarkK10	cM6500 71	ⒻHrttaSue111	Run to theFt 12			
20 Dec⁻5 9FG	6 f :22³ :463¹:124ft	13	122	3³	4³	32½	26	LeBncAR3	ScwS 75	Kitassy122	HenriettaSue 11			
11 Dec75 3FG	6 f :22³ :471 1:132ft	2½	1145	3¹	2¹	1ʰ	24	ClarkK7	Mdn 74	ⒻMissyRed 119	HenritaSue 12			
3 Dec⁻5 1FG	6 ⁻ :224 :47 1:132ft	8½	1075	43½	2½	1ʰ	2ⁿᵒ	C·arkK8	5000 ⁻8	CityDevelomnt115	HnrtaSue 12			
24 Nov75 1FG	6 f :23² :483 1:133ft	50	1085	63½	66½	45	59½	ClarkK12	M7500 67	TryThs frSze119	SwngngE.J. 12			
	Feb 12 FG 3f ft :36bg			Jan 21 FG 3f ft :36⅖bg										

Most racegoers have no trouble recognizing the importance of past performance profiles. The pp shown above is a season's worth of racing history at a glance. The date, distance, track, and track condition for every start; the fractional times of the leader and finishing time of the race winner; the odds, the weight, the running line, the beaten lengths, and finishing position; the jockey, post position, class of race, speed rating, top two finishers, and size of field. An incredible amount of information. But it is not enough. Indeed, it is not even the complete picture provided by other sources of information published in the very same newspaper. The result chart is far more comprehensive, far more valuable.

While every race is being run in North America, a sharp-eyed *DRF* employee known as the "Trackman" gives a horse-by-horse call of the fast-paced action on the track to an attentive assistant. Presto, the result chart is born. Flash, it's over the wires to Hightstown, New Jersey; Los Angeles, California; Chicago, Illinois; and other cities where editions of the *Form* are put together.

At the chart desk at *DRF* offices each horse's running line is extracted from the chart and then added to its past performance profile.

What many fans do not realize about this process hurts them every time they go out to the track.

Because of space limitations much important information is lost in the transmission from chart to profile. And even more of that information is lost if the profile is scheduled for publication in the *Form*'s tabloid-size Western editions. But whichever edition we consider (in this book all past performance examples are taken from the smaller Western editions), there is no reason any of this information should be lost to the player.

Saving a set of chronologically dated result charts for the track(s) in your area is all that's required to fill in the spaces. While each edition of the *Form* publishes complete result charts for all tracks covered by the past performances, the cost-conscious, once-a-week horseplayer can still keep pace with doings at his favorite track through the condensed charts appearing in the sport section of a good local newspaper. Moreover, by not paying some attention to these charts, you will forfeit your best chance to advance your game.

Foolish Pleasure		126	B. c (1972), by What a Pleasure—Fool-Me-Not, by Tom Fool. Breeder, Waldemar Farm Inc. (Fla.).		1976	6	3	0	1	$127,260
Owner, J. L. Greer. Trainer, L. Jolley.					1975	11	5	4	1	$716,278

5 Jly 76 8Aqu	1 3/16 :47 1:11 21 :55 2ft · 2½	125	11½	11½	11	1no	MapleE4	HcpS 85	FoolishPleasure125	Forego 4
20Jun76 8Hol	1¼ :45 41:10 1:58 4ft 9-5	126	69½	74½	76	56½	PincyLJr1	HcpS 90	PayTribute117	Avatar 8
6Jun76 8Hol	1¼ :46 21:10 21 :47 1ft 2-3 ▲128		33	42½	42	33½	PincyLJr2	HcpS 92	Riot in Paris122	PayTribute 5
27Mar76 9GP	1 1/16 :46 41:09 41:40 1fm3-5 ▲129		21½	22	32½	84¼	BaezaB3	HcpS 99	StepForward117 LordHenham 9
6Mar76 9GP	7 f :22 :44 31:21 2ft 1-3 ▲129		43	63¾	1½	13½	BaezaB2	HcpS 97	FoolishPleasre129 PackrCaptn 10
4Feb76 7Hia	7 f :23 :45 41:22 2ft 1-3 ▲119		42½	43	1h	17	BaezaB4	Alw 93	FoolishPleasure119 Dashboard 7
10oct75 8Bel	1 1/16 :46 41:11 1:41 3ft 1-5 ▲120		21½	11½	1h	2no	CordroAJr6	Alw 94	Stonewalk126 FoolishPleasure 6
13Sep75 8Bel	1¼ :47 21:10 42:00 ft 2½	12i	54	66½	66	510	CrdroAJr4	InvH 89	Wajima119	Forego 7

July 22 Bel 4f ft :46⅔h   July 19 Bel 7f ft 1:26⅗b   July 15 Bel 4f ft :46b

When Foolish Pleasure invaded the West Coast in late spring 1976, he was probably unaware of his unpopularity with the top stock at Hollywood Park. Maybe they remembered the way Avatar and Diabolo were "bounced" right out of contention during the stretch run of the 1975 Kentucky Derby. Maybe they wanted to chase Leroy Jolley and his horse back East on the next plane. In any case, Foolish Pleasure's first race at Hollywood Park, on June 6, was much like his second race at Hollywood, on June 20. I think the chart and the Trackman's comments for the latter race tell the story quite graphically.

EIGHTH RACE
Hollywood
JUNE 20, 1976

1 ¼ MILES. (1.58⅕) HOLLYWOOD GOLD CUP. Purse $250,000 Guaranteed. A handicap for 3-year-olds and upward. By subscription of $150 each, to accompany the nomination, $750 to pass the entry box and $2,000 additional to start, with $150,000 guaranteed to the winner, $40,000 to second, $30,000 to third, $20,000 to fourth, and $10,000 to fifth. Weights, Sunday, June 13. Starters to be named through the entry box by closing time of entries.

A Gold Cup of original design will be presented to the owner of the winner. Trophies will be presented to the winning trainer and jockey. Closed Wednesday, June 9, 1976, with 21 nominations.

Value of race $250,000, value to winner $150,000, second $40,000, third $30,000, fourth $20,000, fifth $10,000. Mutuel pool $372,617. Exacta Pool $285,230.

Last Raced	Horse	Eqt.A.Wt	PP	¼	½	¾	1	Str	Fin	Jockey	Odds $1
6Jun76 8Hol2	Pay Tribute	4 117	7	31½	31	3½	31	11½	13½	Castaneda M	13.90
12Jun76 6Hol1	Avatar	b 4 123	8	52	51	6hd	61½	2½	22	McHargue D G	7.50
6Jun76 8Hol1	Riot in Paris	b 5 123	3	4hd	41	41	52	3½	Toro F	a-2.40
31May76 8Hol1	Dahlia	6 121	4	21	22½	21	2½	41	4½	Shoemaker W	a-2.40
6Jun76 8Hol3	Foolish Pleasure	4 126	1	72½	6hd	71½	73	74	52½	Pincay L Jr	1.80
23May76 8Hol1	Ancient Title	b 6 127	5	61	73½	5½	5hd	61	6no	Hawley S	1.70
29May76 6Hol1	Our Talisman	b 4 115	6	12	14	11	1hd	3hd	73½	Olivares F	a-2.40
31May76 8Hol6	Top Command	5 116	2	8	8	8	8	8	8	Mena F	a-2.40

OFF AT 5:53 PDT Start good, Won ridden out. Time, :23⅕, :45⅖, 1:10, 1:34⅗, 1:58⅖ Track fast.

$2 Mutuel Prices:	4–PAY TRIBUTE	29.80	9.40	3.40
	5–AVATAR		9.00	3.60
	1–RIOT IN PARIS (a–entry)			2.40

$5 EXACTA 4–5 PAID $360.00.

Ch. c, by High Tribute—Drummer Girl, by Tompion. Trainer McAnally Ronald. Bred by Elmendorf Farm (Ky).

PAY TRIBUTE taken in hand after a clean break dropped behind the early leaders went up gradually into the far turn, attended the pace to the three sixteenths pole, drew out and into a clear lead under coaxing then stretched his margin in the last sixteenth under a hand ride. AVATAR raced unhurried early, moved nearer leaving the far turn, entered the stretch from between horses in the middle of the track to rally and prompted the winner then lost his full punch. RIOT IN PARIS saving ground raced close enought to the three furlong pole, remained inside pointing for a hole approaching the furlong pole but had to take up when blocked, steered out and around but could not regain his full momentum. DAHLIA broke alertly to be closest the early lead, rallied on the far turn to share the lead to the upper stretch and faded. FOOLISH PLEASURE placed on the rail while being outrun early, checked when blocked into the far turn, remaned without room passing the quarter pole, swung wide for a clear path then could not make up the needed ground. ANCIENT TITLE showed little early speed and came out from the quarter pole while perhaps in light contact with AVATAR and lacked a late rally. OUR TALISMAN set the pace and faltered. TOP COMMAND was always outrun.

Owners— 1, Elmendorf; 2, Seeligson A A Jr; 3, Bradley & Whittingham; 4, Hunt N B; 5, Greer John L; 6, Kirkland Ethel Estate Of; 7, Murty Farm & Schwartzman (Lessees); 8, Martin Mr-Mrs Q & Murty Farm.

Trainers— 1, McAnally Ronald; 2, Doyle A T; 3, Whittingham Charles; 4, Whittingham Charles; 5, Jolley Leroy; 6, Stucki Keith L; 7, Rettele Loren; 8, Whittingham Charles. ¹

Scratched—Mateor (23May76 7Hol¹⁰).

Bettors at Aqueduct on July 5, 1976, probably needed no introduction to Foolish Pleasure. When you win a Derby and $1 million in two racing seasons it's hard not to make an impression. But only chart savers at Aqueduct would have known that Foolish Pleasure's two California races were not as bad as they appeared in the past performances. The Hollywood Gold Cup chart, along with many of the nation's most important stakes race result charts, appears regularly in all editions of the *Daily Racing Form*. I strongly recommend saving these charts too. You will pick winners from them. In the modern age of Thoroughbred racing a trainer will not hesitate to ship a good horse 3,000 miles and back again for a weekend shot at a stakes-class purse.

Fine-line decisions are intrinsic to the handicapping process, and result charts invariably present more clues to the right side of the line than the "p.p.'s." Sometimes these additional clues provide an insight or an excuse for a recent defeat, or force a reappraisal of a horse's physical condition. And sometimes they point out an extra dimension of quality not otherwise detectable from the past performances. The following two race result charts speak volumes to the point I am making. The first is one of my personal favorites. The salient points are underlined.

SIXTH RACE

Garden State

NOVEMBER 9, 1972

1 ⅛ MILES. (1.41) ALLOWANCE. Purse $6,000. 3-year-olds and upward which have not wontwo races of $5,200 at a mile or over since June 15. 3-year-olds, 119 lbs. Older 122 lbs. Non-winners of three races of $4,225 at a mile or over since May 15 allowed 3 lbs. such a race of $3,900 since then, 5 lbs. such a race of $4,225 since April 15, 7 lbs. (Maiden, claiming and starter races not considered). (Originally carded to be run at 1 1/16 Miles, Turf.)

Value of race $6,000, value to winner $3,600, second $1,200, third $660, fourth $360, fifth $180. Mutuel pool $114,235.

Last Raced	Horse	Eqt.A.Wt	PP	St	¼	½	¾	Str	Fin	Jockey	Odds $1
23Oct72 ⁸GS⁵	Laplander	b 5 119	5	5	6	5hd	5⁶	4⁴	1³½	Barrera C	2.70
21Oct72 ⁹CT⁵	Test Run	6 119	3	1	2²	2³	4hd	2hd	2½	Keene J	20.50
21Oct72 ⁸Lrl²	Seminole Joe	4 119	4	3	3¹½	4⁶	1½	1½	3¹	Iannelli F	7.30
21Oct72 ⁶Lrl¹	Duc by Right	b 5 119	2	2	1²	1²	2¼	3hd	4½	Moseley J W	4.40
27Oct72 ⁸GS⁶	Warino	b 4 119	7	4	4²	3½	3¹½	5⁶	5⁶	Hole M	3.30
27Sep72 ⁸Atl⁶	Roundhouse	b 4 119	1	6	5²	6	6	6	6	Tejeira J	16.70
23Oct72 ⁵Aqu³	Prince of Truth	b 4 122	6	7	—	—	—	—	—	Blum W	2.20

Prince of Truth, Lost rider.

Time, :23⅘, :47⅕, 1:12⅘, 1:39⅕, 1:45⅘ Track slow.

$2 Mutuel Prices:

5-LAPLANDER	7.40	4.20	2.80
3-TEST RUN		11.00	4.60
4-SEMINOLE JOE			4.20

B. g, by Assemblyman—Reindeer, by Polynesian. Trainer Kulina J. Bred by Fowler A (Md).

IN GATE AT 2:55; OFF AT 2:55 EASTERN STANDARD TIME Start Good For All But PRINCE OF TRUTH Won Driving

LAPLANDER, forced to steady and steer wide to avoid a loose horse inside of him entering the clubhouse turn, fell back, recovered gradually nearing the end of the backstretch, circled rivals rallying into the stretch, again steadied and moved inside to miss the loose horse, gained command leaving the furlong grounds and gradually drew clear. TEST RUN pressed the early pace, reached close contention from the inside in upper stretch was in tight a furlong out and faltered. SEMINOLE JOE was forced to check lightly by the loose horse entering the clubhouse turn, recovered quickly, reached the lead from the outside nearing the stretch, came in when intimidated by the loose horse a furlong out, was straightened away and faltered. DUC BY RIGHT went to the front at once, drew clear and was tiring when placed in close quarters between horses by SEMINOLE JOE in the drive. A claim of foul lodged by the rider of DUC BY RIGHT against the rider of SEMINOLE JOE was not allowed. WARINO was forced wide into the first turn, was taken in hand, rallied to reach close contention from the outside entering the stretch and tired. ROUNDHOUSE was never a factor. PRINCE OF TRUTH stumbled and unseated his rider at the start, raced with his field and caused repeated interference.

Owners— 1, Buckingham Farm; 2, Oliver & Stanley; 3, Sugar Mill Farm; 4, Haffner Mrs H Y; 5, Nesbitt H J; 6, Brandywine Stable; 7, Tucker J R.

Trainers— 1, Kulina J; 2, Oliver D; 3, Stirling W Jr; 4, Wahler C; 5, Cocks W; 6, Raines V W; 7, Jennings L W.

Scratched—Best Go (18Sep72⁸Atl⁶); Vif (27Oct72⁸GS⁸).

On the day Laplander was playing tag with a riderless horse at Garden State Park, a claiming horse named Third Law was giving Maryland racing fans a first-class impersonation of O. J. Simpson.

FOURTH RACE

Laurel

NOVEMBER 9, 1972

7 FURLONGS. (1.22⅕) CLAIMING. Purse $7,150, of which $650 to breeder of winner. 3-year-olds, Registered Maryland-Breds. Weights, 122 lbs. Non-winners of two races since September 18, allowed 2 lbs. A race since then, 4 lbs. A race since September 11, 6 lbs. Claiming price $12,500; for each $1,000 to $10,500, 2 lbs. (Races where entered for $9,500 or less not considered.)

Value of race $7,150, value to winner $3,900, second $1,430, third $780, fourth $390; $650 to Breeder of Winner. Mutuel pool $87,225.

Last Raced	Horse	Eqt.A.Wt	PP St	¼	½	Str	Fin	Jockey	Cl'g Pr	Odds $1
20Oct72 ⁴Lrl⁶	Third Law	3 116	7 2	7ʰᵈ	7½	4½	1¹	Jimenez C	12500	40.60
29Sep72 ⁸Bel⁶	Admiral Kelly	b 3 118	1 8	2½	1ʰᵈ	2²	2½	Turcotte R L	12500	4.10
24Oct72 ⁵Lrl¹	All Above	3 119	3 1	1ʰᵈ	2¹½	1ʰᵈ	3ʰᵈ	Feliciano B M	12500	1.40
24Oct72 ⁵Lrl⁷	Rigel	b 3 116	4 6	5½	3½	3ʰᵈ	4½	Passmore W J	12500	6.10
4Nov72 ⁴Lrl¹	Gunner's Mate	b 3 113	8 3	6⁴	6²	6³	5¹	Cusimano G	10500	4.90
24Oct72 ⁵Lrl⁸	Go Bet	3 116	2 4	3½	4ʰᵈ	5ʰᵈ	6²½	Kurtz J	12500	22.70
2Nov72 ⁸Lrl⁵	Hoosier Grand	3 116	6 7	8	8	7³	7³½	Wright D R	12500	6.40
3Nov72 ⁵Lrl⁷	Sky Flight	3 116	5 5	4½	5²½	8	8	Alberts B	11500	12.90

Time, :23⅗, :47, 1:13, 1:26 Track fast.

$2 Mutuel Prices:

7-THIRD LAW	83.20	20.60	5.80
1-ADMIRAL KELLY		5.80	3.60
3-ALL ABOVE			3.20

B. g, by Quadrangle—Flighty Jane, by Count Fleet. Trainer Green P F. Bred by Kelly Mrs L C (Md).
IN GATE AT 2:28; OFF AT 2:28 EASTERN STANDARD TIME. Start Good. Won Driving.

THIRD LAW, away in good order but without early speed, had to check stoutly behind horses on the stretch turn, went to the rail entering the stretch, responded strongly when set down, had to pull sharply outside ADMIRAL KELLY for racing room a furlong out but continued strongly to gain command and draw clear in the final seventy yards. ADMIRAL KELLY, away a bit slowly, was hustled up to force the pace inside all above before a quarter, got the lead leaving the backstretch, lost and regained it inside all above in the stretch, then could not resist the winner's closing bid while tiring near the end. ALL ABOVE set or forced the pace outside ADMIRAL KELLY throughout but hung slightly near the end. RIGEL, always in contention, responded between horses in the final quarter but was not good enough. GUNNER'S MATE did not threaten with a mild closing response. GO BET gave an even effort. HOOSIER GRAND showed little. SKY FLIGHT had only brief early speed.

Owners— 1, Master's Cave; 2, Audley Farm Stable; 3, Lee C; 4, Leonard R A; 5, Green Lantern Stable; 6, DiNatale J; 7, Hunt R R; 8, Berry C T Jr.

Trainers— 1, Green P F; 2, Thomas G; 3, Lee C; 4, Hacker B P; 5, Delp G G; 6, Bannon J T; 7, Vogelman R E Jr; 8, Simpson J P.

Overweight: Gunner's Mate 1 pound.

Armed with the Trackman's notes about the winner in each of these two races, we should have no difficulty imagining that Laplander and Third Law were able to step up sharply in company and win with ridiculous ease shortly thereafter. It is not stretching the point to say that a few equally revealing charts a season could more than pay for the cost of a subscription to the *Form*. Frankly, I could fill the rest of this book with four-star Trackman comments that pointed out horses who gave better showings than the past performance profiles revealed. But there are other important result chart clues that never find their way into the past performance profiles. Let's go back to Hollywood Park for an everyday example.

Wool Jacket   **113**   Ro. f (1973) by Try Sheep—French Jacket by Short Jacket.
Breeder, Middle Ranch (Calif.).

Owner, J. Morjoseph. Trainer, G. Jones. $13,000

| | | 1976 | 9 | 2 | 2 | 0 | $12,035 |
| | | 1975 | 4 | M | 0 | 0 | $1,115 |

11Jly76 5Hol	⊤ 1¹⁄₁₆ :47⁴1:12³1:44 fm 8½	113	6³½ 2¹ 65½ 5⁶	MenaF¹⁰	13000 73	ⒻWhyMreWrry116 NvrLetGo 12
27Jun76 1Hol	⊤ 1¹⁄₁₆ :46⁴1:112¹:43²fm 20	114	7⁹½ 53½ 4³ 54½	RamirzR⁹	13000 78	ⒻDallasMiss116 HisBoy'sPia 10
18Jun76 1Hol	1¹⁄₁₆ :47 1:12 1:44²ft 4	114	75½ 9⁶ 9⁹ 8¹¹	NoguezA⁵	14000 62	ⒻSchon116 HisBoy'sPia 10
10Jun76 5Hol	1 :47¹1:13 1:39⁴sl 10	112	55½ 3¹ 1h 1³	NoguezA⁴	12500 67	WoolJacket112 DesertSailor 10
26May76 5Hol	1 :45⁴1:10⁴1:36⁴ft 9	115	10¹⁵ 9¹¹ 9¹⁵ 7¹⁶	PincyLJr²	18000 66	ⒻSave aLittle116 NshuaTryst 10
5May76 2Hol	1 :47¹1:11⁴1:37²ft 9½	116	6⁶ 75½ 5⁶ 4⁶	ToroF⁸	20000 73	ⒻCpriciousDrm121 Sve aLtle 10
21Apr76 3Hol	1¹⁄₁₆ :47³1:12³1:44⁴ft 8-5	*116	44½ 4² 2⁴ 24½	ShokrW⁵	c16000 66	ⒻMajinai116 WoolJacket 6
8Apr76 4SA	6½ f :22³ :46 1:17⁴gd 5½	114	75 53½ 3² 1h	HlyS¹⁰	M20000 84	ⒻWoolJacket114 NowSean 10
18Mar76 3SA	6 f :22¹ :46 1:11²ft 7½	117	10¹⁰ 76¾ 4⁵ 2⁸	MenaF²	M20000 74	ⒻChquitaTryst117 WoolJackt 11
22Dec75 3BM	6 f :22⁴ :46²1:11³gd 30	117	75½ 55½ 52½ 45¾	CaballroR⁴	Mdn 76	ⒻAllWekEnd 117 Portalesisle 12

July 6 Hol 4f ft :49h   June 6 Hol 3 ft :38h   June 1 Hol 4f ft :48²⅗h

---

FIFTH RACE

Hol

July 11, 1976

1¹⁄₁₆ MILES (Turf). (1:39⅗). CLAIMING. Purse $11,000. 3-year-olds and upward. Fillies and mares. 3-year-olds, 112 lbs.; older, 122 lbs Non-winners of two races at one mile or over since April 8 allowed 2 lbs; of such a race since then, 4 lbs.; of a race since then, 6 lbs. Claiming price $16,000. 1 lb. allowed for each $1,000 to $13,000. (Claiming and starter races for $12,500 or less not considered.) Winners prefered.

Value to winner, $6,050; second, $2,200; third, $1,650; fourth, $825; fifth, $275. Mutuel Pool, $209,123. Exacta Pool, $497,210.

Last Raced	Horses	Eqt	A	Wt	PP	St	¼	½	¾	Str	Fin	Jockeys	Owners	Odds to $1
27Jun76 1Hol⁴	Why More Worry	b5	116	9	12	7½	4h	1¹	1³	1²	WShoemaker	M Ritt	2.10
27Jun76 1Hol⁷	Never Let Go	b4	116	11	11	12	10½	7h	4¹	2²	FToro	H T Sheridan	10.30
27Jun76 1Hol³	April's Hope	b4	114	8	10	10¹	9½	6¹	3h	3no	SHawley	Riplyn K Stable	4.50
27Jun76 1Hol⁵	Dallas Miss		5	120	12	5	8¹	7½	5½	2½	4²	OVergara	Daverick Stable	2.50
27Jun76 1Hol⁵	Wool Jacket		3	113	10	9	5½	6h	2h	6½	5¹	FMena	J Morjoseph	8.30
4Jly76 2Hol⁶	Society Kid		6	116	7	4	4²	5¹½	3½	5¹	6¹	RRosales	R F May	19.70
11Jun76 3Hol⁵	Miss Elite		4	110	6	8	9¹½	8¹	8²	7²	7¹½	RMGonz'l'z⁵	N B Hunt	26.80
29Apr76 5Hol⁸	One Chicken Inn		4	114	4	7	6½	11²	9³½	8¹	8³	MCastaneda	Mrs R Sahm	39.00
20Jun76 1Hol⁵	Lady Nephilim		5	110	1	2	2½	1½	4½	9⁴	9⁵	VCalvaJr⁵	Royal Hawaiian Stable	61.30
3Jun76 9Hol⁴	Shirley's Wish	b4	113	2	6	11¹	12	11⁵	10½	10no	RCespedes	Hickory Mill Farm	46.10
4Jly76 2Hol⁵	Sand Storm		5	116	5	3	3²½	3½	10h	11¹²11²⁵	DGM'Hargue	Benford-Smith	16.50
3Jun76 8Hol⁸	Glitter		4	116	3	1	1½	2¹	12	12	12	JGuzman	P Lerner	68.60

OFF AT 4:06 PDT. START GOOD. WON DRIVING. Time, :23, :47⅘, 1:12⅗, 1:37⅖, 1:44. Track firm.

$2 Mutuel Prices {
9-WHY MORE WORRY	6.20	4.40	3.20
11-NEVER LET GO		8.40	5.40
8-APRIL'S HOPE			3.80

$5 EXACTA (9-11) PAID $188.00

Dk. b. or br. m, by Time Tested—Wave of Joy, by Johns Joy. Trainer, R. Frankel. Bred by W. M. Wickham (Ky.).
WHY MORE WORRY was bumped at the start, rallied wide and drew out in the stretch. NEVER LET GO was steadied at the start, took up behind a wall of horses at the quarter-pole, then when clear, closed to the end. APRIL'S HOPE broke slowly, maneuvered for room and improved her position in the drive. DALLAS MISS lost ground and tired after a mild bid. MISS ELITE raced blocked midway and could make little impact. LADY NEPHILIM broke alertly to share the lead along the rail and faltered. GLITTER lost her action.

If you give a careful reading to the chart and compare it with Wool Jacket's July 11 running line, you will discover several missing facts:

1. Specific eligibility conditions for the race ($16,000–$13,000 claiming, and so on).
2. Fractional times for each quarter-mile split (p.p.'s show two splits).
3. Position at the start of the race (missing from the p.p.'s).
4. Position at first quarter-mile split (missing from p.p.'s).
5. Blinkers or no blinkers (available in Eastern-edition p.p.'s).
6. Exact age, weight, odds, jockey, owner, running pattern, and finishing position for entire field (weight and margins of top three finishers available in Eastern-edition p.p.'s).
7. Index date, track, and race number of most recent start by each member of the field.
8. Purse value of the race (missing from p.p.'s).

NOTE: In result charts the margins at each call refer to the horse's margin in front of the *next* horse. In past performance profiles the margins indicate lengths behind the *leader*.

Ordinarily, trackman Jay Woodward includes a comment for each and every prominent horse in the field. For no apparent reason, no remark appears for Wool Jacket, a horse that seemed to make a giant move entering the stretch, only to fall back out of contention in the drive to the wire. Woodward is, however, one of the top chart callers in the country. He, Jack Wilson (New York), Dick Carroll (Detroit), and Bill Phillips (part-time chart caller, full-time columnist) are the four most precise chart callers I have ever had the pleasure of reading. The only unreliable track-man I have ever read has retired and died. May he rest in peace. As for result charts, we have just scratched the sur-face. With a little research and a few investigative tools, we can use the added information to obtain even more substan-tial clues, clues that can increase our understanding of the horse, the track, and the nature of the game itself.

4.
The Bias of
the Racing Surface

Suppose someone walked up to you and said he knew a roulette wheel in a Las Vegas casino that was rigged in the player's favor. The wheel paid the customary 32–1 odds for a correct number but seldom stopped on any number higher than 20. I am sure you would have trouble believing it.

With a few important variations, that is precisely what I am about to tell you about the majority of racetracks in America. *Some numbers rarely win.*

At Pimlico racecourse in Baltimore, Maryland, where the first turn is less than a stone's throw from the starting gate in $1\frac{1}{16}$-mile races, horses with sprint speed and inside post positions have a ready-made shot at saving ground and a clear-cut winning edge. Conversely, horses forced to break from post positions nine, ten, eleven, or twelve in such races have to be far superior and perfectly ridden to remain in contention. And there are many racetracks in America with a bias like that. Aqueduct in New York ($1\frac{1}{8}$ miles on the main track, $1\frac{1}{16}$ miles on the new inner dirt track) is a well-known example. But the Fair Grounds in New Orleans and Churchill Downs in Louisville are rarely considered in a similar light.

Most players approach two-turn races at these two racetracks with an eye toward the fast-closing distance-type runner. It's hard to think otherwise while the two longest stretch runs in American racing are in full view. (Each is over 1,300 feet.) But these are two extremely elongated racetracks, with radically sharp turns. And the starting gate is frequently positioned so close to the first bend that the race is over before the stretch comes into play. A player who knows that about the Fair Grounds and Churchill may not pick the winner of every two-turn race, but very often he will be able to plot the way a race is likely to be run. In addition, he will catch many well-meant speed types outrunning their apparent distance limitations.

And there are other kinds of biases worth knowing

about. At Keystone racetrack in Pennsylvania, Garden State Park in New Jersey, and all other racetracks open for business during cold-weather months, extra layers of topsoil are frequently mixed with antifreeze agents to keep the racing surface from turning into a sheet of ice. The effort is usually successful, but not always; sometimes the rail is like a paved highway, and sometimes it's a slushy path to a quick and certain defeat.

No doubt it would be superfluous to spell out the impact such aberrant track conditions have on horse performance, so I won't. But I will say that a handicapper will probably think about throwing away his *Racing Form* if he doesn't take note of them. Indeed, if there is one pervasive influence on the handicapping experience, track bias comes very close to filling the bill. While it isn't fair to say that all races are won and lost because of the influence of a biased racing strip, the player can hardly hope to make consistently accurate predictions without weighing its significance. For instance, take Saratoga, the beautiful track in upstate New York that annually runs a twenty-four-day August meet.

A decade ago Saratoga had a soft racing surface that was biased in the extreme toward stretch runners and outer post positions. This may have contributed to a considerable extent to the track's reputation as a "graveyard for favorites." Confronted with a typical Saratoga race, most players were naturally impressed with recent winners shipping up from Aqueduct, a track that still tends to get pasteboard hard and front-running fast during July. At Saratoga very few of these horses were able to duplicate their prior good form, and race after race went to horses with the best late kick. In the 1960s observant horseplayers could eliminate a lot of short-priced, front-running horses at Saratoga; they can't do that anymore.

In 1974 a new, faster racing strip was installed, and it has turned Saratoga into a front runner's paradise. Now the player has to respect Aqueduct form; the two tracks are nearly identical. Track biases exist, but they are not necessarily the same from year to year.

When Calder racetrack (Florida) was going through its growing pains with the only artificial racing surface in American Thoroughbred racing, a horse capable of running half a mile on the lead in 46 seconds and change, which is not especially fast time at most racetracks, was a horse in fantastic shape. He couldn't win very many races at Calder —the track was powerfully tilted toward stretch-running speed—but when and if the stable was able to keep such a speedball fit enough to get a crack at Hialeah or Gulfstream Park, it was fat city.

Today the Calder-to-Gulfstream angle still works because Gulfstream has the kind of racing surface that speed horses dream about. At the same time, a fit front runner at Calder is no longer an automatic throwout. Times change, people change, and so do track biases.

But track biases do exist. Every racetrack has its peculiarities. Some are small in circumference, some have pasteboard-hard running surfaces, some card races that place a premium on early speed or post position. And nothing can help to change or create a bias as effectively as a shift in weather conditions. A sudden rainstorm on an otherwise normal racetrack is odds on to force a premium on early speed. On the other hand, a few days of rain, a sudden frost, or extreme heat can have totally unpredictable effects. It's wise to hold onto your money during such drastic changes in weather—unless, of course, you are able to see what is happening firsthand.

Out at the track, any racetrack, it is relatively easy to spot a track bias if you:

Watch the turns.
Observe the running patterns. Are horses able to make up

ground going to the outside or is the rail the only place to be?

Watch the break from the gate. Are horses in certain post positions always a bit late getting into the hunt?

Watch the run to the first turn (especially in route races). Are horses able to settle into contending positions from outer post positions without undue effort?

And watch the top jockeys. Do they consistently steer their horses to one part of the track over another? (Frankly, I'm not at all sure I should mention jockeys in this context, because all but a handful seem unable to recognize a bias until they have lost a bunch of races because of it. Of course, there are exceptions; and if you happen to be at a track where Sandy Hawley, Jorge Velasquez, Angel Cordero Jr., Willie Passmore, Mike Venezia, or Vince Bracciale Jr. are riding, watch them. They will spot a favorable path on the racing strip in two or three runs of the course.)

If you are unable to attend races regularly or are planning an assault on a new track, the only way to spot a bias is through careful reading of the result charts. But even if your on-track observations have detected a bias—it's hard not to notice the presence of one when six races in a row are won wire to wire—you will need to refer to the charts to note those horses that were stuck on the outside, blocked, left at the gate, or handed the race on a silver platter.

A horse stuck on the rail on a dead rail day will have a ready-made excuse. A speed horse that cruised to a front-running victory because it drew into a favorable post may not be as good as it seems. By way of example I am including trackman Jack Wilson's comments and the charts for the first four main-track races run at Saratoga on August 21, 1976. If the player had reviewed charts from preceding days, the front-running accent would have been hard to miss. (During a rainy spell earlier in the meet, speed held up, but the inside was a bog.) On August 18, 19, and 20 the inside part of the racetrack was faster than the outside. The charts for August 21 indicate that the tendency toward inside speed was overpowering.

FIRST RACE
Sar
August 21, 1976

6 FURLONGS. (1:08). MAIDENS. CLAIMING. Purse $7,500. Fillies. 2-year-olds. Weight, 119 lbs. Claiming price, $20,000; 2 lbs. allowed for each $1,000 to $18,000. Value to winner $4,500; second, $1,650; third, $900; fourth, $450. Mutuel Pool, $93,694. Off-track betting, $82,077.

Last Raced	Horse	EqtAWt	PP	St	1/4	1/2	Str	Fin	Jockeys	Owners	Odds to $1
13 Aug76	1Sar3	By by Chicken	b2 115	8	1	1½	2³	1h	1h	JVelasquez	Harbor View Farm	1.70
13 Aug76	1Sar9	Sun Bank	b2 119	5	2	2h	1h	2²	22¼	MVenezia	B Rose	b-4.30
13 Aug76	1Sar8	Mean Katrine	b2 115	1	3	5²	5½	4²	3¾	ASantiago	Robdarich Stable	7.50
		Peach Flambeau	2 117	4	5	4h	4¹½	3½	4¹¾	DMcHargue	J W LaCroix	a-7.40
		I Gogo	b2 112	6	9	6h	6½	6¹	52½	KWhitley7	Brookfield Farm	18.50
13 Aug76	9Sar6	Good Party	2 115	3	4	3²	3½	5½	6no	EMaple	N A Martini	12.50
25 Jly 76	2Del5	Tootwright	b2 119	2	10	7½	7³	7⁴	7⁵	PDay†	D Sturgill	3.00
		North Ribot	2 115	7	8	8²	8¹	8½	8h	MPerrotta	Betty Rose	b-4.30
27 Jun76	9Bel8	Hot Dogger	b2 117	9	6	9¹	9½	9¹½	9½	TWallis	Judith McClung	21.20
13 Aug76	9Sar4	Behavingaise	b2 117	10	7	10	10	10	10	RTurcotte	J W LaCroix	a-7.40

†Seven pounds apprentice allowance waived.
b-Coupled, Sun Bank and North Ribot; a-Peach Flambeau and Behavingaise.
OFF AT 1:30 EDT. Start good. Won driving. Time, :22⅖, :46⅗, 1:12⅘. Track fast.
Official Program Numbers ↘

$2 Mutuel Prices:

7-BY BY CHICKEN	5.40	3.40	2.80
2-SUN BANK (b-Entry)		4.60	3.40
3-MEAN KATRINE			3.60

B. f, by The Pruner—Chicken Little, by Olympia. Trainer, Lazaro S. Barrera. Bred by Carl L. Broughton (Fla.).

BY BY CHICKEN saved ground while vying for the lead with SUN BANK and prevailed in a stiff drive. The latter raced outside BY BY CHICKEN while dueling for command and narrowly missed. MEAN KATRINE finished evenly while saving ground. PEACH FLAMBEAU rallied approaching midstretch but hung. I GOGO failed to seriously menace while racing wide. GOOD PARTY tired from her early efforts. TOOTWRIGHT, off slowly, failed to be a serious factor. NORTH RIBOT was always outrun. BEHAVINGAISE showed nothing. Claiming Prices (in order of finish)—$18000, 20000, 18000, 19000, 20000, 18000, 20000, 18000, 19000, 19000. Scratched—Lots of Flair.

SECOND RACE
Sar
August 21, 1976

1⅛ MILES. (1:47). CLAIMING. Purse $8,500. 3-year-olds and upward. 3-year-olds, 117 lbs.; older, 122 lbs. Non-winners of a race at a mile and a furlong or over since Aug. 1 allowed 3 lbs.; of such a race since July 15, 5 lbs. Claiming price, $12,500; 2 lbs. allowed for each $1,000 to $10,500. (Races when entered to be claimed for $8,500 or less not considered.)

Value to winner $5,100; second, $1,870; third, $1,020; fourth, $510. Mutuel Pool, $131,999. Off-track betting, $95,870.

Last Raced	Horse	EqtAWt	PP	St	1/4	1/2	3/4	Str	Fin	Jockeys	Owners	Odds to $1
7 Aug76	1Sar6	Tingle King	b4 114	1	3	2½	3⁴	11½	15	1⁶	RTurcotte	Vendome Stable	5.40
7 Aug76	1Sar4	O'Rei	7 113	4	5	4h	4h	4⁴	3³	2⁴	TWallis	Mrs L I Miller	3.40
13 Aug76	3Sar1	Mycerinus	b5 122	8	7	7	7	6²	4⁷	3no	MVenezia	Audley Farm Stable	3.40
7 Aug76	2Sar7	Good and Bold	5 117	5	2	3⁴	2½	2³	2½	49½	EMaple	S Sommer	4.00
18 Aug76	7Sar8	Slaw	3 107	7	4	6²	6½	7	5²	5⁸	RD°g°diceJr5†	Betty Anne King	26.40
7 Aug76	1Sar9	Gene's Legacy	b4 106	6	6	5¹	5⁶	5¹½	6¹	66½	KWhitley7	Beau-G Stable	10.40
13 Aug76	3Sar2	Mister Breezy	4 113	3	1	1¹½	1½	3¹½	7	7	JCruguet‡	M M Garren	2.50

†Two pounds apprentice allowance waived. ‡Five pounds apprentice allowance waived.
OFF AT 2:05 EDT. Start good. Won handily. Time, :23⅗, :47, 1:11½, 1:36⅗, 1:50⅖. Track fast.

$2 Mutuel Prices:

2-TINGLE KING	12.80	5.80	4.20
3-O'REI II.		5.20	4.00
7-MYCERINUS			3.40

B. c, by Bold Legend—Miss Tingle, by Avant Garde. Trainer, Flint S. Schulhofer. Bred by D. Shaer (Md.).
TINGLE KING raced forwardly into the backstretch, took over while saving ground into the far turn and drew away while being mildly encouraged. O'REI II., never far back, finished well to be second best without menacing the winner. MYCERINUS, void of early foot, passed tired horses. GOOD AND BOLD, a factor to the stretch, tired. MISTER BREEZY stopped badly after showing speed to the far turn.
Overweight—Tingle King, 1.
Claiming Prices (in order of finish)—$10500, 10500, 12500, 12500, 12500, 10500, 10500.
Scratched—Campaigner.

Daily Double (7-2) Paid $56.60; Double Pool, $303,256; OTB Pool, $515,166.

THIRD RACE
Sar
August 21, 1976

6 FURLONGS. (1:08). CLAIMING. Purse $9,000. 3-year-olds and upward. 3-year-olds, 117 lbs.; older, 122 lbs. Non-winners of two races since Aug. 1 allowed 3 lbs.; of a race since then, 5 lbs. Claiming price, $20,000; 2 lbs. allowed for each $1,000 to $18,000. (Races when entered to be claimed for $16,000 or less not considered.)
Value to winner $5,400; second, $1,980; third, $1,080; fourth, $540.
Mutuel Pool, $157,960. Off-track betting, $94,849. Exacta Pool, $158,817. Off-track betting Exacta Pool, $231,460.

Last Raced	Horse	EqtAWt	PP	St	1/4	1/2	Str	Fin	Jockeys	Owners	Odds to $1
26 Apr76 6Aqu9	Gabilan	4 117	7	2	1h	12	15	13	EMaple	S Sommer	6.20
7 Aug76 2Sar2	Rare Joel	b4 117	1	7	71½	7½	6½	2h	JVelasquez	Elysa M Alibrandi	5.40
25 Jly76 3Aqu5	Snappy Chatter	b4 117	5	5	5h	41	2½	3¾	JAmy	May-Don Stable	8.80
7 Aug76 2Sar1	Commercial Pilot	b4 113	2	4	4½	52	3h	41¾	DMcHargue	Lovir Stable	6.50
10 Jly76 2Aqu6	Odds and Evens	5 108	8	8	8	6h	71½	53	RDelg'riceJr5	Colvie Stable	17.10
7 Aug76 4Sar2	Native Blend	b6 108	4	3	33	21	41	63	KWhitley7	Hobeau Farm	1.60
23 Jun76 7Bel9	Chaulky Long	b4 118	3´	6	65	8	8	72½	BBaeza	A Rosoff	4.40
7 Aug76 4Sar4	What A Lucky Star	b4 117	6	1	2½	32	51	8	PDay	J W LaCroix	14.90

OFF AT 2:45 EDT. Start good for all but ODDS AND EVENS. Won ridden out.
Time, :21⅘, :44⅗, 1:09⅘. Track fast.

$2 Mutuel Prices:

7-GABILAN	14.40	6.20	4.20
1-RARE JOEL		6.00	4.40
5-SNAPPY CHATTER			5.20

$2 EXACTA (7-1) PAID $89.60.

Dk. b. or br. c, by Penowa Rullah—Little Buzzy, by Royal Coinage. Trainer, Frank Martin. Bred by L. P. Sasso (Md.).

GABILAN sprinted clear approaching the stretch and, after opening a good lead, was ridden out to hold sway. RARE JOEL, void of early foot, finished full of run. SNAPPY CHATTER rallied from the outside entering the stretch, lugged in near the final furlong and continued on with good energy. COMMERCIAL PILOT split horses nearing midstretch but lacked the needed late response. ODDS AND EVENS broke in the air. NATIVE BLEND, a factor to the stretch, gave way. CHAULKY LONG was always outrun. WHAT A LUCKY STAR stopped badly after entering the stretch.
Overweight—Chaulky Long, 1.
Claiming Prices (in order of finish)—$20000, 20000, 20000, 18000, 18000, 19000, 20000, 20000.

FOURTH RACE
Sar
August 21, 1976

6 FURLONGS. (1:08). MAIDENS. SPECIAL WEIGHTS. Purse $9,000. Fillies and mares. 3-year-olds and upward. 3-year-olds, 117 lbs.; older, 122 lbs.
Value to winner $5,400; second, $1,980; third, $1,080; fourth, $540.
Mutuel Pool, $223,335.

Last Raced	Horse	EqtAWt	PP	St	1/4	1/2	Str	Fin	Jockeys	Owners	Odds to $1
	Love for Love	3 117	2	4	21	2½	22½	12	PDay	Rokeby Stable	1.10
13 Aug76 5Sar7	Solo Dance	3 117	1	3	72	71½	5½	2no	JVelasquez	Elmendorf	5.60
13 Aug76 5Sar8	Ready Again	b3 117	5	1	12	11	1h	31½	MVenezia	Dogwood Stable	21.10
13 Aug76 5Sar3	Cornish Pet	3 117	6	6	5½	3½	3½	4h	JCruguet	Verulam Farm	5.00
	Skater's Waltz	3 117	4	5	3½	41	61	5h	RCSmith	A G Vanderbilt	16.60
13 Aug76 5Sar2	Like for Like.	3 117	3	2	4½	51½	4½	6no	JARodriguez	Waldemar Farm	6.10
	Naivasha	3 110	8	8	61	8	71½	76¾	KWhitley7	King Ranch	28.50
13 Aug76 5Sar4	Artful Levee	3 117	7	7	8	6½	8	8	RLTurcotte	Whitney Stone	5.90

OFF AT 3:21½ EDT. Start good. Won handily. Time, :22⅗, :46⅘, 1:12⅕. Track fast.

$2 Mutuel Prices:

2-LOVE FOR LOVE	4.20	3.20	3.40
1-SOLO DANCE		4.80	4.40
5-READY AGAIN			6.40

Dk. b. or br. f, by Cornish Prince—Rare Exchange, by Swaps. Tr., Elliott Burch. Bred by Mellon Paul (Va.).
LOVE FOR LOVE prompted the pace into the stretch, took over from READY AGAIN just inside the final furlong and proved clearly best under confident handling. SOLO DANCE, eased back along the inside early, finished well to gain the place. READY AGAIN saved ground while making the pace and weakened under pressure. CORNISH PET made a bid from the outside leaving the turn but hung. SKATER'S WALTZ, between horses much of the way, lacked a late response. LIKE FOR LIKE rallied along the inside leaving the turn but failed to sustain her bid. ARTFUL LEVEE failed to be a serious factor.

I must confess that I was not at Saratoga on August 21, 1976. I was home writing this book. In fact, I missed the entire Saratoga meeting, which is something I'd rather not do again. Saratoga is a special place, a racetrack where the trees outnumber the people, where the best of racing is on display for twenty-four glorious summer days. Oh, it gets hot in Saratoga Springs. Very hot. But with a track bias like the one you just got a peek at, with races and bets like the one you are about to contemplate, a good player will tell time by the coming of the Saratoga season. Frankly, I've enjoyed the experience of writing this book—I might even do another. But I'll be damned if I ever do one during August again.

6th Saratoga

AUGUST 21, 1976

1¼ MILES. (2:01). 107th running TRAVERS. SCALE WEIGHTS. $100,000 added. 3-year-olds. Weight, 126 lbs. By subscription of $200 each, which shall accompany the nomination; $500 to start, with $100,000 added. The added money and all fees to be divided: 60% to the winner, 22% to second, 12% to third, and 6% to fourth. The winner shall have his name inscribed on the Man o' War Cup and a gold plated replica will be presented to the owner. Trophies will also be presented to the winning trainer and jockey. Closed with 22 nominations.

McKenzie Bridge 126

B. c (1973), by Le Fabuleux—Nanticious, by Nantallah.
Breeder, Carver Stable (Ky.).   1976.. 9 2 1 1 $82,566
Owner, Mrs. Douglas Carver. Trainer, J. S. Dunn.   1975.. 4 1 1 0 $9,626

11 Aug76	8Sar	1¼ :46¹¹:103¹:484gd	3	114	10¹⁷ 96¾ 42½ 4³	McHeDM⁶	AlwS 88	FatherHogan114 DanceSpell 10
27 Jun76	8Hol	1¼ :45²¹:093¹:591ft	5½	114	9¹² 66½ 5⁶ 5⁹¼	McHeDG⁵	AlwS 86	MajsticLight114 CrystlWatr 9
5 Jun76	7Bel	1¼ :47 1:11¹2:29 ft	6½	126	9²² 7¹² 37½ 2ⁿᵏ	McHgeD²	ScwS 75	BoldForbes126 McKzeBrdge 10
24 May76	7Bel	1-½ :46²¹:104¹:423ft	3	113	77½ 6⁶ 5¹½ 12½	VasquezJ⁷	Alw 89	McKnzieBridge113 FthrHgn 7
2 May76	6Hol	⑦ 1⅛ :47¹¹:124¹:424fm	3-2	118	5⁵ 21½ 54½ 53¾	ShoakerW⁶	Alw 81	Delta Junction 121 Lean To 6
17 Apr76	8Hol	1⅛ :46 1:093¹:482ft	152	122	9¹³ 7⁸ 66¼ 44½	AlvarezF⁹	SpwS 85	CrystalWater122 Life'sHope 11
28 Mar76	8SA	1⅛ :46 1:10¹1:48 ft	16	120	8¹³ 9⁹ 9¹⁵ 9²¹	HawleyS⁶	SpwS 71	An Act 120 Double Discount 9
17 Mar76	8SA	1⅛ :47¹¹:114¹:484ft	3-2	^118	8¹² 63½ 5⁵ 36¾	ShakerW³	SpwS 81	June's Blazer 118 Pindoro 8
24 Jan76	6SA	1-¹⁄₁₆ :45⁴¹:104¹:43 ft	3½	114	4¹⁰ 4¹ 2h 1⁴	ShoakerW⁷	Alw 87	McKenzieBrdge114 Spoonwd 7
2 Nov75	8SA	1-¹⁄₁₆ :46¹¹:104¹:433ft	21	118	8⁸ 86½ 6⁷ 56¾	OlivresF⁷	SpwS 77	Telly'sPop118 Imcrnishprnce 8
25 Oct75	6SA	6½ f :21⁴ :444¹:16¹ft	4½	118	7¹⁰ 4⁵ 4²½ 24¾	ToroF¹	Alw 87	PntedWgn115 McKnzieBdge 7

Aug 19 Sar 4f ft :48¾b   Aug 10 Sar 4f sy :50½b   Aug 5 Sar 4f ft :49b

Quiet Little Table 126

Gr. g (1973), by Mr. Leader—Grey Table, by Grey Sovereign.
Breeder, Meadowhill (Ky.).   1976 9 5 1 2 $104,781
Owner, Meadowhill. Trainer, P. G. Johnson.   1975 1 1 0 0 $6,000

11 Aug76	8Sar	1¼ :46¹¹:103¹:484gd	2½	^123	57½ 3¹ 6³½ 68¾	Maple⁸	AlwS 82	FatherHogan114 DanceSpell 10
10 Jly 76	8Aqu	1¼ :46⁴¹:36¹¹:49 ft	2½	^111	2h 1½ 1⁵ 12½	Maple⁷	HcpS 90	Quiet Lttle Tble 111 Sir Lstr 8
30 Jun76	8Aqu	1 :45¹¹:084¹:341ft	2	114	3² 5¹¾ 3² 3¹½	TurctteR¹	AlwS 93	Dance Spell 114 Zen 6
5 Jun76	8Bel	1-¹⁄₁₆ :45²¹:10 1:421ft	4½	119	1½ 1½ 1⁴ 12¾	Maple⁴	Alw 91	QuietLittleTable119 KirbyLe 7
26 May76	6Bel	1⅛ :46 1:103¹:491ft	3½	112	2⁴ 2¹½ 1h 1ⁿᵏ	Maple⁴	Alw 81	QuietLittleTable112 Christn 5
17 May76	5Bel	1 :45³¹:094¹:351ft	4-5	^115	22½ 2¹½ 11½ 1³	Maple⁵	Alw 92	QuietLittleTble115 RdAnchr 8
10 May76	6Bel	1-¹⁄₁₆ :46 1:10 1:42³ft	6	111	2½ 1h 2½ 2²	Maple⁸	Alw 87	Sawbones110 QuietLttleTble 8
20 Apr76	5Aqu	1 :45¹¹:45¹¹:101ft	1	^110	4² 4⁵ 3⁴ 11¾	Maple⁴	Alw 92	QuietLittleTble110 Balancer 7
10 Apr76	5Aqu	6 f :22³ :46¹¹:104ft	3½	^117	4⁴ 4⁴ 44½ 33½	Maple⁵	Alw 86	Bonge 117 Distinctively 9
5 Oct75	5Bel	6 f :23 :46³¹:114ft	2	122	3½ 2h 1½ 1²	CstedaM²	Mdn 83	Quie¹LittleTable122 PvtThts 9

Aug 18 Sar 6f ft 1:12¾h   Aug 5 Sar 1¹⁄₁₆m ft 1:53¾b   July 26 Bel 6f ft 1:14½h

Majestic Light 126

B. c (1973), by Majestic Prince—Irradiate, by Ribot.
Breeder, O. M. Phipps (Ky.).   1976..13 6 1 3 $229,123
Owner, Ogden M. Phipps. Trainer, John Russell.   1975.. 7 1 0 2 $8,400

7 Aug76	8Mth	1⅛ :46 1:10 1:47 ft	5½	122	7¹² 5⁴ 1½ 1⁶	HawleyS³	InvH 105	MajesticLight122 Appssnato 10
18 Jly 76	8Hol	⑦ 1⅛ :48 1:12 1:481fm	2	^121	78½ 6⁴ 2½ 1¹	HawleyS⁵	HcpS 95	MajesticLight121 L'Heureux 10
4 Jly 76	6AP	⑦ 1⅛ :48¹¹:122¹:491fm	2½	121	10⁹ 85½ 3² 3¹½	CrdoAJr¹	HcpS 89	Ffth Mrine 121 Mjstic Lght 11
27 Jun76	8Hol	1¼ :45²¹:093¹:591ft	20	114	7¹⁰ 5⁴ 3¹½ 13½	HawleyS⁷	AlwS 95	MajesticLight114 CrystlWatr 9
5 Jun76	7Bel	1¼ :47 1:11¹2:29 ft	14	126	6¹⁶ 59½ 4¹² 4⁹	VelasqzJ⁶	ScwS 66	BoldForbes126 McKzeBrdge 10
15 May76	8GS	⑦ 1 :431fm	6½	117	9¹⁵ 79½ 5¹¾ 1½	BarreraC⁷	Alw 75	Majestic Light 117 Chati 12
5 May76	8GS	⑦ 1 :393fm	2½	115	75½ 6⁴ 41½ 1³½	BarreraC⁷	Alw 75	MajsticLight115 NobleAdml 8
16 Apr76	5Aqu	1 :46¹¹:102¹:36 ft	27	117	8⁹ 7¹⁰ 7¹⁰ 6⁹	BaezaB⁶	Alw 77	BestLaidPlns119 Resilient 9
11 Mar76	8Aqu	1 :46⁴¹:12 1:371sy	5	113	2½ 2¹½ 33½ 58½	CrdoAJr²	Alw 72	Be-A-Son 113 Cabriolet II. 6
28 Feb76	6Aqu	1 :48²¹:133¹:391ft	7-5	^117	3¹ 2h 1h 11½	CordoAJr⁶	Alw 70	MajesticLight117 Resilient 6
20 Feb76	8Aqu	1 :46³¹:113¹:372ft	6-5	^119	6⁸ 4⁶ 4⁴ 31½	CordoAJr³	Alw 78	Kupper 115 Distinctively 8

Aug 17 Sar 7f ft 1:26b

Honest Pleasure 126

Dk. b. or br. c (1973), by What a Pleasure—Tularia, by Tulyar.
Breeder, Waldemar Farms, Inc. (Fla.).

Owner, B. R. Firestone. Trainer, LeRoy Jolley.

| | | | | | | | | 1976 | 8 | 4 | 2 | 1 | $229,172 |
| | | | | | | | | 1975 | 8 | 6 | 2 | 0 | $370,227 |

7 Aug76	8Mth	1¼ :46 1:10 1:47 ft	1 ▲126	2¹½ 11½ 2½	3⁶	PerretC⁴	InvH 99 MajesticLight122 Appssnato 10
27 Jly 76	8Mth	1¼ :46 1:10 1:41¹ft 1-10 ▲115	13½ 11½ 2h	2¹½	BaezaB1	Alw 97 PeppyAddy119 HonestPlsure 6
15 May76	8Pim	1¾ :45 1:09 1:55 ft 4-5 ▲126	2² 2² 4²	57¼	BaezaB⁶	ScwS 87 Elocutionist126 Play theRed 6
1 May76	8CD	1¼ :4541:10²2:01³ft 2-5 ▲126	2⁵ 2½ 2½	2¹	BaezaB⁵	ScwS 88 BoldForbes126 HonestPlesre 9
22 Apr76	7Kee	1¼ :48 1:12 31:49²ft 1-10 ▲121	14 1⁵ 1²	11½	BaezaB²	SpwS 90 HontPlease121 CertnRoman 7
3 Apr76	9GP	1¼ :4641:10³1:47⁴ft 1-20 ▲122	1³ 1³ 13	1³	BaezaB³	AlwS 95 HonestPlsre12 GrtContrctr 6
28 Feb76	9Hia	1¼ :4541:09 1:46⁴ft 1-3 ▲122	12 18 18	111	BaezaB⁷	ScwS 98 HonestPleasure122 IncaRoca 8
11 Feb76	Hia	7 f :23 :4521:22²ft	122 11 14	110 114	BaezaB⁴	AlwS 93 HonestPlease122 ParcForiln 4
Exhibition race; no wagering.
1 Nov75	8Lrl	1¼ :4541:10³1:42⁴ft 1-5 ▲122	11 13 11½	12½	BaezaB³	ScwS 94 HonestPlasure122 Whtsyrple 7
18 Oct75	8Bel	1 :45 1:10¹1:36²sy 6-5 ▲122	1½ 11½ 15	1⁷	BaezaB⁹	ScwS 86 HonestPleasre122 DnceSpell 14
8 Oct75	8Bel	7 f :224 :4521:22³ft	2½ 121 13	14 15 18	BaezaB⁷	AlwS 89 HnestPlsre121 Whtsyrplsure 7
	Aug 19 Sar 4f ft :46½h		Aug 14 Sar 7f ft 1:25h			

Romeo 126

B. c (1973), by T. V. Lark—Gallizzie, by Tiger Wander.
Breeder, P. Madden (Ky.).

Owner, Mary Lou Cashman. Trainer, Paul Adwell.

| | | | | | | | 1976 | 17 | 3 | 2 | 3 | $53,760 |

7 Aug76	7AP	⑦ 1¹ₑ :4741:1241:44¹fm	9 114 12¹⁰ 74½ 7¹⁰ 8¹¹	GavdiaW²	HcpS 77 Effervescing113 Rule theRge 13
29 Jly 76	9AP	1¹ₑ :4711:1121:42¹sy 6-5 ▲115	4¹ 2¹ 1½ 1¾	GavidiaW⁶	Alw 101 Romeo 115 Auberge 7
17 Jly 76	6AP	1¹ₑ :4811:1211:434fm 2½ 115 45½ 2¹ 31½ 43½	GavidiaW⁷	Alw 87 NatvePraise117 Fightmaster 9
4 Jly 76	6AP	⑦ 1½ :4811:1221:491fm 12e 111 34 32 68 69½	SnyderL⁹	HcpS 81 Ffth Mrine 121 Mjstic Lght 11
27 Jun76	8Hol	1½ :4521:09³1:59¹ft 8⅜ 115 37 43½ 45½ 49½	PincyLJr⁸	AlwS 86 MajesticLight114 Crystl Wtr 9
13 Jun76	8Hol	1½ :4631:10³1:47²ft 31 115 68 53 32 2²	Vergra07	HcpS 93 L'Heureux 119 Romeo 7
23 May76	5Hol	⑦ 1½ :4641:1121:423fm 7½ 118 74 41½ 2½ 1no	Vergara07	Alw 86 Romeo 118 Electric Flag 12
7 May76	2Hol	⑦ 1½ :4831:1231:431fm 2 ▲120 43 32 42 43½	McHgeDG⁹	Alw 79 PrinceBoynton115 GasEnrgy 9
25 Apr76	9Hol	⑦ 1¹ₑ :4721:1141:424fm 9 120 64½ 53 53 34½	Vergara05	Alw 80 Today n'Tmrrw117 HdnWrld 10
17 Apr76	5Hol	⑦ 1¹ₑ :4731:1131:43 fm 7½ 120 42 52½ 33 35½	Vergara09	Alw 78 DeltaJnctn120 Tody n'Tmrw 12
	Aug 18 Sar 5f ft 1:00h	July 28 AP 3f ft :37b			

El Portugues ✳ 126

Ch. c (1973), by Gallant Romeo—Miss Swoon, by Swoon's Son.
Breeder, Copelan & Thornbury (Ky.).

Owner, E. Ubarri. Trainer, Lazaro S. Barrera.

| | | | | | | | 1976 .20 | 2 | 6 | 2 | $66,593 |
| | | | | | | | 1975 . 1 M | 0 | 0 | | $152 |

11 Aug76	8Sar	1¼ :4611:10³1:484gd 4½ 114 6¹¹ 5² 3½ 3³	CrdoAJr⁷	AlwS 88 FatherHogan114 DanceSpell 10
31 Jly 76	8Aqu	⑦ 1¼ :4721:1121:492fm 8 1.12 38½ 5¹⁰ 59½ 69½	VelasqzJ⁵	HcpS Mcdred 117 Dream 'n BeLky 7
7 Jly 76	8Pim	1¼ :4631:1041:484ft 7½e 110 76 58 53½ 43½	VelezRl⁴	HcpS 89 AmericanTradr109 OnTheSly 7
4 Jly 76	6AP	1¼ :4811:1221:491fm 15 114 76¾ 74½ 9¹¹ 9¹⁰	GvidiaW¹⁰	HcpS 81 Ffth Mrine 121· Mjstic Lght 11
27 Jun76	10Tdn	1½ :46 1:10³1:494ft 5½e 112 53½ 3¹ 31 43	VelezRl¹⁴	AlwS 88 Return of a Native115 Cojak 14
4 Jun76	8Bel	1 :47 1:1131:434ft 3-5 ▲110 52½ 33 33 23¾	CordroAJr¹	Alw 79 Brown Cat 117 El Portugues 6
23 May76	8Bel	1 :4531:10¹1:36 ft 8-5 ▲116 64½ 53 51½ 2½†	CrdoAJr⁶	AlwS 87 Sir Lister114 El Portugues 9
	†Disqualified and placed third.
8 May76	8Bel	1 :4531:10 1:35 ft 8½ 126 67 54 2² 2½	CrdoAJr²	ScwS 92 Sonkisser 126 El Portugues 6
1 May76	6Aqu	1 :45 1:09 1:343sy 5½ 110 53½ 45½ 38 28½	AmyJ⁷	Alw 84 Cinteelo 104 El Portugues 7
14 Apr76	6Aqu	1 :4521:09 1:35 ft 9½ 113 58½ 57½ 56½ 54¾	VelasquzJ³	Alw 86 NewCllection112 Cplet'sSng 7
	June 24 Tdn 5f ft 1:02b				

Legendaire 126

Ch. c (1973), by Le Fabuleux—Native Guide, by Raise a Native.
Breeder, W. P. Little (Ky.).

Owner, Silk Willoughby Farm. Trainer, J. P. Conway.

| | | | | | | | 1976 . . 8 | 2 | 1 | 0 | $15,157 |
| | | | | | | | 1975 . . 4 | 1 | 0 | 0 | $5,400 |

11 Aug76	8Sar	1¼ :4611:10³1:484gd 19 114· 9¹⁶10⁸¾ 98¾ 7¹⁰	TurctteR⁴	AlwS 81 FatherHogan114 DanceSpell 10
31 Jly 76	6Aqu	⑦ 1¼ :4721:12 1:50 fm 11 112 33 1h 66½ 63¾	TurctteR¹	HcpS FabledMonrch114 Effrvscing 8
20 Jly 76	6Aqu	1¼ :4641:3611:49 ft 9 112 67½ 7¹¹ 7¹⁶ 7¹⁵	VasquxJ⁴	HcpS 75 Quiet Lttle Tble 111 Sir Lstr 8
26 Jun76	8Bel	1¹ₑ :4621:11 1:42 ft 6 113 74½ 3¹ 1¹ 12½	VasquezJ²	Alw 92 Legendaire113 RedAnchor 7
3 Apr76	7Kee	1¹ₑ :4711:1111:431ft 7 113 63½ 69 6¹² 6²⁰	BrumfldD⁵	Alw 70 No Link 121 Inca Roca 6
24 Mar76	8GP	⑦ a 1 1:39 fm 6 116 89½ 63½ 53¾ 44†	MarquzC⁵	Alw 82 Hall ofRean114 Fightmaster 10
	†Placed third through disqualification.
6 Mar76	6GP	1¹ₑ :4721:1121:434ft 2½ ▲122 45 33 2½ 1¾	RuaneJ⁵	Alw 82 Legendaire122 ArchieBmish 11
26 Feb76	7Hia	7 f :4531:4611:24 ft 62 115 10⁹ 66 31½ 2nk	MapleE³	Alw 85 Sonkisser 122 Legendaire 11
21 Nov75	7Aqu	1 :4441:0841:344sy 11 122 9¹⁸ 9³⁰ 9³² 9⁴⁰	CastandaK⁵	Alw 52 Cinteelo 117 Play the Red 9
	Aug 17 Sar 1 ft 1:43b	Aug 10 Sar 3f sy :36b	Aug 7 Sar 5f ft 1:07b		

Dance Spell 126

B. c (1973), by Northern Dancer—Obeah, by Cyane.
Breeder, Christiana Stables (Ky.).

Owner, Christiana Stables. Trainer, J. W. Maloney.

| | | | | | | | 1976 . . 7 | 3 | 1 | 1 | $72,702 |
| | | | | | | | 1975 . 10 | 2 | 6 | 1 | $93,846 |

11 Aug76	8Sar	1¼ :4611:10³1:484gd 3½e 121 2⁵ 1¹ 1h 2¹	VasquzJ⁵	AlwS 90 FatherHogan114 DanceSpell 10
20 Jly 76	8Aqu	1¼ :4641:3611:49 ft 3½ 117 3¹ 2½ 3³⅓	CrdoAJr⁸	HcpS 87 Quiet Lttle Tble 111 Sir Lstr 8
30 Jun76	8Aqu	1 :4511:0841:341ft 3½e 114 1½ 1¹ 12 1¹⅓	CdroAJr³	AlwS 95 Dance Spell 114 Zen 9
12 Jun76	6Bel	6 f :223 :4531:093ft 2¾ 112 2¹½ 32 68 6¹¹	CruguetJ³	Alw 83 QueenCityLd115 VlidAppeal 6
8 May76	8Bel	1 :4531:10 1:35 ft 1 ▲126 2½ 2½ 44 49	CruguetJ³	ScwS 84 Sonkisser 126 El Portugues 6
8 Apr76	8Aqu	7 f :224 :4541:22 ft 2½ 110 2¹½ 2¹½ 11½ 12½	CruguetJ¹	Alw 91 DanceSpll 110 GabeBnzur 7
31 Mar76	7Aqu	7 f :23 :4541:22³ft 8-5 ▲111 3¹½ 1h 1½ 1½	CruguetJ³	Alw 88 DanceSpel 111 Kohoutek 7
4 Nov75	8Aqu	1¼ :4631:10¹1:49¹ft 9½ ▲113 35 31½ 22½ 2½	CrugutJ¹⁰	AlwS 88 Hang Ten 116 Dance Spell 12
19 Nov75	8Aqu	6 f :221 :4511:094ft 2½ 115 2¹½ 2h 22½ 2²½	CruguetJ³	AlwS 92 LordHenribee117 DanceSpell 6
1 Nov75	8Lrl	1¹ₑ :4541:10³1:424ft 7½ 122 31½ 33½ 33½ 3⁶	CruguetJ⁷	SpwS 93 HonestPlsre122 Whatsyrplse 7
	Aug 20 Sar 3f ft :36b	Aug 17 Sar 5f ft :58⅔h	Aug 8 Sar 5f sy 1:02⅕b		

While it's not necessary to handicap this prestigious stakes race in depth to select Honest Pleasure as a front-running stickout, I am also including (below) the chart of the Monmouth Invitational, the race Majestic Light won over Honest Pleasure by six lengths. The Trackman's comments clearly show that Honest Pleasure was regaining his early season form.

Leroy Jolley wisely stopped on Honest Pleasure after the Preakness debacle (May 15) and was patiently reestablishing the horse's speed and staying power. The recent workouts indicate further progress.

Majestic Light is a slow-breaking, fast-closing three-year-old that appreciates true distance racing. Trainer John Russell has done an excellent job, and there is very little doubt that Majestic Light is fit enough or good enough to win. Thus, a good performance, despite the bias, is possible; however, it's not likely. Much depends on whether Majestic Light can get clear sailing on the rail for an uninterrupted rally. Unfortunately, he will need an unusual degree of co-operation from the rest of the field to get that kind of running room. Finally, he will still have to run faster than Honest Pleasure, who is on the improve and likely to have the rail and the lead for the entire race!

Quiet Little Table, a well-managed speed horse, would have a fine winning chance in any good field. But with Honest Pleasure in the race, Quiet Little Table has virtually no chance at all. It is further doubtful that he has enough speed to stop Honest Pleasure from getting a clear lead over the field in the run to the first turn. That's important for two reasons: (1) most front-running types tend to race better when they are able to relax in front of the pack; (2) everything in Honest Pleasure's record says he is a horse that improves dramatically when he is able to make the lead without undue stress.

Dance Spell has generally good form and cannot be completely eliminated.

The shipper Romeo is a stretch runner that has never beaten a good field.

EIGHTH RACE	1⅛ MILES. (1:48). Ninth running MONMOUTH INVITATIONAL HANDICAP. Purse $100,000. 3-year-olds. by invitation only, with no nomination or starting fees. The winner to receive $65,000, with $20,000 to second; $10,000 to third; and $5,000 to fourth. A representative field of those weighted will be invited to participate. The Monmouth Park Jockey Club reserves the right to reassign weight to any horse after the release of the weights. Owner of the winner to receive a trophy.
Mth	
August 7, 1976	

Value to winner $65,000; second, $20,000; third, $10,000; fourth, $5,000. Mutuel Pool, $349,197.

Last Raced	Horse	EqtAWt	PP	St	¼	½	¾	Str	Fin	Jockeys	Owners	Odds to $1
18 Jly 76 8Hol¹	Majestic Light	3 122	3	2	7²	7²	5½¼	1½	1⁶	SHawley	O M Phipps	5.30
31 Jly 76 8Aqu⁵	Appasionato	3 113	7	9	9½¼	9²	9²	5½¼	2ⁿᵒ	RHernandez	F A Luro	27.10
27 Jly 76 8Mth²	Honest Pleasure	3 126	4	1	2²	2⁴	11½	22½	3½	CPerrtt	B R Firestone	1.10
17 Jly 76 8Pim³	Zen	3 118	6	7	6ʰ	5½¼	4½	3³	42½	JVasquez	Pen-Y-Bryn Farm	3.10
25 Jly 76 8Del¹	On The Sly	3 115	2	8	8⁷	8⁶	8⁶	4²	5½¼	GMcCarron	Balmak Stable	6.00
31 Jly 76 8Aqu²	Dream 'N Be Lucky	3 114	5	10	10	10	10	7⁵	6⁶	MSolomone	G A Zimmerman	33.00
17 Jly 76 8Mth⁶	Wardlaw	b3 115	1	3	3ʰ	32½	3²	6ʰ	7⁴	JTejeira	D Lasater	39.30
27 Jly 76 7Mth¹	Best Bee	b3 113	10	6	5½¼	6½¼	7½	8⁴	8⁶	RWilson	Dixiana	65.10
31 Jly 76 7Aks²	Joachim	b3 117	8	5	42½	4¹	6²	9ʰ	9ʰ	SMaple	E Pratt-J C Van Berg	18.90
17 Jly 76 8Pim¹	American Trader	b3 114	9	4	1³	11½	2ʰ	10	10	AAgnello	Mrs B Cohen	19.60

OFF AT 5:57 EDT. Start good. Won driving. Time, :22⅗, :46, 1:10, 1:34⅗, 1:47 (new track record). Track fast.

4–HONEST PLEASURE	2.80

B. c, by Majestic Prince—Irradiate, by Ribot. Trainer, J. W. Russell. Bred by O. M. Phipps (Ky.).

$2 Mutuel Prices:

3–MAJESTIC LIGHT	12.60	6.80	4.20
7–APPASIONATO		19.40	6.20

MAJESTIC LIGHT, taken in hand after the start, angled to the outside leaving the clubhouse turn, remained outside when roused under a flurry of right-handed whipping at the far turn, brushed lightly with ZEN on the stretch turn but continued strongly to gain the lead in the upper stretch, swerved out when struck left-handed at the eighth-pole but continued to draw off with authority and was under only mild encouragement in the final seventy yards. APPASIONATO, outrun for three-quarters, rallied gamely outside the leaders when roused for the drive but could not threaten the winner. HONEST PLEASURE, reserved off the early pace outside AMERI-CAN TRADER, moved willingly to the lead when asked at the far turn, resisted the winner gamely in the stretch but hung in the closing yards. ZEN rallied just inside MAJESTIC LIGHT at the far turn, brushed with that one but finished with good courage. ON THE SLY did not reach contention with a mild closing rally. JOACHIM and AMERICAN TRADER were finished after three-quarters.
Overweight—Dream 'N Be Lucky, 1 pound.

In summary, what we have here is a fit front-running racehorse of obvious quality getting a track he should absolutely relish. The betting crowd made the wrong favorite.

SIXTH RACE	1¼ MILES. (2:01). 107th running TRAVERS. SCALE WEIGHTS. $100,000 added. 3-year-olds. Weight, 126 lbs. By subscription of $200 each, which shall accompany the nomination; $500 to start, with $100,000 added. The added money and all fees to be divided: 60% to the winner, 22% to second, 12% to third, and 6% to fourth. The winner shall have his name inscribed on the Man o' War Cup and a gold plated replica will be presented to the owner. Trophies will also be presented to the winning trainer and jockey. Closed with 22 nominations.
Sar	
August 21, 1976	

Value of race $108,400. Value to winner $65,040; second, $23,848; third, $13,008; fourth, $6,504.
Mutuel Pool, $328,104. Off-track betting, $342,517.

Last Raced	Horse	EqtAWt	PP	¼	½	¾	1	Str	Fin	Jockeys	Owners	Odds to $1
7 Aug76 8Mth³	Honest Pleasure	3 126	4	1²	1⁶	1⁴	1²	1³	1⁴	CPerret	B R Firestone	2.10
7 Aug76 7AP⁸	Romeo	b3 126	5	51½5½1	5¹	4¹	2ʰ	2¹½	BBaeza	Mary L Cashman	49.30
11 Aug76 8Sar²	Dance Spell	3 126	8	4¹	4¹	3½¼	3½	3¹	3³	JCruguet	Christiana Stable	14.70
11 Aug76 8Sar⁶	Quiet Little Table	3 126	2	3¹	3½¼	2¹	2⁷½	4²	4ⁿᵏ	EMaple	Meadowhill	12.50
11 Aug76 6Sar³	El Portugues	b3 126	6	2¹	2ʰ	4½¼	5½	5½	5¹½	JVelasquez	E Ubarri	23.60
11 Aug76 8Sar⁴	McKenzie Bridge	3 126	1	8	7½	7³	7½²	7²⁴	6³	DMcHargue	Mrs D Carter	4.60
7 Aug76 8Mth¹	Majestic Light	3 126	3	7½	6½¼	6²	6¹½	6½	7³⁰	SHawley	O M Phipps	1.00
11 Aug76 8Sar⁷	Legendaire	b3 126	7	6ʰ	8	8	8	8	8	RTurcotte	Silk Willoughby Fm	64.40

OFF AT 4:34 EDT. Start good. Won ridden out. Time, :23⅖, :46⅖, 1:10⅖, 1:35, 2:00⅕ (new track record). Track fast.

$2 Mutuel Prices:

4–HONEST PLEASURE	6.20	5.00	4.20
5–ROMEO	2	.1 00	6.80
8–DANCE SPELL			5.40

Dk. b. or br. c, by What a Pleasure—Tularia, by Tlyar. Trainer, LeRoy Jolley. Bred by Waldemar Farms, Inc. (Fla.).

HONEST PLEASURE dropped over to save ground after outrunning QUIET LITTLE TABLE into the turn, quickly opened a long lead, made the pace while going easily, was roused soon after entering the stretch and drew away under a hand ride. ROMEO, unhurried early, rallied along the inside leaving the far turn and finished with good energy to be second best. DANCE SPELL, reserved early while saving ground, moved outside QUIET LITTLE TABLE to launch a bid at the far turn, raced forwardly into the stretch but weakened during the drive. QUIET LITTLE TABLE, well placed early, went after HONEST PLEASURE approaching the stretch but had nothing left for the drive. EL PORTUGUES, hustled along after the start, was finished approaching the end of the backstretch. McKENZIE BRIDGE was never close. MAJESTIC LIGHT, void of early foot, was sent up outside horses midway of the far turn but lacked a further response. LEGENDAIRE wasn't able to keep pace.

As a footnote to the Travers result chart, you might be interested to know that Dance Spell—the colt that moved outside to launch his bid against the Saratoga bias—came back to win the Jerome Mile in his next start, paying $17.60. That price was inflated by Dance Spell's number-one post position, generally interpreted by most Belmont fans as an unfavorable post. I can well understand that interpretation because the rail is usually dead at Belmont during the fall meeting. Nevertheless, it is my experience with track biases that logic still prevails in such conditions.

A dead rail only eliminates horses that race on the dead rail.

A front runner breaking from post one should be automatically downgraded if not eliminated under such conditions.

A stretch runner breaking from post one may have to give up a length or two at the start. That of course is frequently reason enough to eliminate many stretch runners.

Horses like Dance Spell—those that have tractable speed, speed that frequently permits maneuverability—may yet get trapped along the rail if the jockey is not alert. That's a smaller risk factor, but it cannot be overlooked. Several issues must be balanced against that risk:

How superior is the horse breaking from post one?
How many horses figure to break with him?

How good is the jockey?

Have most of the riders been breaking toward the outside in order to avoid the rail, thus leaving post one with room to maneuver?

What kind of odds are available for the risk?

In my judgment, a set of encouraging answers to these questions, especially to the first and last questions, would suggest buying into the risk.

EIGHTH RACE
Bel
Septemb'r 6, 1976

1 MILE. (1:33⅗). One hundred and seventh running JEROME HANDICAP. $100,000 added. 3-year-olds. By subscription of $100 each, which shall accompany the nomination; $500 to start, with $100,000 added. The added money and fees to be divided: 60% to the winner, 22% to second, 12% to third and 6% to fourth. Trophies will be presented to the winning owner, trainer and jockey. Closed with 30 nominations.

Value of race $111,000. Value to winner $66,600; second, $24,420; third, $13,320; fourth, $6,660.
Mutuel Pool, $560,376. Off-track betting, $193,704.

Last Race	Horse	EqtAWt	PP	St	¼	½	¾	Str	Fin	Jockeys	Owners	Odds to $1
21 Aug76 ⁶Sar³	Dance Spell	3 117	1	4	3½	2½	1¹	1½	13¾	RHernandez	Christiana Stable	7.80
30 Aug76 ⁶Bel³	Soy Numero Uno	3 117	7	2	4½	4¹	31½	31½	2ⁿᵒ	PDay	Strapro Stable	3.00
26 Aug76 ⁸Sar¹	Clean Bill	3 112	5	10	1¹	1²	2ʰ	2¹	3²	JImparato	Tartan Stable	30.60
19 Aug76 ⁸Mth³	Full Out	3 116	4	1	5ʰ	5ʰ	4½	4ⁿᵏ	DMontoya	Buckland Farm	61.90
17 Jly 76 ⁸Rkm⁶	Life's Hope	3 117	3	7	7½	6½	4½	5½	5ʰ	MSolomone	Harbor View Farm	31.50
21 Aug76 ⁶Sar⁴	Quiet Little Table	3 117	2	3	2ʰ	3½	6¹	6½	6³	EMaple	Meadowhill	7.20
18 Aug76 ⁶Sar¹	Sawbones	3 113	10	8	10	9½	81½	7¹	7¾	HGustines	Greentree Stable	5.20
18 Aug76 ⁸Mth²	Sonkisser	3 122	6	6	6½	7ʰ	9½	9¹	8ʰ	BBaeza	H I Snyder	3.10
30 Aug76 ⁶Bel²	Kirby Lane	3 112	8	5	81½	81	7½	8½	9½	ACorderoJr	Gedney Farms	6.30
11 Aug76 ⁸Sar¹	Father Hogan	b3 115	9	9	9ʰ	10	10	10	10	MVenezia	Sea Spray Farms	8.00

Uncoupled for betting purposes: LIFE'S HOPE and KIRBY LANE.

OFF AT 5:53½ EDT. Start good. Won driving. Time, :23⅗, :46⅗, 1:10⅗, 1:35. Track fast.

$2 Mutuel Prices:

1-DANCE SPELL	17.60	7.60	4.60
7-SOY NUMERO UNO		6.00	3.60
5-CLEAN BILL			9.00

B. c, by Northern Dancer—Obeah, by Cyane. Trainer, James W. Maloney. Bred by Christiana Stable (Ky.).

DANCE SPELL, away in good order, moved to the fore when ready while racing well out in the track approaching the stretch and drew away under brisk handling while continuing wide. SOY NUMERO UNO, reserved behind the early leaders, made a bid while racing wide nearing the stretch, lugged in slightly approaching the final furlong and was just up for the place. A foul claim against SOY NUMERO UNO by the rider of FULL OUT, for alleged interference through the stretch, was not allowed. CLEAN BILL, off slowly, rushed through along the rail to take over before going a quarter, remained a factor to midstretch and weakened. FULL OUT, never far back, remained a factor into the stretch but lacked a late response while drifting out. LIFE'S HOPE made a mild bid along the inside nearing the turn but hung. QUIET LITTLE TABLE tired from his early efforts. SAWBONES, outrun early, was sent up between horses leaving the far turn but failed to be a serious factor. SONKISSER, steadied along while in close quarters between horses approaching the end of the backstretch, lacked a further response. KIRBY LANE failed to seriously menace while racing very wide. FATHER HOGAN showed nothing.

Scratched—Fighting Bill.

Dance Spell's next start was in Forego's Woodward Stakes on September 18. Honest Pleasure was also in the field, making his first start since the Travers. Honest Pleasure drew the rail, Dance Spell the extreme outside post in a ten-horse field. There was really no betting issue involved. Forego was a stickout with a tempting 1–1 price, considering his tendency to go off at 1–2. But there is just no margin for profit or error playing horses at those odds.

Because of the post position draw, the second-best horse looked convincingly like Dance Spell; the third choice depended on how much post one would actually cost Honest Pleasure. As the chart below indicates, the Woodward was no less formful than the other two races we have examined in this series of Saratoga-Belmont stakes races.

EIGHTH RACE
Bel
Sept'ber 18, 1976

1⅛ MILES (chute). (1:45⅗). Twenty-third running WOODWARD HANDICAP. $150,000 added. 3-year-olds and upward. By subscription of $100 each, which shall accompany the nomination; $500 to pass the entry box, $1,500 to start, with $150,000 added. The added money and all fees to be divided 60% to the winner, 22% to second, 12% to third and 6% to fourth. Mrs. William Woodward has donated a trophy to be presented to the owner of the winner and trophies will also be presented to the winning trainer and jockey. Closed with 27 nominations.

Value of race, $173,200. Value to winner $103,920; second, $38,104; thirds, $15,588 each. Mutuel Pool, $550,396.

Last Raced	Horse	EqtAWt	PP	St	¼	½	¾	Str	Fin	Jockeys	Owners	Odds to $1
21 Aug76 8Mth³	Forego	6 135	2	10	7h	7h	7²	4³	1¹¼	WShoemaker	Lazy F Ranch	1.10
6 Sep76 8Del⁴	Dance Spell	3 115	10	1	6⁴	5¹½	2½	1h	2²¾	RHernandez	Christiana Stable	7.10
21 Aug76 6Sar¹	DH Honest Pleasure	3 121	1	2	1¹	1¹½	1¹	3²	3	CPerret	B R Firestone	2.10
14 Sep76 4Bel¹	DH Stumping	b6 109	4	7	5¹	6²	5¹	5⁷	3½	JAmy	Hobeau Farm	27.80
6 Sep76 8Bel²	Soy Numero Uno	3 112	5	4	3¹	3½	3²	2½	5⁸½	EMaple	Strapro Stable	11.20
21 Aug76 8Mth¹	Hatchet Man	b5 114	3	9	10	10	8½	7¹	6no	HGustines	Greentree Stable	11.30
21 Aug76 8Mth⁸	El Pitirre	4 112	7	5	9⁴	9½	9h	6½	7³	ASantiago	E Ubarri	29.20
6 Sep76 8Del⁴	Dancing Gun	b4 112	8	2	2¹½	2h	6h	8½	8h	JVelasquez	Gedney Farms	37.30
6 Sep76 8Bel⁸	Sonkisser	3 117	6	8	4½	4½	4²	9¹½	9nk	BBaeza	H I Snyder	37.40
7 Sep76 8Bel⁸	Right Mind	5 114	9	6	8h	8⁵	10	10	10	RTurcotte	Deronjo Stable	70.90
	DH Dead-heat.											

OFF AT 5:45 EDT. Start good. Won ridden out. Time, :23, :45⅗, 1:09½, 1:33¾, 1:45⅘. Track fast.

$2 Mutuel Prices:

2–FOREGO	4.20	3.00	2.20
11–DANCE SPELL		5.40	3.00
1–HONEST PLEASURE (Dead-heat)			2.20
4–STUMPING (Dead-heat)			2.80

B. g, by Forli—Lady Golconda, by Hasty Road. Trainer, Frank Y. Whitley, Jr. Bred by Lazy F. Ranch (Ky.). FOREGO, unhurried after breaking slowly, was steadied along while racing along the inside to the turn, eased out for room approaching the three-eighths pole, moved fast while continuing wide after entering the stretch, caught DANCE SPELL inside the final sixteenth and drew clear under good handling. DANCE SPELL, eased back after breaking in front, moved fast to make his bid while racing well out in the track leaving the turn, took over from SOY NUMERO UNO with a furlong remaining but wasn't able to withstand the winner while besting the others. HONEST PLEASURE sprinted to the front along the inside soon after the start, made the pace while racing well out from the rail, held on well to midstretch and finished on even terms with STUMPING while weakening. STUMPING, never far back, finished with good energy. SOY NUMERO UNO, reserved behind the early leaders, moved through along the inside to gain a narrow advantage nearing the stretch, remained prominent to the final furlong and gave way. HATCHET MAN was always outrun. EL PITIRRE was never close. DANCING GUN was finished soon after going five furlongs. SONKISSER gave way after racing forwardly for six furlongs. RIGHT MIND was always outrun.

Track bias is one of the fundamental realities of racing. There really is a logic to the race, a surprisingly consistent stream of logic. But it can rarely be appreciated without understanding the role of the racetrack itself as it influences the flow of the action from start to finish.

A SAMPLE RACE. The Schuylerville Stakes, July 29, 1974. Opening day at Saratoga. Five of the first six races were main-track sprints and all were won wire to wire. Not one horse made a move on the outside all day and no horse was passed in the stretch. The logical front runner in this race paid $22.40. I'll give you one guess. The winner will be revealed in Chapter 12.

7th SARATOGA   **JULY 29, 1974**

6 FURLONGS. (1:08) Fifty-seventh running SCHUYLERVILLE (1st Division).

My Compliments   116   B. f (1972), by Delta Judge—Granny's Pride, by Roman.
Breeder, R. L. Reineman (Ky.).   1974 3 2 1 0 $11,580
wner, R. L. Reineman. Trainer, W. C. Freeman.

20-74³Mth	5½ f 1:05⅕ft	9-5	▲119	4²	2½	1h	12¾	RuaneJ⁵	Alw 91	ⒻMyComplim'ts119 Q Up Myst'ryM'd	6
6-74³Aqu	5½ f 1:05	ft 6-5	▲117	1½	13	13	12	VeneziaM⁶	Alw 91	ⒻMyC'mpliments117 Aware Q'n'sTurf	7
n25-74³Aqu	5½ f 1:05	ft 15	117	6³⅜	6³¼	3½	2no	VeneziaM⁸	Mdn 88	ⒻLadyP'tia117 MyC'plim'ts M'lyB'ne	10

July 27 Sar 4f ft :49¾b   July 17 Aqu 4f ft :47¾h   July 13 Aqu 4f ft :51b

Our Dancing Girl   116   B. f (1972), by Solo Landing—Amber Dancer, by Native Dancer.
Breeder, Elcee-H Stable (Fla.).   1974 5 1 1 2 $11,793
wner, Elcee-H Stable. Trainer, J. Rigione.

10-74³Aqu	5½ f 1:02⅘ft	11	115	3¹	3⁹	3¹⁴	3²¹	HoleM³	AlwS 78	ⒻRuff'n118 L'gh'gB'dge OurD'c'gGirl	4
1-74⁷Mth	5½ f 1:06	ft 7½	117	1⁴	1h	2¹	3³	GallitanoG⁶	Alw 84	PropMan118 Prev er OurDanc'gGirl	7
n15-74³Bel	5½ f 1:06	ft 3¼	116	1⁴	1⁵	1⁶	14½	HoleM⁴	Mdn 85	ⒻO'rD'c'gG'l 116 Tricks Bl'de ofR's s	10
n 7-74³Bel	5½ f 1:05⅘ft	3½	116	1²	1²	11½	21	HoleM²	M40000 86	ⒻCur!ique116 OurD'c'gG rl SwiftImp	10
y30-74³Bel	5½ f 1:06	ft 4½	114	31	11	21½	47½	HoleM³	M35000 77	ⒻCurtainCall 116 M'snM'se Cl's'gM't	8

July 24 Bel 5f ft :59⅘h   July 8 Bel 4f ft :47¾h   June 29 Bel 4f ft 48¾b

La Bourresque   116   Dk. b. or br. f (1972), by Victoria Park—Nearanna, by Nearctic.
Breeder, J. L. Levesque (Can.).   1974 6 1 2 2 $7,164
wner, J. L. Levesque. Trainer, J. Starr.

14-74⁶WO	6 f 1:11²⅕ft	8e	119	5⁴	55½	54¾	2no	TurcotteN¹	Alw 86	R'son'bleWin119 LaB'r'sque Dap'rS'dy	12
6-74⁵WO	6 f 1:11³⅕ft	15	112	3ⁿk	1h	2½	32½	D'tfashH⁴	HcpS 83	ⒻDeepstar112 M'dow.sw t LaB'r'sque	8
n27-74⁴WO	6 f 1:13³⅕sl	9½	116	5	25³½	5⁶	59¾	RogersC⁴	InvH 65	P'sleyPal 117 H'pe forS'Shine Petrus	7
n 8-74⁴WO	5½ f 1:04³⅕ft	1	▲119	3½	3²	33½	3⁹	RogersC⁶	Alw 87	ⒻKn'tlyPr's119 M'd'sw t LaB'r'sque	6

Some Swinger   116   Ch. f (1972), by Tirreno—Batting a Thousand, by Hitting Away.
Breeder, H. T. Mangurian, Jr. (Ky.).   1972 4 2 0 1 $6,475
wner, H. T. Magurian, Jr. Trainer, T. F. Root, Sr.

8-74⁶Crc	6 f 1:13⅗ft	4-5	▲118	4¾	41⅛	2½	14	GuerinE¹	Alw 85	ⒻSomeSw'g'r118 B'l'rineR'se Whirl It	8
n29-74⁶Crc	5 f 1:00⅘ft	17	118	85¾	83½	5³	31½	GuerinE⁵	HcpS 89	ⒻMyM'mN'h113 W'd a.L'L'g S'eS'g'r	12
n17-74²Crc	5½ f 1:07⅘ft	9	118	3ⁿk	11½	14	13	Gr'nst'nB³	Mdn 88	ⒻS'eS'g'r118 Fl'daN'dies H'K andEye	10
n 5-74²Crc	5½ f 1:07⅘ssy	18	118	9¹⁰	9¹¹	9¹⁶	9¹³	StLeonG³	Mdn 78	ⒻSoloRoyal 118 Sm'l theRoses OldH'n	9

July 25 Bel 4f sy :46hg   July 21 Bel 6f ft 1:16b   July 17 Bel 3f ft :37b

Secret's Out

119 Lt. ch. f (1972), by Royal Saxon—Secret Verdict, by Clandestine.
Breeder, Mrs. M. W. Schott (Fla.).　1974　4　3　0　0　$24,503

Owner, Marcia Schott. Trainer, J. E. Picou.

Jun19-74	8Mth	5½ f	1.04	ft	6	119	2¹	74¾ 69¾ 59½	B'mf'ldD²	AlwS 88	ⓕF'r'Wind 115 Copernica Fant'ticMiss 7
May26-74	9Suf	5 f	1:00⅖sm	3-5	^121	1½	1² 13¼ 13½	W'dh'eR⁹	HcpS 85	Secret'sOut121 Inchiq'l,h Wh t aT'k't 9
Apr24-74	7Kee	4½ f	:53⅕ft	1	^119	2	1³ 1¹ 14½	B'f'ldD¹	AlwS 89	ⓕS'cr't'sOut119 Fl'lPrinc's Ain'tE'sy 8
Mar15-74	3Hia	3 f	:33²ssy	2½	^117	3	1¹ 13½	W'dh'seR¹	Mdn 95	ⓕS'cr't'sO't117 Ebalide W'tATrink't 14

July 17 Bel 5f ft 1:12⅘h　　July 11 Bel 6f ft 1:13h　　June 29 4f ft :48⅘b

Precious Elaine

112 Dk. b. or br. f (1972), by Tom Fool or Advocator—Imgoinaway, by
On-and-On. Br., Mrs. J. R. Pancoast (Fla.)1974　3 M 1 0　$1,980

(Formerly named Idontlikehim).
Owner, A. J. Brodsky. Trainer, J. P. Conway.

Jly 15-74	3Aqu	6 f	1:13	ft	10	117	11½ 11½ 1½ 21¾	S'nt'goA¹	Mdn 76	ⓕGoldB'x117 PrciousEl'ne C'rd nQu'd 11
Jun12-74	8Bel	5½ f	1:03	ft	18	112	6⁴ 6¹¹ 6²³ 6³⁰	Cast'daM⁵	AlwS 70	ⓕRuffian 117 Copernca Jan Verzal 6
May22-74	3Bel	5½ f	1:05	ft	4½	116	2³ 3⁹ 7²¹ 9³⁴	Cast'daM¹	Mdn 66	ⓕRuffian 116 Suzest Garden Quad 10

July 24 Bel 4f ft :49b　　July 10 Bel 5f ft 1:00½h　　July 5 Bel 3f ft :36⅘b

But Exclusive

116 Ch. f (1972), by Exclusive Native—Royal Bit, by Alcibiades II.
Breeder, L. Combs II. (Ky.).　1974　3 1 2 0　$9,470

Owner, W. A. Levin. Trainer, D. A. Imperio.

Jly 12-74	4Aqu	6½ f	1:05⅖ft	3	118	65½ 47½ 3⁶	2⁴	VeneziaM¹	Alw 82	ⓔSc't'shM'l'dy118 B'tExcl ve C's'nlvy 8
Jun22-74	3Bel	5½ f	1:05⅕ft	3-2	^116	64¼ 2²	2½ 1ʰ	VeneziaM⁵	Mdn 89	ⓕButExclu've116 Aw're Sc't'shM'l'dy 9
Jun10-74	4Bel	5½ f	1:05⅕ft	7¾	116	5⁷½ 4⁶	4⁵ 2³½	Ven'ziaM¹	Mdn 85	ⓕFr'chR'lel16 B'tExcl've M'lvB'l'tine 10

July 26 Bel 4f ft :48⅕h　　July 19 Bel 4f ft :47⅖hg　　July 11 Bel trt 3f ft :35⅖h

5.
The Money Tree

Trainer Glenn C. Smith will never make the Hall of Fame at Saratoga. But I doubt seriously that he cares.

Mr. Smith, never more than a part-time claiming-horse trainer with few horses and no following, did quite well during the winter meets at Bowie a decade ago. He also helped to teach a particular struggling student of handicapping an important lesson: You can't really understand this game without taking the role of the trainer into account.

It was February 1, 1963, and I had just had a miserable afternoon at Bowie, a zero-for-nine afternoon, and I was not enjoying the four-hour bus ride back to New Jersey one bit. My handicapping had been awful, but the fellow in the back of the bus who had done considerably better was bent on giving me a headache. He was succeeding more than I cared to admit. In exasperation, I opened up the *Racing Form*— half to punish myself, half to get out of his range. What I saw is what you see below—Trojan Seth, the wire-to-wire winner of the sixth race. A 3–1 stickout trained by Mr. Smith.

Trojan Seth ✳		112	B. h (1958), by Trojan Monarch—Cedquest, by Alquest. Breeder C. B. Caldwell.										
									1962	8	4	0	4	$10,422
Owner, G. C Smith. Trainer, G. C Smith.							$7,500		1961	13	2	3	1	$7,240
Apr27-62⁷Lrl	7 f 1:24⅖ft	5	114• 1²	1½	2²	3²	AddesaE⁵	10000 88 Cycount103 C'ch a'dF'r109 Troj'nSeth 6
Apr18-62⁶Lrl	6 f 1:12⅘ft	3½	114• 1½	2½	2ʰ	3⅜	AddesaE⁵	10000 90 Klinkh'se116 C'h andF'r108 Tr'j'nSeth 10
Apr 7-62⁶Lrl	6 f 1:11⅕sy	3	114• 2ʰ	2½	2½	3²½	AddesaE¹	12000 97 Adorette115 Polyn'nB'ly115 Tr'nSeth 7
Mar28-62⁷Bow	6 f 1:11 ft	6-5	112‡ 1⁵	1⁶	1⁶	1⁵	AddesaE¹	Alw 96 Tr'j'nS'th112 S'r andC'm107 En'shS'le 6
Mar17-62⁷Bow	6 f 1:11⅘ft	3-2e	113 1ʰ	2½	2¹	3⁴†	McKeeC²	Alw 88 Yeuxdoux115 Adorette119 TrojanSeth 7
†Dead heat.								
Mar 5-62⁷Bow	5½ f 1:05⅖ft	2½ ▲117‡12	1½	1ʰ	1ⁿᵒ	AddesaE²	9000 92 TrojanSeth 117 Dollmaker 117 OleKel 6
Feb20-62⁷Bow	6 f 1:14⅗m	2½ ▲113‡ 1³	1¹½	1ʰ	1½	AddesaE⁶	8000 79 Trojan Seth 113 Dollmaker 112 Ji-Jo 6
Feb14-62⁷Bow	6 f 1:14 sy	6-5 ▲108‡ 11½	1⁴	1¹	12½	AddesaE²	7000 81 TrojanSeth108 Dalsax1'4 Tourdan 8
Dec13-61⁶P,m	6 f 1:13 m	12 107‡ 2¹	2²	43½	5⁶	AddesaE⁵	9000 79 Ano rArt114 Giewith116 Barb'raLeeG. 7
Jan 30 Bow 1m ft 1:45⅖b								

According to all the rules of traditional handicapping theory, Trojan Seth should have been a throwout on the grounds of physical condition. The colt had not been out on the track for a race in over nine months. The workout, a single slow mile just two days before the race, could hardly have sharpened the colt's speed. And as the race shaped up, it was not an easy spot.

There were four recent winnners shipping in from the South and two confirmed $8,500 horses dropping down in class. Now, when it was too late, the bottom two races in Trojan Seth's chart barked out their message.

Instantly, it was clear that Trojan Seth was not a horse that needed to be raced into shape. Was Smith, I wondered, the kind of man who made a habit of such doings?

The answer, along with the cure for my headache, came later that night when I compared the past performance records of all Smith's starters from the previous winter. Nine horses. Thirty-two starts. Ten total victories. An excellent 30 percent win record. But there was more, much more. I checked back over the prior year just to be sure.

There was no doubt about it; this little-known trainer brought considerable skill to his craft. Smith had a pattern. An amazing 60 percent win record with first-time starters and absentees, only one of which was a post-time favorite. But the most astounding part of the pattern was the long, slow workout that accompanied six out of his seven absentee winners. All were sprinters, all showed early speed in their past performances, and all but one scored after several months of inactivity.

The lone exception raced in a route, finished out of the money, and then came back five days later to score in a sprint at 16–1. Mr. Smith was a horseplayer's dream. A veritable money tree. He trained all his horses back on the farm, away from the prying eyes of the clockers and the competition. And the long, slow workout was just the final touch of a well-thought-out training regimen.

Each year Smith invaded Bowie with a stableful of razor-sharp claimers, got the money, went back to the farm, and smiled a lot.

I was smiling too. By meeting's end Smith won nine more races to lead the Bowie trainers. His overall win record was an excellent 30 percent. But he was five for nine with the pattern, and I was four for eight. But the moral of the story is not complete without sharing one additional detail.

One of the nonpattern horses that won for Mr. Smith was a cheap but useful three-year-old named Cedar Key. Smith lost him via the claim box for $5,000, took him back for $6,500, and then lost him again at the end of the meeting for $6,500 to Don McCoy, the same trainer who had taken him away from Smith the first time.

McCoy wanted this colt as badly as Smith, but for a very different reason. McCoy's New York client owned a bakery shop with the identical name—the Cedar Key Bakery. Of such motives are champions made.

Over the next two years, while Smith was breaking his back to win $100,000 in purses with his band of hobbled platers, Cedar Key was winning nearly $200,000 in turf stakes coast to coast. That may be one reason Mr. Smith will never make the Hall of Fame at Saratoga. For what it's worth, he has my vote.

6.
Coaching Counts

There are many successful trainers like Glenn C. Smith. Every racetrack has its aces, and each horseman brings to his craft one or more special skills (or winning strategies) that separate him from the rest of the crowd.

Some are small-time operators, patient men who spend months getting cheap, sore-legged horses fit enough to deliver one or two sharp efforts. Others travel the racing circuit first class, commanding large armies of horses on several fronts. And there are a few—throwbacks to the days when racing was truly the sport of kings—who deal only with the best-bred racing stock money can buy.

Because of these vastly different economic situations, because different trainers have rather personal methods, preferences, and skills, there is no single, simplistic formula that can be applied to a reading of physical condition. Although we all tend to forget it from time to time, the Thoroughbred racehorse is an athlete in the purest sense of the word. And to a far greater degree than most people think, the trainer is its coach.

From dawn until well after dusk, 365 days a year, the trainer must watch over the feed tub, consult the veterinarian, study the *Racing Form,* plan the workout schedule, saddle the horses, watch the day's races, make travel arrangements, supervise the stable help, reassure the owners, select the class, distance, jockey, equipment, and date of the race. The horse is a wonderfully fast, woefully fragile creature, and it takes considerable skill, timing, and patience to keep it in competition. (It also costs the owner about $7,500 a year per horse.)

"I can usually tell when a horse is a race away from losing its form," said Allen Jerkens, master horseman and the best coach a thoroughbred athlete could posssibly want. No other trainer in racing is more dangerous with recently acquired stock and no other trainer is more in touch with the subtle day-to-day changes of the horses in his barn.

"There are many signs," explained Jerkens. "Every horse has his own habits. You get to know them pretty well. The ankle doesn't respond as quickly, or the hair on the coat begins to lose its sheen, or he leaves some feed in the tub. You've got to look them over very carefully. Any change makes an impression." Later, Jenkens added, "If you want to save a horse for future racing, the time to stop on him is *before* he stops on you."

A handicapper who happens to be a reporter can learn a lot touring the backstretch.

"A great many good horses are abused at an early stage in their careers," said articulate John Russell, the versatile horseman in charge of the blue-blooded Phipps Stable, a man with a strong winning history with lightly raced horses stretching out in distance, stakes-class three-year-olds, turf routers, and shippers.

Russell amplified his point. "It's a complex dilemma. First, you have to get a two-year-old to develop a little confidence, train him hard enough to be fit so he gets some benefit out of his racing. Second, the money is out of this world for a good two-year-old; and when you've got one, you have to decide how much potential the horse has to remain sound, how far you think he will want to run, and how much you can afford to push him.

"Frankly," Russell added, "I'm not opposed to breaking a horse's maiden in a first or second start—an early win is a magnificent confidence builder, the best in fact—but I'm more concerned with having a horse reach its natural peak in the spring or summer of its three-year-old season."

Not all trainers can afford the luxury of long-range planning. Where cheap horses are concerned, most goals begin and end with the here and now. Nevertheless, at each racetrack there are a few claiming-horse trainers who seem to have more patience and a better sense of timing than many stakes-class horsemen. One such trainer is Richard E.

Dutrow, who has been ripping up Maryland racing since he graduated from Charles Town minor-class racing in West Virginia a few years ago. Another is King Leatherbury, who for fifteen years has been no less a force on the same circuit. Between them, Leatherbury and Dutrow win approximately 350 of the 1,800 races run in Maryland each season. In a very real sense they are at war with each other, but they conduct their operations in the spirit of détente.

Very rarely do they claim from each other. Very rarely do they compare notes or share insights or anything else. But they respect each other's talent and they learn from each other by competing tooth and nail throughout the long Maryland season.

Dutrow used to have difficulty stretching horses out in distance. Leatherbury is an ace at that. Leatherbury used to win most of his races with horses dropping in class. Dutrow likes to push his horses up the class ladder. Today each trainer has incorporated a few of his rival's methods. Leatherbury still has an astounding 60 percent win record with dropdowns coming back after thirty or more days' rest. But he wins more often with repeaters stepping up in class than he used to. Dutrow still wins one race in every four attempts, a record only the top twenty or thirty trainers in America can claim, but he now wins them at any distance with all types of horses.

"I'm not a claiming-horse trainer," Dutrow said to a bleary-eyed reporter one morning. "At least I'm not anymore. Right now I'm training two-year-olds, stakes horses, turf horses, and as many allowance-class runners as I have claimers." What Dutrow didn't say was that most of the allowance horses in his care started out as claimers before he solved their problems and moved them up in class.

King Leatherbury has more than a few allowance runners in his barn too, but it is still the cheap, sore-legged horse that brings out the man's best work. "When you're dealing with cheap horses, you have to be part horseman, part businessman," he explained. "You have to have the patience to wait on a horse; you can't be too aggressive, too forceful, but you can't waste a whole lot of time either. Once the horse begins to respond, you can't be thinking about next year or next week; you've got to put it in a race where it can win . . . dropping it down a notch or two in class is like taking out insurance."

"I agree," said Johnny Campo, the ebullient, oft-quoted, New York-born and -based horseman who decided he wanted to become a trainer the day he saw a Hopalong Cassidy movie in his youth. Campo is the closest thing to a Damon Runyon character on the New York backstretch, and the Belmont Stakes "Alibi Breakfast" would not be the same without him. Almost unnoticed, or perhaps partially obscured by his deceivingly clownish reputation, Campo is one of the most effective trainers of two-year-old fillies in the country, and he has nearly as much skill with allowance-class routers on the main track and with claimers of every age and sex. While Campo is not the most patient trainer of a promising three-year-old, he has trained two juvenile champions—Protagonist and Talking Picture—and has been among the top five trainers in New York since the day he took out a trainer's licence in 1970.

"I can't tell you how interesting it is to be a trainer," Campo said in a serious moment. But that didn't stop him from trying. By the third sentence he was in high form.

"Every horse is different. Some need a long-drawn-out program to get them to do anything; others will kick down the barn to get in a race or a work every three days. But don't get me wrong," he added, "I'm no genius or anything. I don't do nothing special. I just work hard, harder than most, especially on the legs. I learned a lot about legs from working for Eddie Neloy when he had all those top two-year-olds for Wheatley in the sixties. Don't let anybody tell you that top horses don't have leg problems. All horses have leg problems. That's one thing at least that all horses have in common. Fact is," he continued, "the biggest leg problem I've ever seen was on the best horse I've ever had—Protagonist—and not getting him to the Derby was my biggest disappointment so far. He would've won it. I know he would've won it. But I'll get another chance; I've got some pretty good two-year-olds in my barn right now. But what was that question you asked, something about claimers?"

"Yes, claimers, Johnny—what about claimers? Do you like to drop them in class as often as King Leatherbury?"

"Well, it works both ways," Campo responded. "A drop in class has to help most horses. That's just plain common sense. But sometimes I'll drop a horse in class because I'm praying somebody'll take the stiff off my hands. I'm sure Leatherbury does the same thing. It's like poker. Sometimes you've got to bluff and sometimes you're laying there waiting with the best hand at the table."

Phil Johnson, a first-rate public stable trainer who wins most of his races with two-year-old maidens, first-time starters, fillies, turf specialists, and high-priced claimers, had more to say on this subject: "As a rule, I'm very suspicious about dropdowns. There are few bargains and too many bargain hunters. I much prefer to take a horse that has come to life and is being stepped up a notch or two in company. You can always drop it back a bit later, but a sound, improving horse is where the money is."

Anthony Doyle, who trained the rugged Avatar to a victory in the 1975 Belmont Stakes via a series of demanding workouts at various distances, had some poignant insights into the trainer's dilemma a few hours before his greatest victory. "If you see a horse show some speed when you didn't train it hard enough to expect it, that's the time to think you might have something special," said the Irish-born Doyle, a West Coast–based horseman whose winners at every class level usually telegraph their potential via improved workouts. "But," he added, fully aware that Avatar was going to put up or shut up later in the day, "if you do train a horse hard and draw a blank, the horse is telling you something. Maybe you've made a mistake; maybe blinkers would help or a change of scenery or a switch in distance. Maybe you pushed too hard, or not hard enough. Sometimes you have to guess, sometimes the jockey will give you a clue, and sometimes the answer comes in the middle of the night."

In the middle of the night Charles Town ace Wade Johnson is usually just returning from the track. "By the time I get to work with a horse," said Johnson, "it's had maybe ten, twenty, or thirty starts, four or five different trainers, a couple of major injuries, a lot of medication, and everything has been tried already. But every horse has its hole card and every horse—even a sore-legged, eight-year-old, $1,500 claimer—can be treated with patience and respect.

"When I claim a horse like that, I'm betting my time and money that I can straighten it out fast."

Leroy Jolley, controversial, talented, and every bit as articulate as John Russell, was not talking much during Honest Pleasure's troubles in the 1976 Triple Crown chase. But in a calmer period the previous summer he offered several insights into the pressures faced by the trainer of a million-dollar horse. "If you're shooting for a major race like the Derby or the Travers or the Jockey Club Gold Cup, you can't start thinking about it two weeks beforehand," said the trainer of Foolish Pleasure, Honest Pleasure, and Optimistic Gal.

Jolley continued: "You have to know your horse and know what you are trying to do. Every workout, each race, must have a purpose. Good horses tend to be precocious workers and you have to let them test their limits; get them tired and move them out in distance or up in company step by step. The biggest problem," Jolley said with emphasis, "is not getting them fit but *keeping* them fit. One unlucky break or bad step can ruin a month's worth of training or even end a horse's career. I suppose I've been pretty lucky so far, but I've also been very careful."

"I don't know about the Derby. I've never had a horse good enough to think about it," said Ida Mae Parrish, a Midwestern-based horsewoman who annually demolished the Massachusetts fair circuit (40 percent winners) over a ten-year period. "But to get a stableful of cheap claimers ready to win, you have to freshen them up, give them a lot of long, slow gallops, a decent work or a prep race, and crack down hard at the first sign of improvement. If you get too cute or wait too long to put them in a sensible spot, you'll never pay the feed bills, much less win a race."

According to the American Racing Manual and other authoritative sources, there are approximately 7,000 licensed trainers in North America.

More than a thousand failed to win a single race in 1974, 1975, or 1976.

A thousand more failed to win as few as ten races, and another thousand failed to win twenty.

Looking at this picture from the opposite perspective, the top 400 trainers have won approximately 25 percent of all the purse money distributed in each of the past three calendar years. Barely more than 100 were good enough to win one race in every five attempts.

For his own protection alone, the player should know which trainers have winning skill, what that skill is, and which ones can't train their way out of a paper bag.

7.
The Trainer's Window

In the hands of one trainer, a horse with good recent form might be an excellent wager; in the care of another, the horse might be ready to fall apart at the seams.

In the hands of an ace, a horse stepping up sharply in company or stretching out in distance might well be expected to handle the task; in the care of a lesser talent, such a maneuver might only be an experiment or an unnecessary risk.

Naturally, the vast majority of trainers like to bet to overcome their financial difficulties or to take advantage of their skill; but the player is misled if he thinks they are any better at handicapping than they are at their chosen craft. The horse may have a fine turn of speed or suddenly show signs of life; but if the trainer is impatient, sloppy, or incompetent, he will find a way to lose control of the horse and blow the best of opportunities.

Maybe the horse is crying for a route race on the turf, or perhaps he needs a better jockey or a change in equipment or a shorter resting period between starts. Maybe the horse has been too ambitiously placed too often or has left his race on the training track. You'd be amazed how many horses are mismanaged in that fashion.

The positive and negative impact of the trainer on horse performance is all too rarely taken into account by the average horseplayer, who at best glances at the leading trainers' list and automatically assumes universal competence.

But the mistake is easily corrected, and it is great fun.

After all, the past performance profile is not only a summation of horse performance but a window through which the talents, habits, and strategies of the trainer can be seen.

For example, by comparing the past performance records of a dozen or so winners (and losers) trained by Frank Whiteley Jr., the player will know for a certainty that every last horse this man (and his son David) send to the post is a dangerous contender.

There are no frills, no tricks, no wild experiments.

A sprinter is kept sprinting, a stakes horse is given a balanced, well-spaced campaign, and a first-time starter is well prepared and well meant.

Mistakes are made; but they are seldom repeated. Experiments are tried; but if they do not produce improvement or satisfactory results, the horse is promptly returned to familiar conditions.

You can learn a lot about good horsemanship by looking through the Whiteleys' window.

Forego   **137**   B. g (1970) by Forli—Lady Golconda by Hasty Road.
Breeder. Lazy F Ranch (Ky.).   1976   7   5   1   1 $321,481
Owner, Lazy F Ranch.   Trainer, Frank Y. Whiteley, Jr.   1975   9   6   1   1 $429,521

```
18 Sep76 8Bel   1¼ :45³1:09¹1:45⁴ft   1  ^135   7⁶  76½  42½  11½  ShmkrW²   HcpS 98 Forego 135        Dance Spell 10
21 Aug76 8Mth   1¼ :47²1:11²2:00³ft   3-5 ^136  3³   2²   2¹   3¹   VasquzJ⁷  HcpS 98 HatchetMan112    IntrepidHro 8
24 Jly 76 8Aqu  1¼ :46⁴1:11²2:01¹ft   2-3 ^134  6⁸½ 2¹½  2h   1²   CustinsH⁴  HcpS 90 Forego 134       Lord Rebeau 8
 5 Jly 76 8Aqu  1⅜ :47⁴1:11²1:55²ft   2-5 ^134  32½ 21½  31½  2no  GustinsH²  HcpS 85 Foolish Pleasure 125 Forego 4
13 Jun76 8Bel   1¼ :47²1:11²1:48³ft   4-5 ^132  42½ 3²   1h   12¾  VsquezJ¹   HcpS 84 Forego 132       El Pitirre 5
31 May76 8Bel   1 :45³1:09²1:34⁴ft    1  ^130   54½ 44   41½  1h   GustinsH⁴  HcpS 94 Forego 130       Master Derby 6
20 May76 8Bel   7 f :23⁴ :46⁴1:22 ft  1-3 ^126  41½ 3½   1h   11½  GustinesH² Alw 92 Forego 126        Wishing Stone 4
```

Oct 1 Bel 4f sy :46h   Sept 27 Bel 1f ft 1:43½b   Sept 25 Bel 5f ft 1:05b

---

Sarsar   **117**   Ch. f (1972), by Damascus—Durga, by Tatan.
Breeder, A. B. Hancock, Jr. (Ky.).   1974   0 M   0   0   (——)
Owner, W. H. Perry.   Trainer, D. A. Whiteley.
July 15 Bel 5f ft :58h   July 9 Bel 4f ft :49bg   July 4 Bel 4f ft :47⅕h

---

Arabian Law   **108**   Dk. b. or br. c (1973), by Damascus—Lagides by Lacaduv.
Breeder, Mrs. Martha F. Gerry (Ky.).   1976   7   3   3   1 $46,735
Owner, Lazy F Ranch.   Trainer, D. A. Whiteley.   1975   1 M   1   0 $3,060

```
18Jly76 8Aqu   6 f :22¹ :45¹1:10³ft 6-5 ^112  7⁸   68¾ 6⁴   1nk  VasqezJ³  HcpS 90 ArabianLaw112      FullOut 7
 8Jly76 8Aqu   6 f :22² :45¹1:09²ft 8-5  113   63¾ 62¼ 2½   2nk  VasquezJ¹ Alw 96 SoyNumeroUno111     ArabanLw 6
 6Jun76 7Bel   6 f :22⁴ :46¹1:01¹ft3-5 ^115  64½ 6²   1¹   12¾  VasquezJ⁷ Alw 91 ArabianLaw115        TaxBracket 8
20May76 7Bel   6 f :22³ :45³1:09⁴ft3-2 ^114  96¾ 6⁴   43½  2no  VasquezJ¹ Alw 93 KaiserFluff106       ArabianLaw 10
10May76 4Bel   6 f :22⁴ :46 1:10¹ft6-5 ^114  64½ 33   12   16½  VasquezJ¹¹ Mdn 84                      ThirdWorld 12
15Apr76 4Aqu   1 :44³1:09 1:36 ft6-5 ^113  5⁸   5⁹   45½  31½  VasquezJ¹ Mdn 84 RedAnchor112          Gaytense 10
29Mar76 1Aqu   6 f :23¹ :47 1:04⁴ft  8  113   83¾ 5³   31½  2½   VasqezJ¹¹ Mdn 88 Arachnoid114         ArabianLaw 12
21Sep75 4Bel   1 :47⁴1:12⁴1:37⁴m 4½  122   6³¾ 67½ 4¹⁴  4¹⁹  GustinesH⁴ Mdn 60 ArtAboveAll 122       RoyalMssion 10
```

July 15 Bel 4f ft :47h   July 5 Bel 4f ft :46⅘h   June 30 Bel 4f sl :47⅕h

---

Revidere   **118**   Ch. f (1973), by Reviewer—Quillesian, by Princequillo.
Breeder, Claiborne Farm (Ky.).   1976   7   7   0   0 $181,018
Owner, W. H. Perry.   Trainer, David A. Whiteley.

```
 4 Sep76 8Bel   1¼ :46³1:10¹1:47⁴ft       2³  2³   2²   11½  CrdoAJr¹  HcpS 88 ⒻRevidere124       PcificPrincss 5
 5 Jly 76 8Mth  1¼ :48 1:12²1:50³ft  3-5 ^121  2¹  1½   2h   1h   VasquzJ⁷  AlwS 87 Reidere 121        Javabine 8
26 Jun76 7Bel   1⅜ :48²1:13²2:28²ft  2½ 121   2½  1½   2h   1½   VasquzJ⁵  ScwS 78 ⒻRevidere121        OptimisticGal 10
12 Jun76 8Key   1⁄₁₆:47⁴1:12²1:44 ft 3-5 ^118  1n  1h   11½  14   VasqezJ³  AlwS 84 ⒻRevidere 118       Critical Miss 8
11 May76 7Bel   1⁄₁₆ :46 1:10⁴1:43¹ft 6-5 114  2½  1h   12   13   VasquezJ⁷ Alw 86 ⒻRevidere114         Cohabitation 7
22 Apr76 7Aqu   1 :46 1:10³1:35¹ft   6-5 ^114  2½  12   11½  12¾  VasquezJ⁷ Alw 90 ⒻRevidere 114        Perl 7
 5 Apr76 3Aqu   7 f :23² :47¹1:25 ft 1-2 ^112  2¹  2½   11½  17½  VasquezJ⁸ Mdn 76 ⒻRevidere 112        How Pleasing 8
```

Sept 24 Bel 3f ft :35b   Sept 20 Bel 6f ft 1:12½h   Sept 16 Bel 5f ft 1:02⅕b

NOTE: *Honorable Miss' past performance profile is on page 126.*

If you were to perform a similar study on Jack Van Berg, probably the busiest and best trainer in the Midwest, you would also find unmistakable patterns staring you in the face.

Like Whiteley, Van Berg gives stakes horses consistent, thoroughly professional management. But with claimers and modest-class allowance stock, Van Berg operates with an arsenal of maneuvers that produces one winner in every four attempts and a nation-leading total of 350–400 victories per year. It is astounding, perhaps, but Van Berg's three most productive winning patterns account for almost half his total victories and would have produced a flat bet profit over the past ten years.

Along with Dave Vance, who handles a division of the far-flung Lasater Stable, Dick Dutrow (Maryland), Bobby Frankel and the father-son team of F. W. and Gary Jones (California), Ned Allard (New England), Richard Hazelton (Illinois), H. N. Steck (New Jersey), C. P. Sanborn (Florida), W. J. Danner (Ohio), Wade Johnson (West Virginia), Dewey Smith (Louisiana), Laz Barrera, Frank Laboccetta and Joe Trovato (New York), and several other fine horsemen, Van Berg is deadly with repeaters going up in class as well as with recent claims. On the other hand, a Van Berg winner attempting a repeat victory at the same class level or lower is usually a poor risk (approximately one win for every eight attempts). The same is true for most of the other horsemen who tend to win going up the ladder.

Obviously, it takes considerable horsemanship to know that a horse is fit enough and fast enough to beat better competition. And it takes no less skill to spot genuine value in another man's horse. It costs money to claim a horse. Not Monopoly money—*real* money: $5,000, $10,000, $20,000 and up. If a trainer at your favorite track seems particularly skillful with recent claims, it would be worthwhile to pull out a few past performance profiles and compare them. Possibly he likes to give his recent claims a few weeks off, or else break them in with an easy race. Some trainers prefer to wait out the thirty-day "jail" period which most states require. (After a claim, the trainer is forced to race the horse at a price at least 25 percent higher for a period of thirty days.) Perhaps you will conclude that there is no apparent pattern. Don't believe it. That is rarely the case. You're probably not looking at the right clues. For example, the third and most significant Van Berg pattern has nothing to do with past performance records as they appear in the *Daily Racing Form*. It merely has to do with where he is!

To a far greater extent than any horseman I have ever seen, Jack Van Berg is prone to go on incredible winning binges, seemingly at will. In amazing Ripley-like fashion, these streaks invariably coincide with his travel itinerary.

Van Berg has many horses under his wing and operates at two or three tracks simultaneously, often leading the trainers' standings at each racetrack. But if he is not on the grounds to personally supervise the training regimen of his stock, only his recent claims and repeaters win more than their share of races. If he is on the grounds, however, and has indicated control over the situation by winning two races back to back or three out of five, the odds say he'll win fifteen more before he saddles thirty or thirty-five to the post. Sometimes such a streak will last a month or more; sometimes it will be the only clue a player will get.

During the 1974, 1975, and 1976 racing seasons, I'm familiar with at least twenty-five such explosions at a dozen different racetracks. The only dependable form pattern I've detected is the extraordinary reliability of his repeaters stepping up in company. Actually, there is no theory of handicapping or insight into the conditioning process that will explain some of his wins. But don't say I didn't warn you.

Can you imagine the kind of bet Lucky Principio was when he came back April 2 to attempt a repeat victory in the middle of a Van Berg streak?

```
Lucky Principio            112  Dk. b. or br. g (1972), by Sir Ivor—Spar Officer, by Round Table.
                                Breeder, Carver Stable (Ky.).         1976  4 2 0 0    $19,500
Owner. P J. Luckino.  Trainer, J. Van Berg.                          1975  7 3 2 0    $14,744
 2 Apr76 8OP    6 f :214 :4511:093ft   14  115  68¾ 66¼ 52¼ 1no  WhitedDE1   Alw 97 LckyPrncpo115  ChnceLndng  7
27 Mar76 5OP    6 f :213 :4511:11 ft   11  119  63½ 52½ 2h  1no  WhitdDE1   25000 90 LuckyPrincipio119 King'sCre 12
19 Mar76 7OP    6 f :214 :4441:11 ft   28  110  610 68½ 66  73½  MiceliM4   33000 85 JustAWondr112 MilingoEstr  8
28 Feb76 7Hia   6 f :22  :45 1:094ft   14  117  63½ 63½ 85¾108¾  FieslmnJ4  25000 85 LoveReality115 LucayanBrze 10
29 Nov75 9HP    6½ f :232 :4911:23 sy  3½  110  1½  2r  33  49½  JonesK5    HcpS 56 Ske theAnvl 118  Dr'sEnjyDs  6
22 Nov75 3HP    6½ f :232 :48 1:202gq  2 *119 11  1½  16  110  JonesK4    Alw 79 LckyPrincipio119 I CanHcktt  8
13 Nov75 7HP    6 f :243 :4931:16 ft  1-2 *119 21½ 11  14  15   JonesK6    Alw 72 LkyPrincipio119 BelmrLanes  7
 7 Nov75 8HP    4 f :224     :474ft    1 *114  5  33  22  1no  JonesK5    Alw 86 LkyPrincpio114 Whps aDaisy 10
 1 Apr75 4OP    6 f :214 :4511:112ft   3½  113  75¾ 55½ 51½ 2½   LivelyJ4   Mdn 85 BeauMatt113 LckyPrincipio 11
26 Mar75 4OP    6 f :221 :4531:111ft   1 *113 2r  2r  41  44½  StrassRO1  Mdn 84 Galley Ho 113   Beau Matt 12
      April 9 HP 4f ft :49⅗b              March 10 HP 4f gd :53b
```

Winding River (below) was a Van Berg claim on March 27. There was no streak going at Sportsman's Park on April 8, but there was a repeater pattern. Thirteen to one is mind bending. In today's race Winding River remains at the same $8,500 class level. I hope there is something else worth playing in this race because Winding River is going to be the favorite. He may win, but Van Berg knows this horse is not as sharp as he looks. Otherwise he would step him up in class again.

```
Winding River *           116  Dk. b. or br. h (1971). by Crafty Admiral—Santa's Creek, by River War.
                                Breeder, S. Cohn (Md.).               1976  7 2 0 2    $8,640
Owner, J. Van Berg.  Trainer, J. Van Berg.              $8,500       1975  14 0 5 3    $9,383
 8 Apr76 9Spt    1 :4841:1511:411ft  (13) 115  33  2h  11  12¼  TurctteRL5 8500 74 WindgRivr115 Sctch andSda 10
27 Mar76 6FG    1 1/16 :4741:1311:463ft 3½  114  67  36  22½ 1nk  GuajdoA2 (c)500 82 WindingRiver114  FowlLuck  8
21 Mar76 7FG    6 f :22  :4541:11 ft   19  112  87½ 77  54½ 55½  GuajrdoA5  8000 84 Kerry Debby 104    Timoteo  8
10 Mar76 7FG    6 f :222 :4621:114ft   15  114  75¾ 65  33½ 54½  GuajrdoA3  8000 81 Bandwagon114 NationalNote  8
18 Feb76 9FG   140 :4641:1221:403ft   7½  113  56½ 34½ 43½ 39   PowerJ10  c6250 81 Sctch andSda113  CurusKitn 10
 7 Feb76 3FG    1 1/16 :4821:1411:46 ft 3½  113  41¾ 1h  21  34½  DayP8     6300 80 Tumizon 116       Tipo Ke'  8
31 Jan76 5FG    6 f :222 :4621:12 ft   4½  115  85¼ 911 917 910  TrosclrAJ9 7500 75 SpanishState117 FuelPrince  9
14 Sep75 6LaD   6 f :23  :4611:122ft   8½  116  67  57½ 35½ 51¾  DupasR3   13000 101 Peerless Prince 120 Truxton  9
 6 Sep75 7LaD   7 f :234 :4741:272sl   2½ *116  67  67½ 611 59½  FrominM2   1500 89 Amberope118   WindingRiver  6
30 Aug75 6LaD   6 f :231 :4731:134ft    2  116  48  49  37  27¼  FrominM5  16000 88 Bill'sCmet116  Run to theWe  8
      April 16 Spt 5f ft 1:03b            April 5 Kee 5f ft 1:02b
```

The following horse is one of eight stakes winners trained by Jack Van Berg during the first six months of 1976. Looks like Frank Whiteley's work, doesn't it? Obviously, the man knows how to read a condition book and is not afraid to go hunting.

Summertime Promise   **119**   B. f (1972), by Nijinsky II.—Prides Promise, by Crozier.
Breeder, P. Mellon (Va.).

Owner, K. Opstein. Trainer, J. Van Berg.

					1976	9	3	5	1	$139,250
					1975	8	2	1	2	$65,300

7Jly 76	8AP	⑦ 1 :47³1:114¹:38 fm 1-2 ▲122	1½	14	14	1¹	SnyderL7	Alw 85	⒠SmrtmePmise122 Ksaptmus 7
19May76	8Hol	⑦ 1¹⁄₁₆:47²1:113¹:414fm 2¾ ▲119	2¹	2½	2ʰ	3²	LivelyJ7	HcpS 88	⒠MiaAmore116 Bastonerall. 7
8May76	8Haw	⑦ 1 :49²1:142¹:404sf 4-5 ▲120	12½	1ʰ	1³	1³	LivelyJ3	HcpS 67	⒠SmrtimePmise120 MiniGift 10
17Apr76	8Pim	⑦ 1¹⁄₁₆:47³1:112¹:421fm 3¼ 117	1ʰ	1ʰ	1ʰ	2ⁿᵏ	MHeDG9	HcpS 100	⒠Dese duVl 119 SmtmePmse 9
31Mar76	8OP	17⁰:46²1:112¹:403ft 2 119	2¹	2½	12	1ⁿᵏ	McHeDG2	HcpS 93	⒠SumertmePrmise119 Baygo 9
29Feb76	8SA	1⅛:48²1:123¹:492ft 17 114	1¹	3¹	2ʰ	2ⁿᵒ	McHgeDG5	InvH 85	⒠FscntgGrl 115 SmrtmePmse 8
14Feb76	9Hia	⑦ 1⅛ 1:48²hd 3½ 114	2½	21½	2¹	2½	McHgeD1	HcpS 91	⒠YsDrMggy116 SmrtmePmse 14
4Feb76	9Hia	⑦ 1¹⁄₁₆ 1:414fm 4¾ 115	1²	11½	12	2ⁿᵒ	McHeD12	HcpS 89	⒠Redndcy117 SmrtimePrnise 12

No streak, no claim, no repeat, no step-up in class. No play.

Nowata Pride   **117**   Gr. c (1973), by Thermos—Swing Time Too, by Leisure Time.
Breeder, C. E. Stewart (Okla.).

Owner, Mrs. J. Potrykus. Trainer, J. Van Berg.   **$12,500**

					1976	2	1	0	0	$6,400
					1975	3	1	1	0	$3,768

11 Mar76	10P	6 f :22¹ :46²1:13 ft	2 ▲122	4²	3²	42½	51¾	MapleS7	15000 78	Two Rivers 115	Quen Boy 12
24 Feb76	10P	6 f :214 :46 1:113ft	12 116	1½	1¹	13½	1¼	MapleS1	15000 87	NwataPride116	RunForClem 12
22 Nov75	10HP	6½ f :23² :474 1:222gd	4½ 113	12¹	61¹	61²2	41²2³	StraussR8	HcpS 46	Alastair 122	Tidoc 12
11 Nov75	1HP	6 f :25 :49¹¹:161¹ft	3-5 ▲120	1¹	12	13	15	StraussR1	Mdn 71	NowataPre120	NationlArmr 8
29 Oct75	1HP	4 f :23³ :483ft	3¾ 120	4	44½	47½	25	StraussR7	Mdn 77	SenatrKiddoo120	NowtaPde 10

Feb 8 OP 4f ft :49⅗b

Van Berg isn't the only trainer who goes on winning streaks. All good trainers tend to get hot from time to time. It's important to be able to detect such patterns in the making.

Sometimes a trainer will point for a particular meeting, à la Glenn C. Smith or Ida Mae Parrish. Sometimes he must sacrifice a month or two of racing to get ready.

When Frank Martin, a hard man to pin down, went to California for the 1974–1975 winter racing season, he obviously had Aqueduct on his mind. Martin won only two races in fifty-odd starts at Santa Anita, but he returned to New York with a barnful of tigers. Three weeks into his 1975 Aqueduct winter invasion Martin had nineteen winners; eight weeks later he had fifty. An astute player in California or New York, who was willing to look through Frank Martin's window might well have gotten the message by the third racing day.

Just as the best trainers tend to get hot, they also suffer occasional losing streaks. Fortunately, the player can often spot such losing patterns in the making.

Has the trainer abandoned a successful pattern or strategy? Perhaps he has had to push his horses very hard of late in pursuit of extra victories. Maybe horses and trainer need a rest. Or maybe the horseman is trying to shake off the effects of tough recent defeats or a disastrous break. A few years ago John Parisella, a fine horseman, lost most of his horses by fire. Even when he got new stock it took him a full year to get back into a winning groove. And there are some trainers who don't need a disaster to bring out their worst.

Del Carroll, Reggie Cornell, and John Gaver Sr. are three interesting cases in point. For many years Carroll has been a prominent trainer with a decent overall record. His fillies have won many allowance-class sprints in New Jersey, Kentucky, Delaware, and Florida. He is also a consistent winner on the turf course and does quite well with lightly raced two- and three-year-olds in maiden races. But he has a hole in his game. A big hole.

When Bee Bee Bee upset the Preakness field in 1972, leaving Key to the Mint and Riva Ridge in his wake, the sloppy track helped, but the race was no fluke. Carroll had a very fast horse on his hands. In 1970 Carroll got Bushido ready to score a well-deserved and quite predictable upset in the prestigious John B. Campbell Handicap; Bushido looked very impressive that day. In 1974 Carroll had Better Arbitor and Eastern Lord, two genuinely fast three-year-olds in a year that sorely lacked quality. With all these horses, Carroll changed strategies, pointed for silly races, worked his horses too fast and too often, missed numerous opportunities, and won very few races.

I'll consider a Carroll-trained longshot in a stakes event; but once the form of his horse is exposed, I expect it to deteriorate as fast as he developed it. No trainer can lose control of a good horse and expect it to run to its potential.

Although Carroll has squandered opportunities several times, I doubt any trainer has lost control more often than Reggie Cornell. After gaining a noteworthy reputation in 1958 as the man behind the incredible Silky Sullivan (would you believe Silky once won a 6½-furlong race at Santa Anita after breaking *forty-seven lengths* behind his field!), Cornell won some and lost some during the next twelve years without stirring up much fuss. In the early 1970s, however, he was given the top training post at fabled Calumet Farm, once the nation's premier racing stable. It turned out to be a disastrous relationship.

Calumet had been in decline for much of the 1960s but began a strong comeback under Henry Forrest in 1968 with Forward Pass and other promising horses. Cornell inherited a stable on the rebound, a stable that was destined to provide him with more top-class racing prospects during the next few years than most trainers get to work with in a lifetime: horses like Gleaming, Bold and Able, Eastern Fleet, Prince Turian, Turn to Turia, and the freakishly fast Raise a Cup. All these horses won at least one stakes race very impressively to signal championship potential, and at least half a dozen more showed similar ability in their first or second starts. Every spring Calumet seemed loaded for bear. But by

August Cornell had very few sound horses to work with; most, it seems to me, were kept out of races that were all too obviously theirs to win and instead were pushed to the breaking point on the training track. In my opinion, there is no trainer in all of racing who asks so much of his horses in the morning and gets so little for the effort in the afternoon. With first-timers and absentees Cornell, who was fired by Calumet in early 1976, still remains a 20 percent winner. But two or three races and a dozen workouts later the player can begin marking the calendar for the day when he will read of the horse's sudden departure from competition.

John Gaver Sr., who is always dangerous with a first-time starter and has some outstanding victories to his credit, is nevertheless another trainer who tends to put excessive pressure on his horses in the morning. After years of watching him handle the Greentree Stable stock, I am three-quarters convinced the man thinks each horse is or should be Tom Fool, the rugged handicap star Gaver developed in the early 1950s. Some horses need that kind of intense training regimen to get into shape; a few even require it throughout their careers. Most, however, will buckle under the punishment and either sulk or break down. Frankly, my mind boggles at the number of races a patient trainer like Frank Whiteley Jr. or Elliott Burch would have won with some of the horses trained by Carroll, Cornell, and Gaver, horses that flashed signs of brilliance and horses that you and I will never hear about. The player has to be on his guard with trainers like that. The horses they train are liable to run off form or lose races they should win.

Give Burch a promising two-year-old and you may see an early win, but it is doubtful you'll see the true ability of the horse until it turns three on New Year's Day. Like Charles Whittingham, king of West Coast stakes competition, Burch trains horses to run far and to last from one season to the next.

Fast workouts? Definitely. But each workout is designed to complement the horse's progress in actual races—to advance it toward a longer distance, sharpen its speed, or just keep it within range of Burch's control between important engagements. Once top form has been achieved, Burch will decrease the frequency, the speed, or the distance of the workouts (or all three) in direct proportion to the horse's actual racing opportunities. With that kind of sensible management, Elliott Burch frequently gets two, three, or four wins in a row out of his best-grade stock. And he is just as liable to do that with a good grass horse as he is with a three-year-old colt or filly. The player who knows that about Burch's training skill can string along for a very profitable ride.

Glowing Tribute   **121** B. f (1973), by Graustark—Admiring, by Hail to Reason. Breeder, P. Mellon (Va.).

1976   9   5   1   1 $91,825

Owner, Rokeby Stable.   Trainer, E. Burch.   1975   5   1   1   1 $8,460

6 Aug76	8Sar	⊤ 1₁⅟₁₆ :46 1:10¹1:41¹fm	6-5	▲113	2¹½	2¹	1h	1²	DayP8		HcpO 91	ⒻGlowgTribte113 Assmblyn 10
17 Jly 76	6Aqu	⊤ 1⅛ :49 1:13 1:49¹gd	3½	110	1h	2h	1½	1¾	DayP4		HcpS	ⒻGlwngTribute110 Bubbling 6
10 Jly 76	7Aqu	⊤ 1 :47²1:12¹1:36¹fm	4-5	▲111	1¹	11½	14	12¾	DayP4		Alw	ⒻGlowngTrbute111 StdntLdr 8
31 May76	6Bel	⊤ 1₁⅟₁₆ :46²1:10¹1:41¹fm	10	112	1²	11½	13	15	DayP,		Alw 94	ⒻGlowngTrbte112 StdntLdr 9
4 May76	7Bel	6 f :22⁴ :45³1:11 ft	11	111	86¼	98¾	75¾	3³	GustinesH8		Alw 84	ⒻFurling 113 Desert Boots 10
9 Apr76	7Aqu	6 f :23 :46²1:11⁴ft	4½	121	52¾	35½	47	45	GustinesH5		Alw 79	ⒻIn theOffing114 DesertBts 6
29 Mar76	6Aqu	7 f :23 :46¹1:23⁴ft	3	121	55	54¼	43	44¼	VasquezJ6		Alw 78	ⒻFrlssQueen118 In theOffng 9
5 Mar76	6Hia	6 f :22¹ :46 1:11²ft	4¾	116	55	33½	1¹	15	GustinesH9		Alw 86	ⒻGlowingTrbte116 PlsntTne 10
21 Feb76	5Hia	6 f :22¹ :46¹1:12¹ft	5¾	116	3¾	4¾	2h	2¹	GustinesH2		Alw 81	ⒻSecretGss111 GlwingTrbte 9
4 Nov75	6Bel	7 f :23 :46⁴1:24³ft	7¾	113	1³	11½	43½	79¼	MontoyaD5		Alw 70	ⒻZookalu 116 Dalton Road 8
10 Oct75	3Bel	7 f :22³ :45²1:24⁴ft	1	▲121	1h	2³	53½	69	MontoyaD6		Alw 69	ⒻDancer'sVixen121 FstSaw 7

Aug 3 Sar 4f ft :48b   July 7 Bel 5f ft 1:01b   July 2 Bel 6f ft 1:13b

---

Here are the past performances of Arts and Letters as they appeared in early 1969. The workout line shows that Burch was beginning to crank this horse up for major improvement. He got it. Ten months later Arts and Letters was voted Horse of the Year over one of the best crops of three-year-olds I've ever seen.

Arts and Letters 113 Ch. c (1966), by Ribot—All Beautiful, by Battlefield.
Breeder, P. Mellon (Va.).　　　　1969　1 0 0 1　　$550
Owner, Rokeby Stable.　Trainer, E. Burch.　　1968　6 2 1 0　$18,898

Jan25-69⁶Hia	7 f 1:22⅖ft	3½	119	54½ 45	36	36	CruguetJ⁴	Alw 89 AckAck117 Dist'ctive119 A'ts a'dL't'rs 9
Nov 2-68⁸Lrl	1₁₆ 1:44 ft	2¾	122	42½ 22	32	41½	Vel'q'zJ⁷	ScwS 96 King Emperor 122 Dike 122 Mr. Leader 8
Oct15-68⁶Bel	1 1:36⅖ft	9-5	▲122	2½ 12	13	12½	Vel'squezJ⁹	Alw 92 A'ts a'dL'rs122 Hyd't122 K'g of t'eC'e 9
Sep25-68⁵Bel	7 f 1:24½ft	3	▲122	6³ 33	1ʰ	13½	Velasq'zJ⁹	Mdn 86 A'ts a'dL't'rs122 H'd'l'g't122 W'c'tH'ls 12
Sep18-68¹Bel	6 f 1:11½ft	3¾	122	3³ 21½	2½	23	Vel'quezJ²	Mdn 86 K'g of t'eS'a122 A's a'dL's122 El'tW'k 14
Sep11-68⁴Aqu	6 f 1:12⅗sy	2	▲122	57½ 56	45½	44¾	TurcotteR⁶	Mdn 76 Royal Tom 122 Full of Gin 119 Izaak 12
Aug 9-68⁵Sar	5½ f 1:04⅘ft	5	122	3½ 2¹	33½	47	PincayLJr¹	Mdn 86 DixieGus122 Ch'nHarb'r122 B'uBr'm'l 12

Feb 14 Hia 3f ft :35h　　　**Feb 11 Hia 5f ft :59h**　　　**Feb 8 Hia 1m ft 1:37h**

Some trainers are very strong or weak in one type of racing situation, and the player should know that too.

When Anthony Basile saddles a first-time starter in Kentucky during the spring, the results say 60 percent wins or seconds.

When Lou Rondinello puts a first-timer on the track, anytime, anywhere, a 96 percent losing record says throw the horse out.

Mackenzie Miller, an ace with fast-working two-year-olds, is even better than that with grass-racing stock of all ages. Miller has few peers on the turf, and his win record with newcomers to the infield is better than 40 percent. Again, there is no theory of handicapping that will explain Miller's uncanny success on the turf with horses that look like Student Leader and Fun Forever. But knowledge of the man's special talent can surely help us evaluate their chances when we see them.

Student Leader 115 Dk. b. or br. f (1973), by Personality—Class Is Out, by Outing Class.
Breeder, K. Frazheim II. (Ky.).　　1976　3 1 0 0　$6,600
Owner, K. Franzheim II.　Trainer, M. Miller.　　1975　3 1 0 1　$6,480

16 May76 6Bel	① 1 :45³1:09³1:36 fm	5	111	41¾ 34½ 2²	11½	VelsquezJ⁶	Alw 91 StudentLeadr111 PrmsdOne 9
3 May76 4Bel	6 f :22⅖ :46³1:11¹ft	8½	114	8¹² 8¹⁰ 8⁷	64½	VelsquezJ¹	Alw 81 ⑦Desiree 114 Light Frost 8
24 Apr76 5Aqu	6 f :22² :45²1:11 ft	6	114	54½ 66½ 7¹¹ 8¹⁴	VelsquezJ¹	Alw 74 ⑦Furling 118 Swim 8
¹9 Nov75 3Aqu	7 f :23⁴ :47²1:25⁴ft	6-5	▲119⁵	2½ 1ʰ 1ʰ	1¹½	VelasquezJ³	Mdn 75 ⑦StudentLeadr119 InteOfq 7
29 Oct75 1Bel	5 f :23 :46⁴1:13ʰft	5	119	88½ 75½ 45	3⁸½	VelasquezJ⁻	Man 79 ⑥ SweetBernice119 InteOfq 12
13 Oct75 4Bel	6 f :22⁴ :46³1:11²ft	3	121	9¹⁷10¹² 6¹¹	6¹²	VelasqzJ¹²	Mdn 73 ⑦ZooKaly 121 Bite the Dust 12

May 27 Bel trt 5f ft 1:02⅖b　**May 22 Bel trt 4f ft :49h**　**May 13 Bel trt 3f ft :36⅖b**

Fun Forever 117 B. f (1973), by Never Bend—Fairway Fun, by Prince John.
Br., L. Combs II. & Wm. Floyd (Ky.).　　1976　7 1 1 2　$10,960
Owner, W. Floyd.　Trainer, Mac Miller.

20 Aug76 2Sar	① 1₁₆ :46³1:11⁴1:42²fm	4½	117	2¹½ 1¹½ 1³	17¾	VelasqzJ⁴	Mdn 85 ⑦FunFrvr117 Two fr theShw 11
11 Aug76 6Sar	1₁₆ :47¹1:12¹1:50⁴gd	3-2	▲117	33 2³ 4¹³	4²¹	VelsqezJ²	Mdn 60 ⑦Table Hopper 110 Bashful 8
26 Jly 76 5Aqu	6 f :22² :45⁴1:12 ft	6½	116	65½ 44 25	22¾	MartnsG¹²	Mdn 80 ⑦IronPromise116 FunForever 12
29 May76 2Bel	1₁₆ :46²1:11⁴1:44⁴ft	7	1105	2½ 32 7¹⁷	9²²	MartensG⁹	Mdn 56 ⑦LaughingKys115 TbleHppr 9
12 May76 7Bel	1₁₆ :48 1:12³1:44³ft	8-5	▲114	4ⁿᵏ 31½ 67	7¹⁴	VelasqzJ³	Mdn 62 ⑦DonaMaya114 TbleHopper 10
30 Apr76 4Aqu	6 f :22¹ :45³1:11 ft	1	▲114	65½ 56 37½	34½	VelasqzJ⁴	Mdn 83 ⑦SisterJulie112 MissPrism 8
19 Apr76 2Aqu	6 f :22 :45 1:10⁴ft	2e	▲112	44½ 46 53½	32½	VelquezJ²	Mdn 87 ⑦ShnghaiMry114 Qn'sGmbt 10

Aug 17 Sar tc 3f fm :36⅖h　**Aug 10 Sar 3f sy :34⅖h**　**Aug 7 Sar trt 4f ft :48½h**

J. M. Bollero, Joe Pierce, and T. J. Kelly are other trainers who do exceptionally well in grass races, especially in allowance and stakes company. There are, in fact, too many successful turf trainers for me to list, for grass racing has become very popular in recent seasons. Which introduces a digression of sorts.

There is a book on the market, a well-intentioned generally informative book, that tells all the secrets of turf race handicapping. Or so the ads claim. It sells for twenty bucks.

The only problem with this book (ignoring the $20 price) is that it may be five years too late. Turf racing is no longer a one-dimensional game for students of breeding who happen to have a smattering of knowledge about trainers or class. Yes, you can pick winners on the turf by knowing something about bloodlines—some breeds do show a natural affinity for grass racing (see Chapter 13). Yes, you can also pick winners on the turf by paying attention to trainers like Mackenzie Miller and J. M. Bollero. But you should know a great deal about class, track bias, and condition as well.

Turf racing is extremely competitive now. Whereas formerly three-quarters of the horses entered in any grass race could be easily eliminated on the basis of wrong blood or poor turf form, today the majority of grass races include many horses that are well suited to the conditions. To successfully handicap turf races in the late 1970s you need no fewer tools and skills than you do for any other kind of race. End of digression.

Of all the 7,000 trainers in North America, there is one man who seems to be in a class by himself. He is an incredible talent named Allen Jerkens.

In the early 1960s Jerkens revved up a sprint-type named Beau Purple to take the measure of the mighty Kelso, not once, but three times.

Later in the decade he took Handsome Boy, another

sprinter, and developed him into a winner of four straight $100,000 route races.

During that period he was the leading trainer in New York. More wins, more money won, more stakes, highest win percentage. But no trainer has ever had the kind of year that Jerkens had in 1973.

In the early spring Jerkens cranked up a $25,000 claiming filly named Poker Knight to win an allowance sprint. The result was a surprise, for Jerkens had not trained the filly for speed. Building her stamina through long, slow training gallops, he had hoped to stretch her out in distance at a later date. By virtue of her surprising victory, Jerkens realized that Poker Knight was going to be a much better horse than he had thought.

On April 3 Jerkens entered her in another allowance sprint. Another win. He then stepped up his program, working her a mile in modest time four days later—a work too slow to make the clocker's tab. April 10, another sprint race, this time against the fastest three-year-old filly in the country—the undefeated Windy's Daughter.

"I was more curious to see what she would do than thinking she would win," said Jerkens later that summer. What she did was come within a length of beating Windy's Daughter, closing ground in the stretch.

Two weeks later Jerkens was convinced that Poker Knight could beat any filly in the country at a mile or more. In successive races the ex-claimer proved him right, beating Numbered Account and Summer Guest, the two top fillies in America.

A few months later Jerkens was at it again. Onion to beat Secretariat, paying $13.60; although I've made larger wagers, this was the most painful, most professional bet I have ever made.

Onion came into the Whitney Stakes on the first Saturday in August 1973 with a superior sprint race win over the track on the first Tuesday. The great Secretariat came into the same race with subpar workouts, a signal that had tipped off his subpar performance in the Wood Memorial at Aqueduct in April. Onion was the speed of the field, a four-year-old getting a weight concession from a three-year-old. (That's a big edge, bigger than most people know; see page 126.)

Secretariat drew the rail, which was as dead as I had ever seen it at Saratoga. The few horses that had made moves hugging the rail on the far turn during the preceding week of racing were all eligible to improve dramatically in their next starts.

In all my handicapping experiences I have rarely encountered a situation that was more ripe for an upset. But I was torn and I was angry. Secretariat was the most compelling horse I had ever seen. Every race he ran was different, each more dynamic than the one before. I was emotionally involved with this horse. I rooted for him just like I root for other superior athletic talents—not only the ones that hit the home runs, leap higher than anyone else, or shoot the eyes out of the basket, but the ones that step into another dimension of performance when nothing less than that will get the job done. Damascus, Dr. Fager, Kelso, Majestic Prince, and Canonero II had shown me that kind of talent a few times each. Secretariat did it better than any of them, and he did it repeatedly: in his debut, in his second start, in the Sanford Stakes, in the Hopeful Stakes, in each of the Triple Crown races (and later in the Man O' War Stakes on the grass). I was angry because I was spoiled. I did not want to see him at anything less than his best.

Cold logic said the race was even up. Onion and Jerkens versus a potentially subpar Secretariat and Lucien Laurin. No other result seemed possible. But the tote board said Onion.

Actually Secretariat put in a fine race, gaining three

lengths along the deepest part of the track on the final turn. At the top of the stretch it looked like he was going to drive past Onion and win by daylight. My schizophrenia was showing. I forgot about my bet and screamed for him to do it. But he never uncorked his explosive move. Onion stayed in the middle of the track the whole trip and pulled away in the final five strides. I cashed all my tickets save one.

But Jerkens was hardly through. Days later he bought Prove Out, who had been an allowance-class sprinter for the better part of three seasons. Under Jerkens the horse needed but three weeks to begin a new career as the biggest giant killer of them all.

On the next-to-last day at Saratoga, Jerkens cut him loose to defeat Forego in a seven-furlong allowance race, posting a new track record.

Two weeks later Prove Out tied the Belmont Park track mark for $1\frac{1}{16}$ miles. Two weeks after that he was at Bowie, facing the improving True Knight, a bona-fide handicap horse. I was there too, and of course I bet Prove Out even though he went to post at 8–5 odds. By now I was as mesmerized as everyone else. At the top of the stretch Prove Out was in front and beginning to tire when he bounced off the inner rail. There went some of my Onion money.

One week later I decided to skip a Secretariat race for the first time in his career. It was the Woodward Stakes, and Prove Out put in a superior performance, one of the top ten races of the past twenty years. Secretariat ran just a bit below his exceptional Kentucky Derby form and got his head handed to him. Jerkens again. Incredible.

For an encore, Prove Out showed he was no fluke by beating the other half of the Meadow Stable's team, Riva Ridge, in the two-mile Jockey Club Gold Cup.

In day-to-day racing at Aqueduct, Belmont, and Saratoga, Jerkens is a 25 percent winning trainer overall, but he does have a pattern that produces better than 40 percent winners.

What does Allen Jerkens do with an improving horse? Move it up in company as soon as possible. Or stretch it out in distance or put it on the turf course.

How does one spot a ready-set-go Jerkens runner? Very fast recent trials or a sharp race within the past seven days.

Arcadio II. * **114** Dk. b. or br. h (1971), by Granadero II.—Aretina, by Bell Hop.
Breeder, Haras La Companaia (Chile). 1976 6 2 1 2 $17,508
Owner, Hobeau Farm. Trainer, H. Allen Jerkens. 1975 21 3 4 3 $2,448

24 Aug76	8Sar	Ⓣ 1¼ :46¹¹:111¹:414fm	4½	115	44½ 41½ 2½	1no	HerndezR⁴	Alw 88	Arcadio II. 115	Blue Times	7
17 Aug76	5Sar	6 f :22³ :45³¹:101ft	17	115	2¹ 2¹½ 32½ 32½		RolonJ⁴	37500 86	JacksnSqre117	BldandStrmy	8
18 Apr76	6CIH	Ⓣ a 1¼	2:02²fm	3½e	132		Chile	10	UlloaP	Stk Jadar 132	Poccardi 10
7 Apr76	4HCh	a 6½ f	1:19 ft	7½	134		Chile	3³	UlloaP	Stk Piche 134	Venezuela 10
21 Mar76	7Val	Ⓣa 1⅛	1:554fm	4½	106		Chile	2½	GnzlzF	HcpS Royal Fun 110	Arcadio II. 13
4 Jan76	7CIH	Ⓣa 1⅛	1:413fm	1	ᴬ121		Chile	1¹½	RiveraC	Hcp Arcadio II. 121	Espionaje 8
25 Dec75	7CIH	Ⓣ a 1	1:34²fm	3	106		Chile	2²	GnklezL	Hcp Retraido 132	Arcadio II. 9
14 Dec75	5CIH	Ⓣ a 1¼	2:01⁴fm	†	134		Chile	12½	UlloaP	Hcp Arcadio II. 134	Mesurado 5

†No Pari-mutuel wagering.
<u>Aug 22 Sar 3f f :36b</u> Aug 12 Sar 3f ft :37⅖b Aug 4 Sar 4f ft :47⅕hg

---

Tell Me All **121** B. f (1973), by Cyane--Lead Me On, by Native Dancer.
Breeder, Mooring Stable (Md.). 1976 8 5 1 0 $57,355
Owner, Hobeau Farm. Trainer, H. A. Jerkens. 1975 1 M 1 0 $1,760

5 May76	8Bel	7 f :22³ :45³¹:23¹ft	6¾	113	3² 2¹ 2ʰ 1½	RuaneJ⁴	AlwS 86	ⒻTellMeAll 113	DrlyPrcious	5
26 Apr76	4Aqu	1 :46³¹:103¹:35 ft	3-2	ᴬ109	11½ 12 17 11¹	RuaneJ¹	Alw 91	ⒻTellMeAll 109	BusySaxon	5
12 Apr76	5Aqu	6 f :234 :47²¹:112ft	4-5	ᴬ109	1ʰ 1ʰ 1¹ 12½	RuaneJ¹	Alw 86	ⒻTellMeAll 109	FnnyPculiar	6
3 Mar76	9Hia	1½ :46¹¹:102¹:493ft	20	114	1¹ 35½ 714 819	RuaneJ⁸	AlwS 65	ⒻT.V.Vixen116	AnneCmpbll	10
18 Feb76	9Hia	7 f :23 :46 1:23¹ft	4	112	5¹½ 75¾ 66 67¾	RuaneJ⁶	AlwS 81	ⒻT.V.Vixen11	FortyNineSnsts	11
7 Feb76	6Hia	7 f :234 :47 1:242ft	2-3	ᴬ116⁵	3½ 1ʰ 1¹ 1¹	VelezR1⁸	Alw 83	ⒻTellMeAll 116	Cohabitatn	10
24 Jan76	6Hia	7 f :23 :45⁴¹:232ft	7-5	ᴬ109⁵	3² 2³ 1¹ 14	VelezR1³	Alw 88	ⒻTell Me All 109	Polipeg	12
16 Jan76	3Hia	6 f :214 :45¹¹:102sy	9-5	ᴬ121	2¹½ 2¹½ 2½ 2¹	BaezaB⁸	Mdn 90	ⒻMisukaw 121	Tell Me All	11
24 Sep75	3Bel	6 f :22³ :46³¹:112sy	3¾	121	63¾ 31½ 24 27¾	SthRC⁹	M45000 77	ⒻXalapaSnrse121	TellMeAll	10

May 21 Bel 3f ft :34½h May 18 Bel 6f ft 1:12⅖h <u>May 4 Bel 3f ft :34½h</u>

Clean 'Em Up **112** Dk. b. or br. c (1973), by Handsome Boy—Mopkins, by Bolero.
Breeder, Hobeau Farm (Fla.). 1976 4 1 1 0 $7,380
Owner, Hobeau Farm. Trainer, H. Allen Jerkens.

19 May76	5Bel	6 f :224 :46¹¹:10¹sy	3	114	4¾ 1ʰ 2ʰ 1³	MapleE⁷	Mdn 91	Clean 'EmUp114	ThirdWorld	8
15 May76	3Bel	7 f :234 :45⁴¹:242ft	7-5	ᴬ114	2ʰ 1ʰ 11 2¾	GustinesH⁶	Mdn 79 Azirae 114	Clean 'Em Up	8
26 Jan76	4Hia	6 f :22 :45 1:11 ft	9-5	ᴬ122	6⁵ 45 43½ 56¾	GustinesH⁶	Mdn 81	LittleFishrmn122	DancgThf	11
19 Jan76	4Hia	6 f :22² :45³¹:113ft	3¾	122	73½ 99¾ 69 76¾	GustinesH³	Mdn 78	GaitorRatn122	Knight ofLve	12

May 31 Bel 7f ft 1:24½h May 26 Bel 1m ft 1:39⅖h May 25 Bel trt 5f ft 1:02⅕h

---

How can a player uncover the special winning abilities of new trainers operating at any racetrack, or simply formulate intelligent judgments about the present form of any horse entered in any race at any track? A single past performance profile may well answer all the fundamental questions. The trick is to recognize the implications of the evidence. The examples in the next chapter may help to crystallize this point.

8.
"What's He Doing in Today's Race?"

The horse has had ten starts; his last race was a strong performance; the trainer is somebody we have never heard of, or somebody who wins a few races now and then but we don't know how he wins them. How do we decide whether the horse is going to improve, run the same race, or fail to make an impression? What clues in the past performances will help us rate this horse in this field today?

The answer is all the clues we can get—the result charts, the workout listings, and the past performance records of other horses trained by this man or woman. If we had occasion to do that kind of research before we came out to the track, we would be able to make a confident assessment.

In a single past performance profile there are important clues about the fitness of the horse, its class, distance capabilities, and soundness. And in fact about the trainer too.

---

6 FURLONGS—MAIDEN SPECIAL WEIGHT, HIALEAH, FEBRUARY 18, 1976

Nancy's Robert 122 B. c (1972), by Subpet—Sonodra, by Midpassage.
Breedtr, H. E. Robinson (Fla.).

Owner, H. E. Robinson. Trainer, G. Zateslo.

| | | | | | | | | | | | | 1976 | 2 M 0 1 | $600 |
| | | | | | | | | | | | | 1975 | 5 M 0 0 | $165 |

3 Feb76 2Hia	6 f :22³ :46 1:10³ft	71	1175	2h	65	54	34½	DruryMA⁴	Mdn 86 OldFrankfrt122 DbleMerger 10
27 Jan76 3Hia	7 f :23 :46 1:23¹ft	51	122	10¹²	9¹⁵10¹⁵10¹⁶			BrussrdR⁹	Mdn 73 SunnyClime122 DoubleTudor 12
10 Oct75 1Mth	6 f :22³ :45⁴1:10⁴ft	36	1117	3¹	52¾	54¾	65¼	DruryMA¹	Mdn 81 BalTalk118 SparklingSuccs 7
27 Aug75 5Mth	1⁷⁰ :47 1:13¹1:44²ft	13	115	42	43½	57¼	61⁵	ThornbgB⁵	Mdn 81 Doc Rofus 115 West End 8
20 Aug75 3Mth	6 f :22¹ :46¹1:12¹gd	42	117	76½	73¾	58½	58½	ThornbgB⁸	Mdn 71 HigherMarks 117 WestEnd 9
13 Aug75 3Mth	6 f :22¹ :45²1:11²ft	37	117	41½	56½	51²	71⁴	MacBthD¹	Mdn 69 RoyalPower117 IrishOuting 8

Feb 14 GP 5f ft 1:01⅗h   Jan 25 GP 3f ft :37b   Jan 16 GP 6f sy 1:15⅗b

---

Notice the August 1975 races and the six-week gap until Nancy's Robert was able to get back on the track.

The October 10 race was an encouraging effort; but there was no follow-up race to take advantage of the horse's slight but real improvement. Obviously, this sparsely raced colt has had his physical problems.

On January 27, 1976, Nancy's Robert returned to competition but did very little, running in back of the pack.

Without checking the result chart for the race, we

might consider the possibility that there was interference at the start. In any case, this bad trip didn't put Nancy's Robert out of commission again. In fact, his trainer put him back on the track for another race the following week and gave him a five-furlong workout just four days before today's race.

The February 3 race was a marked improvement, the best race of Nancy's Robert's interrupted career. The workout that followed was also good. A positive sign of health, a touch of speed, and a logical move toward better condition.

The evidence says that trainer Zateslo has done a fine job straightening this horse out, and there is every likelihood that Nancy's Robert is on the verge of reaching his peak. We don't know what that peak is, we don't know how long he will be able to hold it, and we don't know whether he will reach it today. But we do know that he is already competitive at this class level and distance, and we have a right to think he's going to run a stronger race, his best to date. Our optimism for this horse's winning chances would be tempered by other strong contenders, but this is a typical maiden race—only two other horses in the field look like they can run. One has had fourteen previous maiden races and three seconds. The other is a well-bred first-time starter that has been training well enough to be dangerous. Nancy's Robert, who should have been a 9–5 favorite, paid $12 to win. The first-timer ran second, beaten by four lengths.

6½ FURLONGS—$8,500 CLAIMING, HAZEL PARK, NOVEMBER 15, 1975

Toolin Around	117	B. g (1968). by Tooley—Saragino by Cosmic Bomb. Breeder. A. J. Algeri (Ky.).		1975	14	2	3	1	$11,073
Owner, Standen Stable. Trainer, A. Blundell.		$8.500		1974	4	1	0	1	$8.000

8 Nov75	5HP	4 f :224	:474ft	4	1175	6	76½ 76¾ 77½	GarciaJR7	Alw 78 WinsomeWine119 RightPckt 7
1 Nov75	5HP	6½ f :223	:4711:204ft	4	1125	2½	1½ 13 31	GarciaJR4	10000 76 Fast Left 112 I Can Hackett 7
18 Oct75	4HP	6½ f :223	:4721:20 gd	9-5	▲1125	44½	32 1h 24	GrciaJR3	10000 77 OwnPower119 ToolinAround 6
11 Oct75	5HP	6½ f :224	:4631:184ft	3¾	1125	54¼	1½ 13 2¾	GrciaJR5	10000 86 Bandwagn119 ToolinAround 9
4 Oct75	7HP	4 f :221	:464ft	26	118	5	85½ 75½ 71¾	MillerS7	Alw 89 FastTrackMiss115 BoldDggr 9
20 Sep75	6HP	6½ f :23	:4731:211hy	17	117	42	23 24 610	MillerS6	10000 64 LightCharger117 FamsPatrt 8
13 Sep75	7HP	6½ f :224	:4641:*92ft	15	117	2h	2½ 68½ 710	BreenR5	12500 74 Brunate 115 Light Charger 8
30 Aug75	5HP	6½ f :232	:4831:232m	4¾	117	55½	56 713 816	MillerS5	10000 48 LightCharger110 Chest Eqle 3
23 Aug75	5HP	6½ f :232	:4811:21 m	3	120	33	32 23 615	MapleS2	12500 61 WavetheFlag115 LdyRchelle 7
9 Aug75	5HP	6½ f :222	:4621:184ft	4-5	▲*20	53½	54 45 711	MapleS1	15000 76 E'Omer 115 Fast Fun 8
Oct 30 HP 3f ft :38⅘b					Oct 2 HP 3f ft :36⅖h				

After two wins and one second no longer appearing in the current past performance profile (see consistency box in upper right corner), Toolin Around was unable to sustain his speed throughout August and September.

Instead of resting this useful gelding, trainer Blundell tried an unusual strategy. If it hadn't worked we might have had reason to think Blundell was off his rocker or at least out of touch with his horse; but the maneuvering did work, so we ought to take a closer look.

On October 4 Blundell ran the already fast-breaking Toolin Around in an ultrashort four-furlong race against some of the fastest-breaking horses on the grounds. The betting public dismissed him at 26–1, and it was right. But one week later Toolin Around was back in top form, the form he maintained without winning in his next two starts at $10,000 claiming.

On November 8, one week before today's race, Blundell repeated the same four-furlong prep race strategy, but this time, unfortunately, the betting public was unaware of the trainer's intentions.

The "go" part of the pattern is today's race, an $8,500 claimer, a slight but important drop in class. This time Toolin Around should (and did) get back on the winning track. Put Mr. Blundell's name down for future reference. He has some unusual methods and was slow to realize the need for a drop in class, but he did use his head with this horse. At $7.60 Toolin Around was a steal.

---

6 FURLONGS—$20,000 ALLOWANCE PURSE, BELMONT PARK, JUNE 7, 1976

Desert Boots   **107**   B. f (1973), by Ridan—Signal Flag, by Restless Wind.
Breeder, Mrs. Barbara Joslin (Fla.).

Owner, W. M. Joslin. Trainer, S. DiMauro.

		1976	7	1	4	1	$16,300
		1975	2	1	0	0	$5,940

17 May76	7Bel	6 f :22	:44¹:103ft	7¾	106⁵	11½	11½	12	2½	MartinJE⁴	Alw 88 ⒻFurling 114 Desert Boots 7
4 May76	7Bel	6 f :22⁴	:45³¹:11 ft	6¼	105⁵	1½	1ʰ	2ʰ	2¹½	VelezRI⁶	Alw 86 ⒻFurling 113 Desert Boots 10
9 Apr76	7Aqu	6 f :23	:46²¹:114ft	2	⁴113⁵	1²	14	15	2ʰ	VelezRI⁶	Alw 84 ⒻIn theOffing114 DesertBts 6
15 Mar76	7Aqu	6 f :22¹	:45³¹:11¹ft	2½	118	1½	12	13	3²	BaezaB³	Alw 85 ⒻAncntFbles114 Rsn frTrce 9
3 Mar76	8Aqu	6 f :22²	:45²¹:101ft	4¾	114	1½	2ʰ	24	78¼	HoleM⁴	AlwS 84 ⒻToughElsie116 LightFrost 13
14 Feb76	6Hia	6 f :21³	:44³¹:112ft	4-5	⁴116	1½	13	14	11½	BaezaB⁵	Alw 86 ⒻDesertBoots116 She'sTrble 8
31 Jan76	6Hia	6 f :22	:45¹¹:111ft	2¾	114	1½	13	11½	22½	MapleE⁸	Alw 84 ⒻDaltonRoad114 DesrtBoots 12
1 Sep75	3Bel	5 f :22¹	:45⁴¹:1¹²ft	3	⁴119	11½	14	1⁷	18½	BracleVJr⁹	Mdn 85 ⒻDesertB'ts119 Sw'tB'rn'e 12

June 3 Bel trt 1m ft 1:46⅖b   May 29 Bel trt 1m ft 1:45⅕b   May 23 Bel trt 1m ft 1:46⅖b

With two champs in the barn (Wajima and Dearly Precious), Steve DiMauro had quite a season in 1975. In 1976 things were not all that bad, but this particular horse must have driven DiMauro crazy.

Desert Boots is a one-dimensional speedball that simply refuses to keep something in reserve for the stretch run. DiMauro is trying to solve her problem through a program of long, slow, stamina-building workouts. The prescription might work and it might not, but it is sensible. In this case it did not work.

Perhaps a route race would get the message across better than the workouts. But there is a chance too that nothing will work. Desert Boots could have congenital wind problems that will always keep her from beating good horses at six furlongs.

In a game like racing we have a right to go our separate ways with a horse like this.

Some may be willing to give DiMauro the benefit of the doubt. I prefer not. Not unless there is a track bias operating in the horse's favor. I want proof that DiMauro has overcome Desert Boots' problem or insurance if he hasn't— insurance of a track bias or proof only a winning race can provide. And I also want a big price.

Although horses with strong early speed are always dangerous and Desert Boots could well win at any time, I'm willing to give her up to the rest of the crowd until she learns to carry her speed to the wire.

Horses that quit in race after race are notorious money burners.

6 FURLONGS—$10,500 CLAIMING, BELMONT PARK, SEPTEMBER 1, 1976

Panda Bear 113 B. g (1973), by My Dad George—Gold Threat, by Infidel.
Breeder, Martha Broadbent (Fla.).

												1976	7	2	1	1	$12,770
Owner, B. Combs II. Trainer, J. Martin. $10,500   1975   3   1   1   1 $5,865

11 Aug76	2Sar	6 f :22² :46²1:11²m	4½	119	32½ 31½ 52½ 53½	BaezaB⁴	12500 80	Chompchomp 117	I'mProud 7
18 Jly 76	2Aqu	6 f :22⁴ :46³1:12²ft	8-5	▲117	31½ 32½ 22 1ⁿᵏ	BaezaB⁷	10000 81	PandaBear117	TakeYourBts 7
16ʲJun76	9Bel	7 f :23 :46⁴1:25²ft	3	117	21½ 21½ 3ⁿᵏ 36½	CrdroAJr⁶	12500 69	Fling 119	Spotted Gem 8
22 May76	9Bel	6 f :22³ :46 1:113ft	4½	119	3ⁿᵏ 3½ 42½ 76½	CrdoAJr⁸	16000 77	Cayman Isle117	Mgie'sPride 11
13 May76	2Bel	6 f :22³ :46²1:113ft	2½	117	11½ 11½ 1ʰ 1½	CdroAJr⁵	12500 84	PandaBear117	CaymanIsle 9
8 May76	4Bel	6 f :22⁴ :46¹1:113ft	2½	▲112⁵	41½ 41½ 5² 4³	MrtinJE⁸	14000 81	HowiesHeat117	TakeYrBoots 8
15 Apr76	7Aqu	6 f :22³ :46 1:12²ft	2½	▲117	3¹ 1ʰ 2ʰ 21½	HerndzR⁷	12500 79	Break theLock115	PndaBear 11
12 Jly 75	9Tdn	5 f :23² :48 1:00³ft	2½	114	2¹ 1ʰ 3ⁿᵏ 32½	WeilerD³	AlwS 85	FierceRuffian115	HpyMircie 7
2 Jly 75	9RD	5½ f :22 :45 1:04¹ft	3½	113	2ʰ 2¹ 3ⁿᵏ 2⁷	RieraRJr³	AlwS 87	ChanningRoad113	PndaBear 9
21 May75	3CD	5 f :22² :47 :59⁴ft	5½ₑ	122	2½ 11½ 1½ 1ʰ	RieraRJr⁷	Mdn 90	Panda Bear 122	Sam's Act 11

Aug 30 Bel trt 3f ft :37b   Aug 24 Sar trt 3f ft :37⅖b   Aug 19 Sar trt 4f ft :54b

If you've never encountered a horse trained by Jose Martin before, this one should be enough to convince you of his skill with claimers.

In the spring Panda Bear was a solid $12,000 racehorse. During the summer Martin found out she was able to beat only $10,000 stock.

Up and down the class ladder Panda Bear won two races and $12,770. Each time Martin dropped the horse to her proper level, she delivered an improved effort.

Three workouts on the deeper training track leading up to today's race assure us of Panda Bear's fitness. Today's drop in class tells us Martin is thinking win. If you're thinking the same thing after you get through with the rest of the field, you'll catch a $9 mutuel.

6 FURLONGS—$9,500 CLAIMING, BELMONT PARK, SEPTEMBER 1, 1976

Tacky Lady   **116** Ch. f (1973), by Nail—Lady Cavan, by Cavan.
Breeder, Mrs. W. A. Kelley (Del.).   1976..11 3 1 0 $15,930
Owner, Stu-Al Stable.   Trainer, Frank Laboccetta. $9,500   1975.. 2 1 0 0 $2,280

Date	Track	Dist	Time							Jockey	Claim	Sp		
24 Aug76	3Sar	7 f :23	:46³1:244ft	3	116	4²	2²	4²	45¾	VelasqzJ8	15000 75	ⒻJrry'sMona116 JyeuxNeill.	8
6 Aug76	2Sar	6 f :23¹	:46⁴1:12 ft	3½	118	62½	63½	63¾	65½	CdroAJr²	20000 74	ⒻShawi 111 Jerry's Mona	9
15 Jly 76	7Aqu	6 f :22⁴	:46¹1:114ft	2½	▲114	3²	21½	1h	1ⁿᵒ	TurtteR⁹	19000 84	ⒻTackyLady114 JoyousPlsre	9
4 Jly 76	1Aqu	7 f :23²	:46⁴1:24 ft	3½	116	2²	2¹	11½	12¾	MapleE10	15000 81	ⒻTackyLady116 FineAsWne	10
20 Jun76	1Bel	6 f :22⁴	:46⁴1:113ft	2½	▲116	1½	1½	1¹	2ⁿᵒ	MapleE¹	12500 84	ⒻDela Pet 121 Tacky Lady	7
9 Jun76	3Bel	6 f :22⁴	:47²1:124ft	17	113	3²	31½	13	13½	MapleE²	7500 78	ⒻTackyLady113 Encapslate	9
13 May76	1Bel	7 f :23¹	:46³1:261ft	5½	114	43	45½	67½	81²	TurcotteR⁴	8500 59	ⒻFiredRed111 NeverFlow	12
4 May76	1Bel	6 f :23²	:47³1:124ft	3½	116	74	105½	83¾	67¾	CruguetJ²	8500 70	ⒻGldnSl 113 StkeUp theBnd	10
20 Apr76	7Aqu	7 f :22⁴	:46 1:25¹ft	6	116	117½	10¹¹10⁹	10⁶½	CrguetJ¹¹	15000 68	ⒻHoldingOn116 FineAsWine	12

Aug 19 Sar trt 5f ft 1:03⅗b   Aug 2 Sar 3f sy :36b   July 27 Aqu 5f ft 1:02⅖b

Barely six weeks before today's race Tacky Lady was winning against horses worth twice as much as those she is facing today. Tacky Lady is dropping down sharply in class, and the bettors at the track think she's a mortal lock, a 3–5 betting favorite. If they were willing to question why this horse is being discounted so suddenly they might make her 3–5 to wind up being carted off the track in a hurry-up wagon.

This is what is known in the trade as a negative drop in class. A horse that is deteriorating so fast that the owner and trainer can't wait to get rid of her. The player should not be so hasty; there are some trainers who win races with horses like this, but in this specific case, all the signs are negative.

Tacky Lady's best races came when trainer Laboccetta had confidence in her ability. He successfully stepped her up in company four straight times.

This is the second steep drop in class in two weeks. Instead of resting this horse, trainer Laboccetta can't wait to get rid of her. I don't think his loss of confidence should be taken lightly. Throw the horse out.

---

1 1/16 MILES (turf)—$10,000 CLAIMING, ARLINGTON PARK, SEPTEMBER 20, 1976

Manager Ed 113   B. c (1973), by Dust Commander—Amberly, by Ambiorix.
Breeder, R. E. Lehmann (Ky.).   1976   5   0   1   1 $2,774

Owner, A. J. Wozneski.   Trainer, John C. Wozneski. $10,000   1975   12   1   1   2 $4,798

10 Sep76	9AP	⊤ 1 :481 1:142 1:40²fm	3½	114	99¾	99	87¾	86	FiresE⁹	11500	67	BlckCrw114	Knck'sOlympus 11
26 Aug76	5AP	1⅟₁₆ :48 1:122 1:441ft	2	▲114	35½	33½	3½	21½	StoverD¹	11500	90	Lex Legio 112	Manager Ed 7
12 Aug76	7AP	1⅟₁₆ :472 1:1141:434ft	20	112	58½	58	44	44½	StoverD²	13500	88	Sum Chipper 113	Fleet Flit 8
27 Jly 76	7AP	⊤ a 1⅟₁₆ :463 1:1441:442fm	25	1075	51³	615	69½	33¾	RdgzDP⁴	10500		SumChipper114	UnitdKngdm 7
16 Jly 76	6AP	6 f :22 :46 1:12²ft	29	1085	10121113	10121	1012	RdrgzDP⁴	10000	69	Demon Run 113	Ahga Mag 11
13 Nov75	9Haw	6½ f :22² :454 1:181ft	9½	118	87	56	21½	2nk	StoverD⁸	7500	82	Key Sa 117	Manager Ed 10
4 Nov75	9Haw	6 f :22² :461 1:12 sy	8	118	910	79	711	79¾	StovrD¹⁰	10000	76	Lil'sTommie117	SumChipper 11
20 Oct75	7Haw	6 f :22² :453 1:10²ft	26	114	67	612	614	620	CoxR¹		Alw	74	Elocutionist 119	Irish Port 6
14 Oct75	3Haw	6 f :22² :454 1:124ft	13	118	911	98½	63½	44¾	StoverD⁹	10000	77	Jim James 116	Rich Passion 9
29 Aug75	4AP	5½ f :224 :472 1:074sy	6-5	▲122	41½	33½	21	1nk	PatsnG¹	cM7000	76	Manager Ed 122	Kid Louie 12

Sept 20 AP 4f ft :51⅜b   Aug 19 AP 4f ft :50b   Aug 3 AP 3f ft :36⅘b

---

Following eight months of inactivity and a terrible six-furlong race on July 16, Manager Ed delivered a vastly improved performance on July 27. It was Manager Ed's first try beyond a sprint distance, his first try around two turns, and his first attempt on grass. We have no way of knowing whether trainer John Wozneski knew his horse was fit enough to perform as well as it did, but he had a right to feel proud of his work. I suspect, in fact, that it went to his head.

On August 12 Wozneski stepped Manager Ed up in company and switched him back to the main track. The horse ran its best but had to settle for fourth money after failing to gain ground in the stretch. We can excuse the trainer for trying to upgrade his horse on that occasion, but the result was not very encouraging.

On August 26 Wozneski dropped the horse a notch, keeping him on the main track, at a level slightly higher than the prior good race. Again, Manager Ed raced to the full limit of his apparent talent, only to lose momentum in the final yards. He did finish second, but that loss of ground marked the second straight wasted opportunity, a sign that trainer Wozneski misjudged his horse's class or distance capability.

Two weeks and *no* workouts later Wozneski decided to try Manager Ed on the grass again. While everything in the horse's record indicates the preference for a slightly cheaper race, the most plausible explanation for the horse's lackluster performance is that trainer Wozneski has blown it. Today's $10,000 race on the turf is not likely to help this horse's chances. Wozneski had a fit horse on his hands but overestimated its talent. The evidence says this horse has lost its edge in condition and will need every break possible to earn a piece of the purse.

1¼ MILES—$350,000 PURSE, HOLLYWOOD PARK, JULY 20, 1974

Chris Evert 121 Ch. f (1971), by Swoon's Son—Miss Carmie, by T. V. Lark.
Breeder, Echo Valley Horse Farm (Ky.). 1974 4 3 0 1 $159,789
Owner, C. Rosen. Trainer, J. A. Trovato. 1973 5 4 1 0 $93,012

Jun22-74⁸Bel	1 1-2	2:28⅖ft	4-5	▲121	2ʰ	1ʰ	11½	13½	Vel'q'zJ1	ScwS 76	ⒻChrisEvert121	F'staLibre	M'dM'll'r 10
Jun 1-74⁸Bel	1 1-8	1:48⅜sy	2⅜	121	3²	2½	1ʰ	1½	Vel'ezJ14	ScwS 84	ⒻChrisEvert121	M'dMulier	QuazeQ'lt 14
May11-74⁸Aqu	1	1:36 ft	9-5	▲121	2¹	4³	31½	1⅓	Vel'q'zJ1	ScwS 87	ⒻChrisEvert121	ClearC'py	FiestaLibre 9
May 1-74⁸Aqu	7 f	1:24⅖ft	2	▲118	74½	66½	67½	34½	Vel'q'zJ10	AlwS 74	ⒻClearCopy113	ShyDawn	ChrisEvert 10
Nov14-73⁸Aqu	1	1:36⅖ft	4-5	▲121	2ʰ	2ʰ	11	11½	Pi'yLJr11	AlwS 85	ⒻChrisEvert121	Amb'lero	Kh'd'sK'er 11
Nov 3-73⁸CD	7 f	1:25⅕ft	6-5	▲116	9¹¹	9¹³	43½	11¼	Pin'yLJr2	AlwS 81	ⒻChrisEvert116	B'ndl'r	KissMeD'rlin 13
Oct 6-73⁷Bel	1	1:36⅖ft	6¼	121	9⁴	31½	4¹	2½	Cas'aM11	ScwS 85	ⒻBundler121	ChrisEvert	I'm a Pl's're 14
Oct 2-73⁶Bel	6 f	1:10½ft	3	120	5²½	4⁴½	3½	12¾	Pinc'yLJr10	Alw 92	ⒻChrisEv'rt120	Symp'th'tic	F'h'gL'dy 10
Sep14-73³Bel	6 f	1:11 ft	3½	120	3¹½	3³	2½	11½	Pin'yLJr10	Mdn 88	ⒻChrisEvert120	M'dMuller	MamaKali 13

July 18 Hol 4f ft :46⅖h   July 14 Hol 1m ft 1:38⅖h   July 9 Hol 6f ft 1:15b

Here from top to bottom is a well-managed, top-grade racehorse at her seasonal peak. Notice the way trainer Joe Trovato established a solid foundation in 1973 and stretched Chris out in distance with each succeeding start in 1974. A fine piece of work by a man who knows how to get a horse to produce and keep producing.

These were the past performances of Chris Evert prior to her fifty-length "upset" victory over the speedy Miss Musket on July 20, 1974 in one of the richest match races of all time. Although the key to her winning performance was in the workout line, it was not possible to know that without searching for other clues published in that day's edition of the *Form*.

For Saturday stakes races, and especially for championship-caliber events, the *Daily Racing Form*'s reportage is often excellent. For the Kentucky Derby, for instance, Joe Hirsch does an incredible job, logging the daily doings of all the key eligibles for the two months leading up to the race. Every player should take some time to read the news items and columns in the *Daily Racing Form;* there are many useful tidbits and insights that can be gleaned from them.

Deep within the pages of the July 20, 1974, edition of the *Form*, California correspondent Pat Rogerson reported on the fractional times for the latest workouts of both horses. Although he was most impressed with Miss Musket's blazing one-mile training trial in $1:35\frac{1}{5}$, the astute player might have noted that Chris' first quarter-mile fraction in her one-mile workout was noticeably faster. On July 17 Miss Musket worked a half-mile in 48 seconds, a relatively slow move compared with Chris' final workout on July 18. "I told Velasquez to break Chris sharply from the starting gate and not to be worried about getting her tired," said Trovato in Rogerson's report. The significance of Trovato's instructions could hardly be lost on the player who knew that 85 percent of all match races have been won wire to wire. The player may not wish to spend his time researching trainer patterns, but he surely can read his *Racing Form* between races at the track.

9.
The Key Race Method

In late October 1972 I was faced with a unique problem. I had just moved to Columbia, Maryland, and was going to conduct a daily five-minute seminar on handicapping over WLMD radio in the Washington-Baltimore area.

Based on my private results, I thought that I could pick 50 percent winners, show a flat bet profit in the thirteen-week test period, and explain handicapping in the process.

The format was simple. I would handicap races at Laurel racetrack and explain the theories behind the best betting opportunities of the day.

There was one catch. I had been to Laurel racetrack only once, on opening day, October 2. And because I had just joined the staff of *Turf and Sport Digest,* I knew I would not be able to go out to the track more than once a week. I had some familiarity with the leading trainers and their patterns, but I didn't know the horses, the track, or very much else about the local conditions. And I only had a week to prepare myself. In desperation, I did further trainer research, studied post positions, pulled out past performance records and workout listings, and studied the result charts as if I were preparing for an examination before the bar.

A brand new racing surface complicated the problem. Wild upsets were taking place every day as the maintenance crew fought to stabilize conditions. Horses with late speed seemed to have a built-in edge during this period, but it was not easy to tell from the past performance records which horses would be able to produce that late speed. I solved the problem by using a simple research tool I had developed a few years earlier, one that investigates the relationship between a race over the track and future winning performance.

Strange as it may seem, almost every stretch-running Laurel winner with a prior race over the track had displayed one major characteristic: a sign of increased speed on the turn in the previous Laurel race. The implications were too powerful to ignore. The turn was the roughest piece of real estate in Maryland. Any horse in good enough shape to make a move on it was a horse worth tabbing for improvement next time out.

Admittedly, as form settled down and the track stabilized, I was forced to handicap races more thoroughly than that. But I got past the first four weeks with 45 percent winners, including some outrageous longshots. And I was on the air to stay.

It is also true that this was a particularly unusual set of conditions, yet the investigative tool has served me well for many purposes, as it might well serve you. Here is how to set it up. Again you will need to work with a set of chronologically dated result charts.

First, with the most recent race on top, check the index date and race number of the winner's last race: see below, 6Aug76 [1]AP[3] Windy City Butch means Windy City Butch last raced in the first race, August 6, and finished third.

THIRD RACE		6 FURLONGS. (1:08⅗). MAIDENS. SPECIAL WEIGHTS. Purse $7,000. 2-year-olds. Weight, 119 lbs.

AP
August 23, 1976

Value to winner $4,200; second, $1,400; third, $770; fourth, $420; fifth, $210.
Mutuel Pool, $144,583.

Last Raced	Horse	EqtAWt	PP	St	¼	½	Str	Fin	Jockeys	Owners	Odds to $1
6 Aug76 1AP3	Windy City Butch	2 119	6	5	7¹	6½	5³	1nk	MGavidia	S Berry C Scott	2.80
	Cornucopian	2 119	5	6	5h	5²½	4h	2½	GPatterson	E A Cox Jr	a-1.80
14 Aug76 3AP2	Hinkston	2 119	3	4	4³	3½	1½	3⁵	EFires	Levitch-Stone	3.30
29 Jly 76 5AP7	Bask	2 119	9	3	3¹	2¹	2¹	4h	LSnyder	Reineman Stable Inc	a-1.80
	Wellspoken	2 119	7	9	2	9	7²	5h	RBreen	EJmendorf	20.60
1 May76 1Sun4	Knotty Knave	b2 119	1	7	6¹	7¹	6¹½	6³½	JLively	M Ross et al	6.30
6 Aug76 4AP7	East Union	b2 119	4	2	1²	6²½	3¹	7½	JPowell	B-G Bromagen	17.20
23 Apr76 3Kee7	Count Tumiga	2 119	8	8	8²	8¹	8	8²	RSibille	G'ld'n Ch'nce F'm Inc	36.10
11 Aug76 3AP2	Debarcation	b2 119	2	1	2¹	4¹½	8¹	9	JDBailey	S Laser	9.90

Coupled, a-Cornucopian and Bask.
OFF AT 2:53 CDT. Start good. Won driving. Time, :22⅘, :46⅘, :59⅕, 1:11⅘. Track fast.

$2 Mutuel Prices:	6-WINDY CITY BUTCH	7.60	3.40	2.40
	1-CORNUCOPIAN (a-Entry)		3.20	2.40
	4-HINKSTON			2.60

Ch. c, by Lurullah—Christy Blue, by Porterhouse. Trainer, Clifford J. Scott. Bred by Estate of Charles Cunningham (Ky.).

WINDY CITY BUTCH was unhurried early, rallied wide leaving the upper stretch to run down CORNU-COPIAN in the final strides. The latter was unhurried early, drove inside the leaders leaving the eighth pole to wrest the lead late in tht drive but was unable to contain the winner approaching the finish. HINKSTON circled rivals coming out of the turn to take the lead a furlong out, faltered late in the drive. BASK moved between horses coming out of the turn, lacked a closing rally. WELLSPOKEN had to steady while in tight quarters leaving the gate, rallied mildly late to pass tiring rivals. KNOTTY KNAVE went evenly. EAST UNION sprinted out o a clear lead in the early running, tired leaving the upper stretch. COUNT TUMIGA was always outrun. DEBARCATION was through after a half.
Scratched—Dravir.

Next, thumb back to the date and race number indicated to see what the winner did in his last race. But whatever he did, *circle his name*. That circle will forever mean that Windy City Butch won his *next* start.

FIRST RACE
AP
August 6, 1976

6 FURLONGS. (1:08⅗). MAIDENS. SPECIAL WEIGHTS. Purse $7,000. 2-year-olds
Weight, 119 lbs.
Value to winner $4,200; second, $1,400; third, $770; fourth, $420; fifth, $210.
Mutuel Pool, $64,776.

Last Raced	Horse	EqtAWt	PP	St	¼	½	Str	Fin	Jockeys	Owners	Odds to $1
21 Jly 76 5AP8	Fiddlefish	b2 119	4	2	1h	13½	12½	11½	APatterson	Mary Lou Cashman	5.00
29 Jly 76 1AP6	Barely Safe	2 119	9	6	5½	3½	21½	22½	RSibille	Golden Chance F'm Inc	8.40
21 Jly 76 5AP2	Windy City Butch	b2 119	8	5	62½	4h	32½	35	WGavidia	S Berry-C Scott	2.00
	Victory Flag	2 119	6	3	4½	51	64	4½	EFires	Elmendorf	14.00
29 Jly 76 1AP5	Gordon Pasha	b2 119	3	1	33	21	41½	5½	RLTurcotte	D A Hess	2.70
21 Jly 76 5AP5	Beau Dustin	b2 119	7	7	78	76	5½	61½	CStone	Mary Zimmerman	16.50
	Selaru	b2 119	2	9	9	8h	71½	72	PRubbicco	Bar R J's Stable	22.10
	The Stinger	2 119	5	8	81	9	82	82½	HArroyo	R F Salmen	15.90
29 Jly 76 5AP2	Coldwater	2 119	1	4	2h	6½	9	9	RBreen	R Russell	9.00

OFF AT 2:00½ CDT. Start good. Won driving. Time, :22⅗, :46⅖, :58⅘, 1:11⅗. Track good.

Official Program Numbers ↘

$2 Mutuel Prices:

5-FIDDLEFISH	12.00	6.60 4.00
10-BARELY SAFE		7.80 3.80
9-WINDY CITY BUTCH		2.80

Ch. c, by Piko—Noholme's Gal, by Noholme II. Tr., Paul T. Adwell. Bred by Fontainebleau Farm, Inc. (Ky.).

FIDDLEFISH broke alertly to vie for the lead outside two rivals, drew out in the turn and won under a strong hand ride. BARELY SAFE circled rivals coming out of the turn and was gradually getting to the winner. WINDY CITY BUTCH was outrun early, rallied strongly between rivals after a half but was no threat to the top pair. VICTORY FLAG went evenly. GORDON PASHA pressed the early lead while between rivals, faltered leaving the turn. BEAU DUSTIN had no excuses. SELARU and THE STINGER were always outrun. COLDWATER had brief early speed along the rail.

Scratched—Brach's Honey, Promising Dream, Uncle Jett, Restless Rascal.

If you repeat this simple exercise for the most recent fifty or sixty races (you can go back as far as you wish) and if you continue the process every day, you will be adding exceedingly valuable information to dozens of result charts. The data may help you distinguish patterns that are not otherwise detectable.

Maybe you will discover, as I did, that the majority of route race winners at Hazel Park and Latonia racetracks had a prior sprint race for a jumpoff effort. Maybe you will observe that horses shipping from California to New York during the early spring win an astounding percentage of races first crack out of the box. Perhaps you will note that horses coming off the turf course at Delaware Park and other tracks tend to show improved early speed in their next try on the dirt. The possibilities are without limit. Without really trying, you will automatically create the Key Race method, a powerful tool that isolates especially well-run races at every class level.

For example, the three horses circled in the following chart came out of the race to win their very next starts. A Key Race.

FIRST RACE
Aqu
July 15, 1976

1⅛ MILES. (1:47). CLAIMING. Purse $7,500. For 3-year-olds and upward. 3-year-olds, 116 lbs.; older, 122 lbs. Non-winners of a race at a mile and a furlong or over since July 1 allowed 3 lbs.; of such a race since June 15, 5 lbs. Claiming price $8,500; if for less, 2 lbs. allowed for each $250 to $8,000. (Races when entered to be claimed for $7,000 or less not considered.)

Value to winner, $4,500; second, $1,650; third, $900; fourth, $450. Track Mutuel Pool, $106,946. OTB Pool, $87,971.

Last Raced	Horses	Eqt	A	Wt	PP	St	¼	½	¾	Str	Fin	Jockeys	Owners	Odds to $1
25Jun76 6Bel3	Charms Hope	b5		113	1	2	4⁴	4³	4⁷	3½	1nk	MVenezia	J J Stippel	2.50
7Jly 76 1Aqu1	Finney Finster	b4		117	3	7	6⁸	5²	3¹½	2h	2¹¼	ASantiago	Camijo Stable	5.60
9Jly 76 1Aqu1	Good and Bold			110	4	1	1⁴	1⁶	1⁶	1³	3¹³	BDiNicola5	Emmarr Stable	3.00
9Jly 76 1Aqu6	Just Like Pa	b3		109	2	4	3½	3¹½	2h	4⁸	4⁹	DMontoya†	Audley Farm Stable	8.50
8Jly 76 1Aqu1	Wave the Flag		6	115	5	6	7	7	7	5⁶	5⁴½	RHernandez	O S Barrera	3.40
1Jly 76 2Aqu1	Jolly Mister	b4		113	6	5	5¹	6⁷	6½	6¹²	6²²	PDay	Stan-Mar Stable	7.30
9Jly 76 3Aqu5	Acosado II.		4	117	7	3	2⁵	2³	5¹	7	7	JVasquez	Bellrose Farm	11.90

†Five pounds apprentice allowance waived.

OFF AT 10:30 PDT. START GOOD. WON DRIVING. Time, :24; :47⅕, 1:12⅗, 1:39⅗, 1:53⅖. Track fast.

$2 Mutuel Prices:

1-CHARMS HOPE	7.00	4.00	2.60
3-FINNEY FINSTER		6.20	3.60
4-GOOD AND BOLD			2.80

B. h, by Abe's Hope—Cold Dead, by Dead Ahead. Trainer, F. J. Horan. Bred by Criterion Farms (Fla.).

CHARMS HOPE, unhurried early, rallied approaching the stretch and outfinished FINNEY FINSTER. The latter, off slowly, advanced steadily to loom a threat near midstretch and continued on with good courage. GOOD AND BOLD tired from his early efforts. JUST LIKE PA rallied leaving the far turn but lacked the needed late response. WAVE THE FLAG was never close. JOLLY MISTER was always outrun. ACOSADO II tired badly.

Charms Hope claimed by M. Garren, trainer G. Puentes; Good and Bold claimed by S. Sommer, trainer F. Martin.
Claiming Prices (in order of finish)—$8000, 8500, 8250, 8250, 8250, 8000, 8500.

Wave the Flag won a $5,000 claimer on July 21. Charms Hope won an allowance race on July 23. Good and Bold won a $10,000–$12,000 claimer on July 31. In addition, Just Like Pa ran fourth on July 29, encountering traffic problems, and won a $9,000 claimer on August 18.

Coincidence might dilute the impact of the added information, but nine out of ten times there is a better explanation. Either this race was superior to the designated class or else it contained an unusually fit group of horses. In either case, that's important information.

Indeed, after Wave the Flag's easy score at $5,000 claiming and Charms Hope's five-length victory in allowance company, the Key Race method would have certainly pointed out the merits of Good and Bold at 9–1 in a six-furlong race on July 31 (note the running line of Good and Bold in the Key Race chart). Observant race watchers and chart readers might similarly have made a strong case for Just Like Pa when he went to the post at 6–1 on August 18.

The Key Race method has many applications, but it is simply sensational in pointing out above-average fields in maiden races and turf events.

Maiden races are a mixed bag. Very few horses entered in such races have established their true class level. Some maidens will turn out to be useful racehorses; others will be little more than walking feed bills. Sooner or later, most often sooner, the best of the maidens wind up in the winner's circle. With deadly precision the Key Race method points out those maiden races that contained the fastest nonwinners on the grounds.

Maybe the winner of a maiden race returns to win a stakes race. Maybe the fifth horse in the maiden race comes back to graduate in its next start. If so, I would begin looking for the second, third, and fourth horses to come out of that maiden race. There could be little question that they had raced against above-average stock. Naturally, I would not suspend the handicapping process. I would still want to know what the rest of the field looked like, whether there was a prevailing track bias, what type it was, what if any trainer patterns were present, and so on. I would, however, surely upgrade the chances of any horse coming out of such a strong field.

Similar logic explains the effectiveness of the Key Race method in classifying turf races. Regardless of a horse's record on dirt, its ability to compete on grass is never established until it has raced on grass. In effect, the horse is a maiden on the turf until it wins on the turf. Again, the Key Race method will isolate the stronger fields.

Every once in a while you will encounter the phenomenon of a result chart with six, seven, or more circled horses —a Key Race in the ultimate sense of the word. My research says this occurs at least once in every 500 races. By the time four horses come out of the same field to win their next starts you should get the message.

The Key Race at Saratoga on August 5, 1972, is my personal favorite. The circles are not included. They aren't necessary. Every last horse provided a winning effort.

EIGHTH RACE
Saratoga
AUGUST 5, 1972

1 $\frac{1}{16}$ MILES.(turf). (1.39 2/5) ALLOWANCES. Purse $15,000. 3–year–olds and upward which have not won three races other than maiden, claiming or starter. Weights, 3–year–olds, 117 lbs. Older, 122 lbs. Non–winners of $7,200 at a mile or over since July 1, allowed 2 lbs. $6,600 at a mile or over since June 17, 4 lbs. $6,000 at a mile or over since May 15, 6 lbs. (Maidens, claiming and starter races not considered inallowances.)

Value of race $15,000, value to winner $9,000, second $3,300, third $1,800, fourth $900. Mutuel pool $128,695, OTB pool $70,388.

Last Raced	Horse	Eqt.A.Wt	PP	St	$\frac{1}{4}$	$\frac{1}{2}$	$\frac{3}{4}$	Str	Fin	Jockey	Odds $1
23Jly72 8Del2	Scrimshaw	4 116	2	2	7¹	7½	4¹	1³	1⁴	Marquez C H	2.40
20Jly72 6Aqu4	Gay Gambler	3 108	8	8	9¹½	9⁵	9⁸	8¹½	2¹½	Patterson G	5.60
22Jly72 6Aqu3	Fast Judge	b 3 111	7	7	6²	6¹	6½	4hd	3hd	Velasquez J	10.00
28Jly72 6Aqu1	Straight To Paris	3 115	9	3	2½	2¹½	2½	2½	4no	Vasquez J	2.70
25Jly72 9Aqu1	Search the Farm	b 4 116	3	9	8¹½	8¹½	8¹	6hd	5no	Guadalupe J	11.20
23Jly72 8Del3	Chrisaway	4 116	4	6	5¹½	4hd	7½	7½	6²	Howard R	25.30
25Jly72 9Aqu5	Navy Lieutenant	4 116	1	1	3½	5¹	3½	5¼	7⁴	Belmonte E	10.90
25Jly72 7Aqu4	Head Table	b 3 113	10	5	4¹	3¹	5½	910	8²	Baeza B	7.50
17Jly72 8Del3	Mongo's Image	3 111	5	4	11½	1½	1¹	3hd	910	Nelson E	28.70
21Jly72 7Aqu5	Chartered Course	b 4 116	6	10	10	10	10	10	10	Arellano J	16.70

Time, :23⅕, :46⅖, 1:09⅘, 1:34⅗, 1:40⅖ (Against Wind in Backstretch). Course firm.

$2 Mutuel Prices:

2–(B)– SCRIMSHAW	6.80	3.60	3.20
8–(H)– GAY GAMBLER		7.00	4.80
7–(G)– FAST JUDGE			5.60

B. g, by Jaipur—Ivory Tower, by Hill Prince. Trainer Lake R P. Bred by Vanderbilt A G (Md).

IN GATE AT 5.23; OFF AT 5.23 EASTERN DAYLIGHT TIME. Start Good Won Handily

SCRIMSHAW, taken back after breaking alertly, swung out to go after the leaders on the far turn, quickly drew off and was never seriously threatened. GAY GAMBLER, void of early foot, was unable to split horses entering the stretch, altered course to the extreme outside and finished strongly. FAST JUDGE, reserved behind the leaders, split horses leaving the far turn but was not match for the top pair. STRAIGHT TO PARIS prompted the pace much of the way and weakened during the drive. SEARCH THE FARM failed to menace. CHRISAWAY raced within easy striking distance while outside horses much of the way but lacked a late response. NAVY LIEUTENANT, a factor to the stretch while saving ground, gave way. HEAD TABLE was finished leaving the far turn. MONGO'S IMAGE stopped badly after showing to midstretch.

Owners— 1, Vanderbilt A G; 2, Whitney C V; 3, Wygod M J; 4, Rokeby Stable; 5, Nadler Evelyn; 6, Steinman Beverly R; 7, Sommer S; 8, Happy Hill Farm; 9, Reynolds J A; 10, Camijo Stable.

Trainers— 1, Lake R P; 2, Poole G T; 3, Nickerson V J; 4, Burch Elliott; 5, Nadler H; 6, Fout P R; 7, Martin F; 8, Wright F I; 9, Reynolds J A; 10, King W P.

Overweight: Head Table 2 pounds.

On August 12 Scrimshaw won the first division of the Bernard Baruch Handicap. One half-hour later Chrisaway took the second division at 50–1. A few days later Chartered Course won a daily double race paying $25. On the same card Gay Gambler—probably the best bet of the year—took the sixth race. Straight to Paris shipped to Monmouth for his win; Fast Judge, Search the Farm, and Navy Lieutenant raced out of the money in their next starts at Saratoga but won on the rebound at Belmont in September. Mongo's Image won a high-class allowance race at the end of the Saratoga meeting at 8–1.

The only horse that didn't race back during this period was Head Table. For weeks I hunted through the *Racing Form* hoping to find his name among the entries. I was prepared to fly anywhere. But he never showed up.

Believe it or not, Head Table returned to the races on April 21, 1973, nine months after the Key Race. Yes, you guessed it: Head Table won by six. That's weird.

10.
An Edge in Class

At Charles Town racetrack in West Virginia, where the racing is cheap and the betting action takes exotic forms, the horseplayer seldom has a chance to see a top-drawer horse in action. Nevertheless, the player would be making a serious mistake if he failed to incorporate notions about class into his handicapping.

On a typical racing program at a minor-league track like Charles Town, the majority of races are for $1,500–$2,000 claiming horses—the lowest level of horsedom. These are horses that have seen their better days or are just not fast enough to compete in the higher-class claiming events found at the major one-mile racetracks.

Actually, that is not quite true. A respectable number of Charles Town horses can run fast—and a select few can run very fast—but they are too short-winded or too battle-scarred to be able to sustain their speed in three-quarter-mile races at the majors. After all, there are no four-furlong races for three-year-olds and up at Arlington Park, and there are no six-furlong races for $1,500 horses either.

For all the wrong reasons, major-track handicappers tend to have a snobbish attitude toward their compatriots at the minors, thinking perhaps that the cheaper racing is less formful, less predictable. I can assure you, however, that there are more winning players per capita at "bull ring" tracks like Charles Town than there are at Aqueduct or Hollywood Park.

Far from being the indecipherable mess that it seems on the surface, minor-track racing offers some of the most attractive betting opportunities in all of racing. Examining the class factor will show exactly why this is so, and for the astute player the applications extend to a large body of races at the major tracks as well.

The first step toward success at Charles Town is to use the result charts to construct a record of the eligibility conditions of all the cheapest races. About 90 percent of Charles

Town claiming events have restrictive clauses which resemble the eligibility conditions found in allowance (nonclaiming) races at the major one-mile tracks.

For example, the third, sixth, eighth, and tenth races at Charles Town on August 4, 1976, were $1,500 claiming races for three-year-olds and up, but any bettor who assumed that these races were for the same class of horse was on his way to a disastrous evening of betting.

The first $1,500 claiming race was limited to horses "which have not won a race in 1976"; the second, "for nonwinners of three races in 1976"; the third, "for nonwinners of two races lifetime"; and the final $1,500 race, "for nonwinners of a race in 1975 or 1976," the lowest $1,500 race in captivity.

The next evening there were four more $1,500 claiming races with four additional sets of eligibility conditions. Confusing? Perhaps. But it turns out that there is a measurable difference between each of the restricted $1,500-class races. This difference is not only reflected in the average winning times for each separate restricted class but is greater than the difference between the average $1,500 and $2,000 race. In other words, it is more difficult to advance within the same $1,500 claiming class than it is to step up to the $2,000 claiming level!

Whenever a $1,500 horse wins at Charles Town, it loses its chance to compete in the same restricted class. The claiming price remains the same—even the purse tends to be the same—but the horse must now face other horses that have also graduated from the lower restricted level.

Naturally, the next level (within the same $1,500 claiming class) will include other horses with recent victories. This makes for much tougher competition.

Indeed, most Charles Town horses have a very hard time scoring two wins back to back, and some never advance until all the better $1,500 horses win their way into the next level of competition. In a very real sense, the slower horses are hopelessly trapped, and some remain trapped for months.

For the purpose of identification, it is helpful (if not essential) to formulate a classification system for all $1,500 and $2,000 races. (At the major tracks, where allowance races are written with similar restrictive eligibility clauses, the purses attached to each race are scaled in proportion to the quality of the field. A classification code is therefore unnecessary, provided of course that the player refers to the charts to note the purse values. The purse values are in themselves a ready-made classification system.)

CHARLES TOWN CLASSIFICATION CODE FOR $1,500 OR $2,000 CLAIMING RACES

O—open race, unrestricted eligibility (top class)

A—Nonwinners of 2 races in the past two months
or 3 races in the past three months

B—Nonwinners of 2 races in three to five months

C—Nonwinners of 2 races in six to nine months
or 3 races in nine to twelve months

D—Nonwinners of 2 races in nine to twenty-four months

E—Nonwinners of a race in nine to twenty-four months

M—Nonwinners lifetime (maidens)

As you can see, the increments *between* class levels at the same $1,500 claiming price are quite steep. It takes a pretty decent $1,500 horse to make its way up the ladder during a calendar year.

The easiest class jump is maiden to E class (nonwinners of a race in nine to twenty-four months). It is no coincidence that the majority of Charles Town repeaters occur at this rock-bottom level. Most E-class horses have very little ability and are always forced to meet recent maiden graduates. Generally speaking, a recent maiden graduate, especially a lightly raced maiden graduate, is a very dependable Charles Town bet. At the very least, the recent victory is a positive sign of current condition. In the spring of 1976 I charted two months of Charles Town races and found fifteen repeaters of this type in thirty-four E-class races. The average mutuel payoff was $8.60.

With minor revisions, the Charles Town classification code will prove useful at any minor-class racetrack and at any major track where similar eligibility conditions are written into the cheapest races.

Tracks like River Downs, Thistledown, Waterford Park, Lincoln Downs, Green Mountain Park, Penn National, Finger Lakes, Commodore Downs, Longacres, and Fonner Park all fit into this category, and there are at least a dozen others spread across the country.

From practical experience at a few of these minor race-tracks, I cannot stress enough the value of the classification code. Of course, you might have to set up slightly different categories depending upon the particular eligibility conditions of races in your area, but you will reward yourself many times over for the effort. Some results will in fact astound you.

At Green Mountain Park, for example, where I enjoyed many an evening during the mid-1960s while working as a counselor at nearby Camp Watitoh, one of the most satisfying bets of my entire career came in the first week that I put the classification code to work.

To my amazement I spotted a 14–1 shot in a $2,000 D-class race that had flashed some high early speed in a $1,500 A-class race. Believe it or not, despite the apparent raise in claiming price, the horse was dropping down sharply in company. He won by nine lengths!

And if you're wondering how this classification code works in today's overexpanded racing marketplace, a good friend of mine, Dick White, has been using this method at Charles Town for the past two years, and he confirms that the identical "dropdown" phenomenon takes place every few weeks.

There are other fundamental applications to consider as well. Very often a $1,500 horse will be entered in an A- or B-class race when it is still eligible for a weaker C- or D-class event. Such a horse can be safely and automatically thrown out. The horse is just out for the exercise, or the trainer is purposely trying to darken its form. (If the horse is really that good, the trainer will invariably raise its selling price.)

Conversely, horses that have been showing signs of life in A- or B-class races make excellent wagers when they are properly placed in less demanding D- or E-class events. This type of hidden class maneuver is the most powerful dropdown angle in all of racing, and you can also expect to see it in a slightly different form at the major tracks.

An allowance race at Aqueduct or Santa Anita or any other major track is probably the toughest kind of race for the novice or intermediate horseplayer. In order to handicap such a race properly, the player must have a fix on the local pecking order. He must know which horses on the grounds are the best sprinters, the best routers, the best turf horses, the best three-year-olds, and so forth. He must also know the approximate breaking point when a claiming race is equal to or better than the allowance race in question.

Allowance race conditions like those $1,500 claiming races at Charles Town are restricted events. A two-time stakes winner or a three-time winner of a $10,000 purse is not allowed into any field that is designed for a band of recent maiden graduates.

Moreover, the major-track trainer of an allowance horse will often do what the Charles Town trainer of a

$1,500 claimer does. He will race the horse against more experienced winners and then drop it back to a level where its best race could make it a top contender. Because the major-track trainer can sometimes hide this maneuver by using top-price claiming events ($40,000+ in New York and California, $25,000+ in Illinois and New Jersey, $15,000+ in Maryland and Michigan, and so on), he can often fool the unsophisticated bettors into thinking the horse is stepping up in company when it goes from a claiming to an allowance race. Many times over the opposite is true.

FIFTH RACE

AP

June   8. 1976

6 FURLONGS. (1:08⅗). ALLOWANCES Purse $8,500 Fillies. 3- and 4-year-olds which have never won two races other than maiden or claiming, 3-year-olds, 115 lbs.; 4-year-olds, 123 lbs. Non-winners of a race other than maiden or claiming since April 13 allowed 3 lbs.; such a race since March 13. 5 lbs.

Value to winner $5,100; second. $1.700; third, $935; fourth, $510; fifth, $255. Mutule Pool, $128,595.

At Arlington Park in June and July 1976 there were thirty such allowance races. Fourteen were won by horses that showed good form in claiming races. It shouldn't surprise you to learn that the purse values for all $25,000 claiming races at Arlington are higher than the purse value listed for this category of allowance race. Without result charts, the Arlington player might never have known that. The suspicion is that few people do, because the average price paid by those fourteen winners was $9.

The same sort of oversight happens at Aqueduct and Santa Anita, where a solid $45,000 claiming winner can usually beat three-quarters of the allowance horses on the grounds. A solid $30,000 claimer can similarly handle the weaker allowance horses. Smart trainers know this, and without result charts to expose the true class levels of each race, the player is at the trainer's mercy.

The chart below refers to Caspar Milquetoast's most recent race, a $60,000 claiming event with a purse of $15,000.

```
Caspar Milquetoast      113  Dk. b. or br. c (1973), by Our Michael—Backseat Driver, by Traffic
                                  Judge.  Breeder. C. Wetherill (Ky.).    1976  12  5  1  2   $45,020
Owner, Leonard Henry.  Trainer Philip G. Johnson.                        1975   5  1  1  0    $7,340
10 Aug76 2Sar    7 f :222 :4511:242sy 8-5 ▲122  34   35   31   121  MapleE1    60000 83 CsprMilqetst122 Adm'sActn  5
16 Jly 76 6Aqu   1 :4531:1011:354sy 8-5 ▲113  591 451 21  11½  MapleE1    55000 87 CasparMilqtst113 MldNedle  6
 2 Jly 76 7Aqu   1 :4641:1111:354ft  3½  112  481 441 341 32¾ SantiagoA4 Alw 84 Political Coverup 112  Bakor  6
24 Jun76 2Bel    7 f :231 :4611:231ft  4½e 122  88  612 44  1no MapleE4    40000 86 CasparMilqutst122 Rbrt'sBy  6
 6 Jun76 4Bel    7 f :231 :4641:23 ft  3½e 117  32  31  1h  1no MapleE6    40000 87 CsprMilqtst117 FnncialWhiz  7
19 May76 6Bel    7 f :232 :47 1:24 sy   4   117  53  43  22  13  VasqezJ3   30000 82 CasparMilatst117 ArcticLck  8
 6 May76 5Bel    1 :4621:1131:371ft  3¾  117  431 2h  1½  2½  VasqezJ4   30000 81 Mr.Interntnl117 CsprMilotst  9
23 Apr76 4Aqu    7 f :231 :4631:25 gd  8½  117  66  671 561 41¾ VsquezJ2   35000 74 ForestStrm117 Drover'sDwn  7
10 Apr76 5Aqu    6 f :223 :4611:104ft   24  115  55  55  55½ 55¾ HoleM3     Alw 83 Bonge 117       Distinctively  9
18 Mar76 7Aqu    1 :4531:1021:363ft  6½  115  713 711 79¼ 69½ HoleM7     Alw 73 HailLiberty115 HenryBrooks  9
 6 Mar76 6Aqu    1 :47 1:1131:363ft 8-5 ▲115  961 761 48  46½ CordroAJr3 Alw 77 Resilient 115    Ship Trial  9
      Aug 24 Sar trt 4f ft :49h        July 27 Bel 6f ft 1:14⅖h        July 11 Bel trt 4f ft :49⅘b
```

The next chart is the result chart for the race in which Caspar was entered with the past performances as shown at top this page. Note the lower purse value and the restriction built into the eligibility conditions. This is a classic example of the hidden class dropdown, expertly manipulated by trainer P. G. Johnson.

SECOND RACE 7 FURLONGS. (1:21). CLAIMING. Purse $15,000. 3-year-olds. Weight, 122 lbs. Non-winners of a race since July 15 allowed 3 lbs.; a race since July 1, 5 lbs. Claiming price, $60,000; for each $2,500 to $55,000, allowed 2 lbs. (Races when entered to be claimed for $50,000 or less not considered.)

Sar

August 10, 1976
Value to winner $9,000; second, $3,300; third, $1,800; fourth, $900. Mutuel Pool, $66,701.
Off-track betting, $61,941.

Last Raced	Horse	EqtAWt	PP	St	¼	½	Str	Fin	Jockeys	Owners	Odds to $1
16 Jly 76 6Aqu1	Caspar Milquetoast	b3 122	1	5	32	32	35	12½	EMaple	L D Henry	1.60
5 Aug76 7Sar1	Adam's Action	b3 118	2	1	24	1h	1½	2nk	JVelasquez	Exeter Stable	2.10
2 Aug76 2Sar1	Austin	b3 113	5	2	1h	25	2½	37½	ACorderoJr	Harbor View Farm	2.60
1 Aug76 7FE3	Salim Alicum	3 122	3	3	4h	4½	41	4	RTurcotte	G R Gardiner	6.00
10 Jly 76 7Aks9	Le Punch	b3 117	4	4	5	5	5 Eased.	RHernandez	E C Cashman	10.00

OFF AT 2:01 EDT. Start good. Won driving. Time, :22⅖, :45⅕, 1:11, 1:24⅖. Track sloppy.

$2 Mutuel Prices:
2-CASPAR MILQUETOAST	......	5.20	2.80	2.20
3-ADAM'S ACTION	....		2.80	2.20
6-AUSTIN	....			2.20

Dk. b. or br. c, by Our Michael—Backseat Driver, by Traffic Judge. Trainer, Philip G. Johnson. Bred by Cortright Weterill (Ky.).

CASPAR MILQUETOAST raced wide into the stretch while rallying and drew clear after catching ADAM'S ACTION near the final sixteenth. The latter saved ground while vying for the lead with AUSTIN to midstretch and weakened. AUSTIN weakened from his eary efforts. SALIM ALICUM was always outrun. LE PUNCH, outrun to the stretch, was eased during the late stages.

Corrected weight—Salim Alicum, 122.
Claiming Prices (in order of finish)—$60000, 55000, 55000, 60000, 60000.
Scratched—Buttonbuck, Gabe Benzur.

SEVENTH RACE
Bel
August 31, 1976

6 FURLONGS. (1:08⅖). WISE MARGIN PURSE. ALLOWANCES. (Purse $10,000.) 3-year-olds and upward which have never won a race other than maiden, claiming or starter. 3-year-olds, 118 lbs.; older, 122 lbs. Non-winners of a race other than claiming since Aug. 1 allowed 3 lbs.; such a race since July 15, 5 lbs.
Value to winner $6,000; second, $2,200; third, $1,200; fourth, $600.
Mutuel Pool, $138,757. Off-track betting, $96,245. Exacta Pool, $177,505. Off-track betting Exacta Pool, $191,008.

Last Raced	Horse	EqtAWt PP St	¼	½	Str	Fin	Jockeys	Owners	Odds to $1
10 Aug76 2Sar1	Caspar Milquetoast	b3 113 6 5	7½	4½	2½	1¹¾	EMaple	L D Henry	1.90
20 Aug76 7Sar3	Bold Needle	b3 113 5 4	4½	5⁷	5⁵	2¾	PDay	Willwynee Stable	7.20
28 Jly 76 6Aqu2	Balancer	4 117 9 1	2⁷	2¹½	3h	3¾	MVenezia	Mrs D E Kerr	5.10
23 Aug76 7Sar3	Master Jorge	3 115 8 2	3¹	3¹	4¹½	4¹	JVelasquez	E Ubarri	5.40
23 Aug76 7Sar7	Private Thoughts	b3 113 2 3	1½	1h	1h	5⁵½	TWallis	R L Reineman	7.40
7 Aug76 9Sar7	Ferrous	3 113 4 6	8²	8³	6½	6¾	ACorderoJr	J Allen	6.10
31 Jly 76 4Aqu1	Irish Era	4 119 1 7	5½	6½	7²	7⁴	RHernandez	V J Cuti Jr	9.30
6 Aug76 1Sar1	Uphold	b4 117 7 8	6h	7h	8²	8¹½	HGustines	Darby Dan Farm	44.70
20 Aug76 1Sar1	Iroquois Tribe	3 118 3 9	9	9	9	9	GMartens	T Veale II	18.60

OFF AT 4:38 EDT. Start good. Won ridden out. Time, :23, :46⅗, 1:11⅕. Track fast.

$2 Mutuel Prices:

6-CASPAR MILQUETOAST	5.80	3.60	2.60
5-BOLD NEEDLE		6.80	3.80
9-BALANCER			3.60

$2 EXACTA (6-5) PAID $49.20.

Dk. b. or br. c, by Our Michael—Backseat Driver, by Traffic Judge. Trainer, Philip G. Johnson. Bred by Cortright Wetherill (Ky.).

CASPAR MILQUETOAST raced wide into the stretch while rallying and proved clearly best under intermittent urging. BOLD NEEDLE, between horses to the stretch, finished with good energy to gain the place. BALANCE raced forwardly to midstretch and weakened. MASTER JORGE made a run between horses leaving the turn but hung. PRIVATE THOUGHTS was used up making the pace. FERROUS raced very wide. IRISH SEA saved ground to no avail.

Corrected weight—Master Jorge, 115.
Scratched—Clean 'Em Up, Kool as Ice.

Occasionally, an aggressive trainer will take a recent graduate or a limited winner and step it right up to top allowance-class or stakes competition. In most cases this is not beneficial to the horse, but unlike the cheap races at Charles Town, the player should not automatically assume that the horse is out for the exercise. That is the most likely explanation, but a careful look at one horse's brief career suggests a different story.

6th Belmont Park

SEPTEMBER 6, 1975

WIDENER TURF COURSE
1 1-16 MILES
BELMONT PARK
FINISH

1¹⁄₁₆ MILES (turf). (1:40⅕). TUDOR ERA PURSE. ALLOWANCES. Purse $20,000. 3-year-olds and upward which have not won four races other than maiden, claiming or starter. 3-year-olds, 118 lbs.; older, 122 lbs. Non-winners of $25,000 at a mile or over since July 12 allowed 2 lbs.; $15,000 at a mile or over since July 2, 4 lbs.; $9,000 at a mile or over since July 26, 6 lbs. (Claiming races not considered in allowances.) 3-year-olds which have never won at a mile or over allowed 3 lbs.; older, 5 lbs.

COUPLED: SHREDDER and DROLLERY; JACQUES WHO and CHRISTOFORO; NALEES RIALTO and BRANFORD COURT.

*Appell II.
111 B. c (1971), by El Centauro—Amichevole, by Tatan.
Breeder, Haras Arjo (Argentina).

Owner, Green Mill Farm. Trainer, T. J. Gullo.

				1975	5	0	2	0	$7,136
				1974	9	4	2	0	$19,978

31 Aug75	4Bel	6 f :231 :46 1:103ft	31 116	621 631 43 53	TurcotteR3	Alw 86 Ramahorn 113	Townsand 6
6 Aug75	7Sar	7 f :23 :46 1:33 ft	21 114	11 31 32 66	TurcotteR6	Alw 89 QueenCityLad120	BigMoses 6
28 Jly 75	4Sar	7 f :221 :4421:223ft	21 116	21 211 32 531	TurcotteR6	Alw 89 OurTalisman112	Christoforo 8
17 Jly 75	8Bel	6 f :223 :4531:101ft	81 113	21 441 421 21	TurcotteR6	Alw 91 NativeB'end 113	Appell II. 8
6 Jan75	9Maro	a 1	1:351ft	119	Uruguay	221 Stk Brac 119	Appell II. 12
24 Nov74	7Pal	a 1	1:354ft 3-4 ▲118	Argentina	1nk SangttiV Stk Appell II. 118	Get Sun 6
9 Nov74	6S.I.	⑦ a 1	1:332fm	3 119	Argentina	541 SangttiV Stk Grand Guignol 119	Ctona 19
1 Sep74	6Pal	a 13	2:15 ft	3 126	Argentina	925 SangttiV Stk El GranCapitan 126	Envite 10
4 Aug74	6Pal	a 1	1:353hy 8-5 ▲123	Argentina	41 SangttiV Stk Telefonico 123	Pinino 21
20 Jly 74	6Pal	a 71	1:29 ft	2 121	Argentina	15 SangttiV Stk Appell II. 121	Pinino 8

Aug 28 Bel 4f ft :49⅘b   Aug 16 Sar 3f ft :36½b   Aug 14 Sar 3f ft :36⅘b

Shredder
112 Ch. c (1972), by Stage Door Johnny—Cut It Up, by Tudor Minstrel.
Breeder, Greentree Stud, Inc. (Ky.).

Owner, Greentree Stable. Trainer, J. M. Gaver.

				1975	2	1	0	0	$5,400
				1974	2	M	0	0	$2,160

23 Aug75	1Sar	⑦ 11 :47 1:1041:463fm	61 117	111 111 14 19	BrccleVJr1	Mdn 94 Shredder 117	CopprKingdm 12
16 Aug75	9Sar	6 f :222 :46 1:104ft	9-5 ▲118	75 86 68 513	BracleVJr2	Mdn 73 YuWipi118	SomethingGold 11
Sep 9-743Bel		6 f 1:11½ft	1 ▲121	Turc'tteR	Mdn 84 Doug 121	Lucky Limey	Shredder 11
Sep 2-743Bel		6 f 1:10⅖sy 7-5 ▲121	1h 1h 2h 34	Turc'tteR7	Mdn 87 Lefty 121	Co Host	Shredder 7

Sept 5 Bel 4f ft :47b   Sept 1 Bel 5f ft 1:03b   Aug 28 Bel 5f ft 1:02b

Candle Stand
116 B. c (1971), by Round Table—Terentia, by Bold Ruler.
Br., W. H. Perry & Claiborne Farm (Ky.).

Owner, W. H. Perry. Trainer, D. A. Whiteley.

				1975	6	2	1	0	$19,800
				1974	5	2	1	0	$9,576

31 Aug75	8Bel	⑦ 7 f :223 :45 1:222fm	12 110	910 983 893 610	WdhuseR5	HcpS 82 BeauBugle113	RibotGrande 10
26 Jly 75	7Bel	⑦ 11 :48 1:13 1:463sf	4-5 ▲116	37 42 21 1nk	VasquezJ1	Alw 68 Candle Stand 116	Meon Hill 6
5 Jly 75	9Bel	⑦ 11 :4521:0941:412fm	7 116	591 35 633 22	MapleE1	Alw 92 PamperdJbnh116	CndleStnd 10
7 Jun75	5Bel	11 :47 1:12 1:432ft	51 116	77 64 651 661	VasquezJ7	Alw 79 Christoforo 116	Co Host 8
15 May75	8Aqu	1 :4521:0921:344ft	7-5 ▲116	481 451 441 441	VasquezJ7	Alw 87 Hunka Papa 114	Phrenology 8
18 Apr75	8Aqu	6 f :222 :45 1:101ft	81 116	541 55 52 111	VasquezJ5	Alw 92 Candle Stand 116	Erwin Boy 8
Sep18-742Ayr		⑦ 11 2:25⅘sf 6-5 ▲119	Ireland	1 CarsonW Stk CandleSt'nd108	Jimsun Mids'mer Star 7
Aug13-743Cur		⑦ 11 2:43⅘yl 41 108	Scotland	481 BurnsTP Stk Rich'dGrenville122	ConorPass Mistigri 9
Jun 1-741Leo		⑦ 11 2:10⅘gd 112 ▲126	Ireland	43 PiggottL Stk Conor Pass 133	Silk Buds Klairvimy 7
May15-743Cur		⑦ 11 2:38²gd 14 122	Ireland	2no MurphyT Stk Klairvimy 139	Candle Stand Tameric 6
Apr 6-746Cur		⑦ 1 1:45 gd 6-5 ▲119	Ireland	11 Pigg'tL Mdn C'dleSt'd126	Archd'eFerd'de Retr'ved 26

Aug 30 Bel 3f ft :37b   Aug 28 Bel 3f ft :36b   Aug 24 Bel 4f ft :48½b

Intrepid Hero
118 B. c (1972), by Forli—Bold Princess, by Bold Ruler.
Breeder, O. M. Phipps (Ky.).

Owner, O. M. Phipps. Trainer, J. W. Russell.

				1975	8	4	2	1	$143,110
				1974	1	M	0	0	(—)

2 Aug75	8Mth	⑦ 11 :4621:1021:493ft	41 115	32 21 2h 2nk	ShmkerW7	InvH 92 Wajima 118	Intrepid Hero 8
13 Jly 75	8Hol	⑦ 11 :4821:1342:29 fm	71 126	131 11 111 12	PierceD5	InvSc 83 Intrepid Hero 126	Terete 7
21 Jun75	8Atl	⑦ 11 :47 1:1021:413fm	4 110	31 2h 11 12	WoodheR2	AlwS 98 IntrepidHero110	King ofFls 8
16 Jun75	7Bel	⒯ 11 :4911:1412:004gd	31 114	11 1h 1h 2h	TurcotteR1	Alw 86 BrianBoru116	IntrepidHero 6
2 Jun75	7Bel	11 :4611:10 1:421ft	71 114	21 31 42 35	TejadaV4	Alw 86 Nalee'sKnght118	AllOurHpes 6
30 Apr75	5Aqu	⑦ 11 :4911:1341:504fm	36 121	311 1h 1h 1no	TejadaV7	Alw 81 Intrepid Hero 121	Northerly 9
12 Apr75	5Aqu	11 :4821:1221:504ft	6 122	321 43 35 471	TejadaV2	Alw 74 Old Vic 122	Gunpowder 6
6 Mar75	3Aqu	1 :232 :4531:371ft	23 116	211 23 21 11	TejadaV2	Mdn 80 IntrepidHero116	NobleRctor 7
Dec14-744Aqu		6 f 1:12⅘ft 15 122	771 812 711 711	Mont'yaD	Mdn 68 Cockbird 122	Alishamar	Trounce 8

Sept 1 Bel tc 1f fm 1:39⅗b   Aug 22 Sar trt 5f ft 1:07b   Aug 17 Sar trt 5f ft 1:03b

Nalees Rialto
112 B. c (1972), by Ribot—Nalee, by Nashua.
Breeder, Mrs. G. M. Humphrey (Ky.).

Owner, Mrs. G. M. Humphrey. Trainer, E. Burch.

				1975	8	2	2	1	$26,340
				1974	7	1	4	1	$14,620

16 Aug75	8Sar	11 :4721:1121:511ft	21 108	34 33 21 13†	MontoyaD2	Alw 79 Nalees Rialto 108	First Slice 6
†Disqualified and placed second.							
12 Jly 75	8Bel	11 :4531:0931:482sy	71 112	851 881 710 712	MontyaD8	HcpS 73 Valid Appeal 110	Wajima 8
7 Jun75	7Bel	11 :48 1:1222:281ft	19 126	55 611 711 817	MntyaD9	ScwS 62 Avatar 126	Foolish Pleasure 9
26 May75	7Aqu	11 :4831:1221:494ft	2 110	13 12 13 123	MontoyaD4	Alw 86 Nalee'sRlto110	TrmpterSwan 7
17 May 5	7Aqu	11 :4721:1121:494ft	2 ▲114	55 421 211 121	MontoyaD6	Alw 86 Nalee's Rialto 114	HvnForbd 11
19 Apr75	7Aqu	11 :47 1:1031:483ft	9-5 ▲113	211 22 22 221	MontoyaD1	Alw 89 KaysRoman115	Kp thePmise 8
4 Apr75	9Aqu	11 :49 1:1421:524ft	51 114	32 21 44	MontoyaD8	Alw 67 Media117	Keep thePromise 7

Sept 3 Bel 5f ft :58⅘b   Aug 30 Bel 5f ft :59⅘b   Aug 27 Bel 3f ft :33⅘b

Drollery
116 Dk. b. or br. g (1970), by Tom Fool—Persian Garden, by Bois Roussel.
Breeder, Greentree Stud, Inc. (Ky.).

Owner, Greentree Stable. Trainer, J. M. Gaver.

				1975	11	1	3	4	$61,785
				1974	6	1	1	1	$13,800

20 Aug75	8Sar	⑦ 11 :4831:11 2:42 fm	3 111	21 32 32 32	BccleVJr8	HcpS 77 SnowKnight 118	GoldenDon 8
10 Aug75	8Sar	⑦ 11 :4831:1231:494fm	7e 112	812 871 54 313	BrcceVJr7	HcpS 76 SaltMarsh116	WardMcAlstr 8
5 Jly 75	8Bel	⑦ 11 :4921:14 2:134fm	91 112	24 311 691 67	BrcleVJr4	HcpS 89 Brigand 112	Prod 9
14 Jun75	8Bel	⑦ 11 :51 1:4212:321fm	33 113	521 521 311 21	BrcleVJr5	HcpS 58 Barcas 113	Drollery 8
2 Jun75	8Bel	⑦ 11 :4811:13 2:03 gd	71 114	511 691 46 211	BrcleVJr4	AlwS 84 Telefonico 120	Drollery 9
10 May75	8Pim	⑦ 11 :4831:1542:332yl	71 124	1225 912 611 361	BrcleVJr1	HcpS 89 Outdoors 114	Outdoors 13
6 Apr75	7SA	a 13 :4721:1122:521yl	12 115	812 621 54 453	BracleVJr4	InvH 60 La Zanzara 114	Astray 12
26 Mar75	8SA	⑦ 11 :4741:1232:261fm	31 120	64 421 42 2no	BrcleVJr2	HcpS 84 El Botija 117	Drollery 6
4 Mar75	9Hia	⑦ 11 2:272fm 9-5e▲111	710 891 661 423	SmithRC5	HcpS 91 Outdoors 112	Barcas 13

Sept 5 Bel 4f ft :48⅘b   Sept 1 Bel 7f ft 1:29b   Aug 25 Bel 5f sy 1:02⅘b

The conditions for the above race clearly suggest a top-drawer field. It was in fact more than that. The field was loaded with stakes-class stock, including some of the nation's best grass horses, several of which appear along with the race winner.

Shredder, a recent graduate of a maiden race, was a lead-pipe cinch. And the best bettors in the crowd knew it. Coupled in the betting with the multiple stakes winner Drollery, Shredder's mutuel price was naturally reduced by a few points. But on the evidence of his lone turf race win, there was no way he would have paid more than 4–1 no matter what he was going to run against.

Shredder was a freak. A champion that never got crowned. In the Eclipse Award balloting, I voted him the top turf horse of 1975, simply on the basis of his two grass races. And I don't think I overstated his credentials. They were both incredible performances. Let's examine them.

In his maiden victory romp Shredder ran on his own courage throughout, raced to a nine-length victory under wraps. Jockey Bracciale never moved a muscle. And if you weren't there to see it, the following two result charts tell an interesting tale.

24th Day. WEATHER CLEAR. TEMPERATURE 73 DEGREES.

FIRST RACE

Saratoga
AUGUST 23, 1975

1 1/16 MILES.(turf). (1.45%) MAIDEN SPECIAL WEIGHT. Purse $9,000. 3- and 4-year-olds. Weight: 3-year-olds, 117 lbs., 4-year-olds, 122 lbs.

Value of race $9,000, value to winner $5,400, second $1,980, third $1,080, fourth $540. Mutuel pool $101,518.

Last Raced	Horse	Eqt.A.Wt	PP	St	1/4	1/2	3/4	Str	Fin	Jockey	Odds $1
16Aug75 9Sar5	Shredder	3 117	1	1	11½	11½	11½	14	19	Bracciale V Jr	6.30
3Aug75 5Sar2	Copper Kingdom	b 3 117	6	12	12	7hd	34	21½	21½	Cruguet J	2.70
3Aug75 5Sar3	Spasoje	3 117	8	11	10hd	9½	6hd	52	3no	Velasquez J	9.50
18Aug75 1Sar2	Braulio	3 117	7	4	4½	5hd	41½	41½	42½	Amy J	13.90
9Aug75 9Sar7	Count Nijinsky	b 3 117	5	7	111½	11½	8½	62	5nk	Turcotte R	a-8.00
13Aug75 1Sar5	Jack Barrett	b 3 117	2	2	31½	2½	2hd	31½	63¾	Hole M	8.30
12Aug75 1Sar7	Off The Record	b 3 110	3	5	8½	6½	101	74	73	Campanelli T7	a-8.00
4Oct74 6Bel7	Vincent	b 3 117	4	3	7hd	8½	9½	8hd	81½	Ruane J	12.20
13Aug75 1Sar2	Blue Cross	b 3 117	12	8	6½	12	12	101½	91½	Baeza B	5.10
9Aug75 2Sar4	Sweet Basil	b 3 117	9	10	9²	101	112	12	10nk	Maple E	9.80
13Aug75 1Sar10	Bridaled Tern	b 3 110	11	9	51½	41	5½	9hd	116	Long J S7	48.00
16Aug75 9Sar3	The Irish Lord	3 110	10	6	2½	3½	71	111½	12	Martens G7	13.00

a-Coupled: Count Nijinsky and Off The Record.

OFF AT 1:30 EDT. Start good, Won ridden out. Time, :22%, :47, 1:10%, 1:35, 1:46% Course firm.

Official Program Numbers

$2 Mutuel Prices:

2-(B)-SHREDDER		14.60	7.60	5.20
5-(G)-COPPER KINGDOM			4.60	3.20
7-(I)-SPASOJE				4.20

Ch. c, by Stage Door Johnny—Cut It Up, by Tudor Minstrel. Trainer Gaver J M. Bred by Greentree Stud Inc (Ky).

SHREDDER sprinted right to the front, made the pace under good handling and drew away rapidly after entering the stretch. COPPER KINGDOM, outrun away from the gate, moved around horses to reach contention racing into the far turn but was no match for the winner. SPASOJE rallied mildly. Barulion, well placed early, lacked a late response. COUNT NIJINSKY, very wide into the stretch, failed to be a serious factor. JACK BARRETT raced forwardly to the stretch and flattened out. OFF THE RECORD saved ground to no avail. BLUE CROSS was through early. SWEET BASIL was always outrun. BRIDALED TERN gave way after going five furlongs. THE IRISH LORD, a factor to the far turn, stopped badkly.

Owners— 1, Greentree Stable; 2, Live Oak Plantation; 3, Tartan Stable; 4, Blum P E; 5, Hexter Stable; 6, Rokeby Stable; 7, Reineman R L; 8, Hobeau Farm; 9, Sturgis J R; 10, Rosenthal Mrs M; 11, Humphrey Mrs G M; 12, Phipps Ogden.

Trainers— 1, Gaver J M; 2, Kelly T J; 3, Nerud J A; 4, Jerkens S T; 5, Freeman W C; 6, Burch Elliott; 7, Freeman W C; 8, Jerkens H A; 9, Veitch S E; 10, Johnson P G; 11, Miller Mack; 12, Russell J W.

Scratched—Paul's Impulse (13Aug75 ¹Sar¹¹); Special Project (3Aug75 ⁵Sar⁴); Triple Optimist (9Aug75 ⁹Sar⁵); Survey (16Aug75 ¹Sar¹⁰); Rapid Transit II (16Aug75 ¹Sar¹¹); Red Grasshopper (18Aug75 ¹Sar⁴).

An allowance race later that day.

SEVENTH RACE	1 1/16 MILES.(turf). (1.39⅖) ALLOWANCE. Purse $15,000. 3–year–olds and upward which
Saratoga	have not won three races other than maiden, claiming or starter. Weight: 3–year–olds, 117 lbs., Older, 122 lbs. Non–winners of $9,000 at a mile or over since July 26 allowed 2
AUGUST 23, 1975	lbs., $7,200 at a mile or over since July 12, 4 lbs., $6,000 twice at a mile or over since June 25, 6 lbs. (Claiming races not considered in allowances.) 3–year–olds which have never

won at a mile or over allowed 3 lbs.; older, 5 lbs.

Value of race $15,000, value to winner $9,000, second $3,300, third $1,800, fourth $900. Mutuel pool $165,739, OTB pool $82,881. TrackExacta Pool $140,551. OTB Exacta Pool $180,996.

Last Raced	Horse	Eqt.A.Wt	PP	St	¼	½	¾	Str	Fin	Jockey	Odds $1
6Aug75 ³Sar²	Great Above	3 101	5	2	22½	21½	13	12½	1nk	Velez R I⁷	3.70
28Jly75 ⁶Sar¹	One On The Aisle	b 3 115	8	7	7½	41	2½	22	26	Maple E	2.00
16Aug75 ⁶Sar²	American History	3 110	6	4	5½	6hd	6¹	4½	31¾	Velasquez J	3.00
28Jly75 ⁶Sar³	In The Swing	b 4 116	7	5	41½	3½	32	34	4nk	Bracciale V Jr	13.00
6Aug75 ³Sar³	Co Host	b 3 113	4	6	81	8	73	52	55	Vasquez J	5.60
25Jly75 ⁸Bel⁵	Port Authority	3 111	3	3	12	1hd	5½	63	63	Turcotte R	12.20
8Jly75 ⁷Com¹	Montsalvat	3 111	2	8	8	71½	42	74	73½	Ruane J	13.50
6Aug75 ³Sar⁵	Campaigner	4 116	1	1	3¹	5½	8	8	8	Cruguet J	17.20

OFF AT 4:53, EDT. Start good, Won driving. Time, :23⅖, :48, 1:11½, 1:35½, 1:41½ Course firm (≈1:40)

$2 Mutuel Prices:	5–(E)–GREAT ABOVE	9.40	4.80	2.80
	8–(I)–ONE ON THE AISLE		3.60	2.40
	6–(F)–AMERICAN HISTORY			2.80

$2 EXACTA 5–8 PAID $28.80.

dk b or br. c, by Minnesota Mac—Ta Wee, by Intentionally. Trainer Nerud J A. Bred by Tartan Farms Corp (Fla).

GREAT ABOVE prompted the pace in hand, took over when ready racing into the far turn, quickly sprinted clear and lasted over ONE ON THE AISLE. The latter, unhurried early, rallied from the outside approaching the stretch and finished strongly. AMERICAN HISTORY, steadied along between horses nearing the end of the backstretch, was going well at the finish. IN THE SWING, never far back, made a run approaching the far turn, remained a factor to the upper stretch and flattened out. CO HOST lacked room between horses midway along the backstretch and failed to be a serious factor. PORT AUTHORITY tired badly from his early efforts. MONTSALVAT, sent around horses racing into the far turn, continued wide and lacked a further response.

Owners— 1, Tartan Stable; 2, Rokeby Stable; 3, Mangurian H T Jr; 4, Brookfield Farm; 5, Schiff J M; 6, Cody M; 7, Steinman Beverly R; 8, Garren M M.

Trainers— 1, Nerud J A; 2, Burch Elliott; 3, Root T F; 4, Kelly E I; 5, Kelly T J; 6, Preger M C; 7, Fout P R; 8, Puentes G.

Overweight: American History 2 pounds; Co Host 2.

Scratched—Grand Salute (13Aug75 ⁶Sar⁶).

On a time-comparison basis, Shredder wins hands down. It was the third fastest 1⅛-mile turf race ever run at Saratoga. Note the final eighth-mile in 11⅗ seconds. That is superhorse time. Most horses are incapable of running the last eighth in 12 seconds flat.

Now let's look at what Shredder did to all those top-drawer stakes horses he met in his next start, his final appearance of the season.

| SIXTH RACE **Belmont** SEPTEMBER 6, 1975 | 1 1/16 MILES.(turf). (1.40½) ALLOWANCE. Purse $20,000 3-year-olds and upward which have not won four races other than maiden, claiming or starter. Weights 3-year-olds, 118 lbs.; older, 122 lbs.; non-winners of $25,000 at a mile or over since July 12, allowed 2 lbs.; $15,000 at a mile or over since July 2, 4 lbs.; $9,000 at a mile or over since July 26, 6 lbs. (Claiming races not considered in allowances.) 3-year-olds which have never won at a |

mile or over allowed 3 lbs.; older, 5 lbs.
Value of race $20,000, value to winner $12,000, second $4,400, third $2,400, fourth $1,200. Mutuel pool $439,287, OTB pool $93,203.

Last Raced	Horse	Eqt.A.Wt	PP	St	1/4	1/2	3/4	Str	Fin	Jockey	Odds $1
23Aug75 1Sar1	Shredder	3 112	2	2	2³	2¹½	1hd	1³	1⁵	Bracciale V Jr	a-1.40
31Aug75 8Bel6	Candle Stand	4 116	4	4	6hd	6¹	4¹	4¹½	2½	Vasquez J	12.10
2Aug75 8Mth2	Intrepid Hero	3 118	5	5	5½	4¹½	3¹	2¹	3²½	Cordero A Jr	1.20
31Aug75 4Bel5	Appell II	4 111	1	1	1½	1½	·21	3½	4½	Turcotte R	12.00
29Aug75 8Bel7	Jacques Who	b 5 111	3	9	9	9	71	·5³	5nk	Martens G5	23.60
20Aug75 8Sar3	Drollery	5 116	9	6	8⁵	8²	6½	7¹²	6⁴	Velasquez J	a-1.40
16Aug75 8Sar2	Nalees Rialto	b 3 112	6	8	7²	5hd	5³	6½	7¹⁵	Maple E	7.40
31Aug75 4Bel6	Bold and Fancy	b 4 116	7	3	3¹	3½	8⁴	8¹	8nk	Castaneda M	44.80
13Aug75 6Sar6	Grand Salute	b 4 118	8	7	4¹	7³	9	9	9	Ruane J	56.80

a-Coupled: Shredder and Drollery.

OFF AT 4:18, EDT. Start good, Won handily. Time, :22⅘, :46⅘, 1:11, 1:35⅘, 1:41⅘ Course firm.

$2 Mutuel Prices:

1-(B)-SHREDDER (a-entry)	4.80	3.60	2.20
5-(D)-CANDLE STAND		8.80	2.60
6-(E)-INTREPID HERO			2.20

Ch. c, by Stage Door Johnny—Cut It Up, by Tudor Minstrel. Trainer Gaver J M. Bred by Greentree Stud Inc (Ky).

SHREDDER, eased back off APPEAL II soon after entering the backstretch, moved through inside that rival to take over on the turn and drew off with authority. CANDLE STAND finished with good courage along the inside to gain the place. INTREPID HERO, unhurried early, loomed a threat from the outside approaching the stretch but weakened during the drive. APPELL II tired badly from his early efforts. DROLLERY was always outrun. NALEES RIALTO rallied nearing the stretch but lacked a further response. BOLD AND FANCY was through soon after going a half. GRAND SALUTE showed some early foot.

Owners— 1, Greentree Stable; 2, Perry W H; 3, Phipps O M; 4, Green Mill Farm; 5, Wimpfheimer J D; 6, Greentree Stable; 7, Humphrey Mrs G M; 8, Vogel Marcus; 9, Steinman Beverly R.

Trainers— 1, Gaver J M; 2, Whiteley D A; 3, Russell J W; 4, Gullo T J; 5, Sedlacek W; 6, Gaver J M; 7, Burch Elliott; 8, Barrera L S; 9, Fout P R.

Scratched—Christoforo (31Aug75 8Bel4); T. V. Newscaster (29Aug75 7Bel6); Branford Court (31Aug75 8Bel7).

I would not like to leave this brief look at allowance races with the notion that all winners come from dropdown maneuvers or have Shredder-type records. The truth is in many allowance races neither factor comes into play. Such allowance races cannot be handicapped without considering track bias, trainer patterns, and other relevant data. Nevertheless, the player who appreciates the subtle power of the hidden class dropdown and is able to incorporate purse values, classification codes, and Key Race studies into his handicapping is almost certain to move many lengths ahead of the crowd. And that's what the game is all about.

11.
$E = MC^2$

In the previous chapter I made a point to introduce the importance of time as it relates to class. At Charles Town the cheapest $1,500 claiming race is usually run in slower time than the next step up in the classification code. At Arlington Park an allowance race for limited winners is usually run somewhat slower than a $20,000 claiming race. And at Saratoga Shredder proved he was no ordinary maiden graduate by running the fastest race of the day.

Although this orderly relationship between class and final times extends through every class level at every racetrack in America, it is nevertheless true that the official time of a race is worthless information by itself.

In order to make sense out of time, in order to make it a meaningful piece of information, the player must be able to answer four intriguing questions:

1. What is a good time or slow time for that distance and that class at that track?
2. How fast or slow was the racetrack the day the race was run? That is, to what extent must the time of the race be adjusted to compensate for the speed of the track itself?
3. To what extent, if any, is final time influenced by track bias, by fractional times, or by unusual pace tactics? And to what extent is it possible to detect a fluky time?
4. When is it most useful to know how fast the horse ran and under what conditions is time a waste of time?

Very few fans ever bother to take these questions seriously. It's an understandable failing. The majority of so-called experts don't do it either. Besides, the past performance profiles seem to provide ready-made answers in the track condition labels, in the speed ratings, and in the track variant figures published in some editions of the *Form*.

Jose Eduardo	117	Gr. g (1972), by Drone—Fleet Ailine, by Count Fleet.

Breeder, R. W. Wilson, Estate (Ky.).   1975 25 5 3 5 $42,900

Owner, Lady Luck Stable. Trainer, W. F. Schmitt. $40,000

21 Nov75	6Aqu	1 :45¹1:09³1:36²sy	3-5 ▲117	1½ 1¹ 1³ 17¾	PcayLJr³	30000 84	JoseEduardo117 Abve theBlt 7
8 Nov75	4Bel	1¹⁄₁₆:45³1:10 1:42¹sy	4½ 117	2¹½ 2¹½ 4² 2¹½	PncyLJr⁵	30000 89	FramptnDlight110 JseEdrdo 8
1 Nov75	3Bel	6 f :22⁴ :46⁴1:11²ft	2¼ ▲117	2ʰ 8²½ 7¹¹ 7¹⁶	VenziaM²	32500 69	JacksonSqre117 CardinlGrge 8
18 Oct 75	5Bel	6 f :22² :46²1:10²sy	3 117	2¹ 2¹ 2½ 13¾	PincyLJr⁵	27500 90	JoseEduardo117 RealGeorge 6
9 Oct 75	7Bel	6 f :22³ :46 1:11³ft	9-5 ▲116	2½ 2ʰ 2ʰ 1½	PincyLJr⁵	27500 84	JoseEduardo 116 MacCorkle 11
1 Oct 75	9Bel	6 f :22³ :46¹1:11³ft	4¾ 116	1ʰ 2½ 3½ 3ʰ	PincyLJr¹	30000 84	Balancer 116 Danny Boy 12
22 Sep75	2Bel	6 f :22⁴ :46²1:11 gd	9½ 112	1¹½ 1¹½ 1½ 2¹	VenziaM³	27500 86	CenturyGold116 JseEduardo 8
7 Sep75	9Bel	7 f 22⁴ :46 1:25²ft	7½ 116	1ʰ 1½ 1¹ 1½	VneziaM⁸	22500 75	JoseEduardo116 TingleKing 12

Unfortunately, a "fast" racetrack can have a wide range of speed conduciveness—from lightning fast to not very fast at all. And there are so many flaws built into the *Daily Racing Form*'s speed ratings and track variants that they border on the ridiculous. They can also cost the unsuspecting player a lot of money.

Speed ratings are the *Daily Racing Form*'s attempt to provide the player with a means of comparing the speed of different horses at different distances. The ratings earned by Jose Eduardo, for example, were computed by comparing his time in each race with the appropriate track record for the distance. In the *DRF* speed-rating system, the track record is always worth 100 speed-rating points, and one point is deducted for each fifth of a second slower than the track mark. According to the time-honored notion that a length equals a fifth of a second, Jose Eduardo's worst race (November 1, 1975) was computed this way:

Belmont 6-furlong track record	= 1:08⅖ = 100 speed rating
Time of race winner	= 1:11⅖ = 85 speed rating
Beaten 16 lengths (deduct 16 points)	= 1:14⅗ = 69 speed rating

Here is a partial list of Belmont Park track records in effect for the 1976 racing season. Each track record is worth 100 speed-rating points. Each horse racing at Belmont earned its speed ratings by comparisons with these times.

There are several things wrong with this method. Two of the most important appear below the chart.

TRACK RECORDS AT BELMONT PARK

DISTANCE	HORSE	AGE	WGT.	TIME	DATE
5½ Furlongs	Raise a Cup	2	118	1:03	June 8, 1973
6 Furlongs	Sailor's Watch	5	114	1:08⅖	July 3, 1975
6½ Furlongs	Cohasset Tribe	4	114	1:15⅕	May 19, 1973
7 Furlongs	King's Bishop	4	114	1:20⅖	May 19, 1973
1 Mile	Stop the Music	3	122	1:33⅗	May 19, 1973
1¹⁄₁₆ Miles	Everton II	4	112	1:40⅖	Aug. 28, 1973
1⅛ Miles	Secretariat	3	124	1:45⅖	Sept. 15, 1973

First, some track records are set on extremely fast racing days, by horses of varying ability. Although each track record equals 100 speed-rating points, at Belmont Park it is considerably more difficult for a horse to earn an 85 rating at seven furlongs and 1⅛ miles than it is at any other distance. King's Bishop and Secretariat ran much faster races to establish their track records than Cohasset Tribe and Everton II did to establish theirs.

Second, a length does not equal a fifth of a second at all distances and at all rates of speed. Mathematically speaking, a length equals a fifth of a second only when horses travel a furlong in 15 seconds. The only horses that go that slow charge 10 cents a ride.

Not surprisingly, the same sort of inconsistencies among track records can be shown to exist at most racetracks. And the error is compounded in the editions of the *Form* that feature track variant figures.

These variants—which purport to measure the relative speed of the track—are computed by averaging all winning speed ratings earned at that track that day. The average for the day is then subtracted from 100 to produce the track variant.

If the average winning speed rating for November 1, 1975, was 88, then the *DRF* track variant would be listed as 12. In the Eastern edition of the *Form*, Jose Eduardo's past performance line for that race would include his 69 rating, but it would read 69–12.

The only time these *DRF* variants provide any worthwhile information is when the variant is very large or very small. A variant above 30 would clearly indicate a slow racing strip. A variant under 10 would suggest a concrete highway. Otherwise these figures are useless to serious students of time because it is impossible to tell whether a moderate variant was the result of fast horses racing over a slow track or slow horses racing over a fast track. So much for *Daily Racing Form* speed ratings.

Those of you who are genuinely interested in winning may well achieve that special level of skill without studying the subject of time in great detail. There are other windows to look through, other methods to determine which horse is best suited to the task and most likely to win. But if you are mathematically inclined and wish to explore the racetrack puzzle from a semiscientific base, you will need to become familiar with speed figures—an ingenious process that translates the answers to the first two questions about time (see page 106) to a workable set of numbers, par times, and parallel time charts.

SPEED FIGURES

The very best speed-figure method I have ever seen was created by Sheldon Kovitz, a math wiz who divided his time at Harvard in the early 1960s between his classes, the track, and the nearest IBM computer. I never met Kovitz, but my good friend Andy Beyer learned the method firsthand and refined it for practical use ten years later. In its present form, it involves a two-step research project that may seem tedious but will do a great deal to broaden your understanding of the hows and whys of racing in your area. And if you're as crazy about handicapping as I am, you might even love it.

STEP 1: Using a complete set of result charts from the previous meeting, compile a list of all final times recorded on "fast" racetracks at every class level and distance. If back copies of the *Form* are unavailable, or too expensive to consider, a trip to the nearest library file of daily local newspapers will suffice. *Daily Racing Form* chart books, costing $22.50 per month, are another alternative.

For the purpose of this research project you are not concerned with anything but age, sex, class of race, distance, and fast-track final times. But for dependable results you should study a minimum of fifteen races at each class and distance. Obviously, the more races you use to work up the data, the more reliable the data will be.

STEP 2: Obtain the *average* winning time for each class and distance.

Logically, to determine a good time for a six-furlong, $8,000 claiming race, you must determine the *average* time for that class and distance. These averages will then serve as the par, or standard, for each class and distance. The following is a sample of six-furlong average times for New York tracks:

Three years and up stakes - - - - - - - - - - - - - - - 1:10
Three years and up $20,000 allowance - - - - - - 1:10⅖
Three years and up $15,000 claiming - - - - - - - 1:11⅗
Maiden special weight (all ages) - - - - - - - - - 1:12

The average winning times at several distances at another racetrack produced the following results:

$15,000 CLAIMING RACE—KEYSTONE RACETRACK				
6 FURLONGS	6½ FURLONGS	7 FURLONGS	1 MILE, 70 YARDS	1¹⁄₁₆ MILE
1:11⅗	1:18	1:24⅗	1:44⅗	1:46⅕

These average winning times are the building blocks for establishing an accurate track variant. They are all equal to a single measurement of average speed—the average speed of a $15,000 claiming horse at Keystone racetrack. We may now compare all final times at Keystone with that average or we may go a step further and plot the averages for every class and construct a parallel time chart, a chart that could help us make accurate time comparisons swiftly.

For convenience, Kovitz created a mathematically sound rating system to simplify comparisons between horses running different times and distances. In this rating system the value of a fifth of a second is proportionately greater in faster races and at shorter distances. It also assigns the appropriate number of points for each beaten length.

I will spare you the mathematics behind this idea and refer you to the Appendix for a step-by-step method to compute a satisfactory version of the Kovitz-Beyer speed-figure system. For those of you who are interested in this subject, I strongly recommend Beyer's beautifully written book *Picking Winners*, which is one of the few handicapping books worth serious attention. The time charts, class pars, ratings, and beaten-length charts for New York racetracks included in the Appendix of this book were adapted from *Picking Winners*, reproduced with Andy's special permission. And if you wonder whether the effort to learn how to derive speed figures is worth the trouble, the next chapter should set your head straight.

12.
The Race Is to the Swift

When is time important? How potent is speed-figure handicapping? What about fractional times? Does "pace make the race," as so many handicappers believe?

It is rare that a horseplayer gets a chance to confront a major mystery of the racetrack puzzle. Being naturally bent toward such mysteries helps. I confess. I am always willing to put my most effective handicapping methods aside and experiment with new tools and test out new ideas.

It was in that spirit that I incorporated Andy Beyer's speed figures in my handicapping in 1972, and it was in the same spirit that I stopped using them in the second year of my handicapping broadcasts in 1974.

In the first season the results said 176 winners in 310 picks. Fifty-three percent. A flat bet profit in all categories.

Of course, I relied on numerous handicapping concepts, but so long as speed figures were available on a daily basis, I wasn't sure how much they contributed.

I designed an informal test to find out.

For the first three months of the new season I continued using figures and made note of when they seemed to be the major reason for a selection. For the next three months I operated without using them at all. And for the remainder of the year I used them only when the results of previous use suggested their relevance. Fortunately, I was able to keep my 50 percent win record intact throughout the experiment.

Certainly, a more scientific survey needs to be done here, but in the meantime I think the results I obtained under fire are worth keeping in mind.

These are my present thoughts on the subject.

1. Speed figures, by definition, tell how fast the horse ran at a given racetrack at a given distance on a given day. They do not automatically tell how fast a horse *will* run, especially at a different distance. But the top speed-figure horse in the race does win approximately 35 percent of the

time at a slight loss for every $2 wager. With no handicapping at all, speed figures produce more winners than public favorites and at slightly better prices.

2. By computing the *par times* for each distance and class at a specific racetrack, the player will know which claiming horses have been meeting better stock than the allowance horses. He will know at a glance whether a $10,000 claiming race is better than a low-grade allowance race without having to consult the purse values in the result charts. He will also know at what class a field of fillies is faster than colts.

3. By computing speed figures on a regular basis, the player will have an important handicapping tool in the following cases.

When maiden graduates are entered in races for winners, their speed figures will often indicate their suitability to the class. The horse that graduates with a mediocre speed figure is not likely to repeat the feat in higher company. The graduate that has earned a superior speed figure may not be overmatched in any company. Below is the past performance record of a horse that graduated with an extremely high speed figure. Here he is entered in the 1975 Belmont Futurity against the best two-year-olds in the country. He ran the same speed figure as his maiden win and won by daylight.

Soy Numero Uno

122 B. c (1973), by Damascus—Tasma, by Crafty Admiral.
Breeder, Nuckols Bros. (Ky.).   1975 1 1 0 0 $5,400

Owner, J. R. Straus. Trainer, H. C. Pardue.

25 Aug75 4Bel   6 f :22² :45²1:09⁴ft 4-5 ▲120 3¹ 2ʰ 1² 1⁴ VasquzJ¹⁰ Mdn 93 SoyNumeroUno120 SecretCll 10
      Sept 5 Bel trt 3f ft :36⅗b   Sept 1 Bel 5f ft :58⅗h   Aug 24 Bel trt 3f ft :37⅖b

---

When a field of maidens is mixed between horses with minimum racing experience and first-time starters, the figures for the horses who have already raced will tell how difficult it will be for the first-timer to win. If the horses with racing experience have been producing above-par figures for the class, the first-timer has to be a tiger to compete. If the figures are subpar, a nicely bred, fast-working first-timer could be an excellent wager.

When a horse has consistently produced superior figures—when its *lowest* figure is better than the *best* figure of the competition—it will win at least 80 percent of the time! (This happens approximately once in every 250 races.)

If the top speed-figure horse in the race is also the horse most likely to get a clear early lead, it deserves a solid edge, providing of course it is not racing far beyond its normal distance capabilities or is not pitted against a stretch-running track bias. On a front-running track bias this kind of horse will usually outrun its apparent distance limitations.

4. Speed figures can be used effectively in the following circumstances.

Prior speed figures can be a valuable clue in spotting the inherent weakness of a betting favorite. If the figures are low for the class or low versus the competition, the player must have well-thought-out reasons to select such a horse at short odds—trainer pattern, visual evidence, vastly improved workouts, and so on.

When a horse is stepped up in claiming price, prior speed figures can be an important clue to its winning potential. If it has run fast enough in the past, the class raise may only be an illusion. Most of the time there will be additional evidence to support the class raise.

See Chapter 18 for an illustration of the value of speed figures in spotting horses in the above two situations.

5. If a horse is likely to get a clear early lead for the first time in its recent racing record, the player should expect a minimum of two lengths' improvement over its customary speed figures. Even more important, whenever such a horse is in a particularly slow-breaking field or has a bias in its favor, no other horse in the race can be played with confidence. An example of this type of straightforward betting situation is also presented in Chapter 18.

6. The traditional handicapping notion that "pace makes the race" is only true in special circumstances.

In the vast majority of sprints the early fractional times do not seem to affect the final time of the race winner. But if the pace is contested by two or more horses, regardless of the early fractions, the chances are good that the leaders will tire in the stretch. Some horses, however, respond to competition by running harder, and the player should have no trouble spotting these game creatures in the past performance records.

Pension Plan ✳   **116** Dk. b. or br. g (1970), by Olden Times—Lo May, by Khaled.
Breeder, R. C. Ellsworth (Ky.).

Owner, B. Federico. Trainer, K. Grusmark.

| | | | | | | | | | | | 1975 | 15 | 6 | 4 | 2 | $60,601 |
| | | | | | | | | | | | 1974 | 24 | 6 | 9 | 3 | $86,370 |

13 Oct75 8Bel	6 f :22³ :45³¹:09⁴ft	17	134	1ʰ	2ʰ	2½	4³	CaplboP²	HcpS 90 Honorable Miss 133 No Bias 15
5 Oct75 9Suf	6 f :22¹ :45²¹:11¹ft	3-5	▲124	1ʰ	1ʰ	1ʰ	1ⁿᵏ	CapalboP¹	Alw 85 Pension Plan 124 Bow Ski 7
22 Sep75 9Suf	6 f :22 :45¹¹:11 ft	6-5	▲126	1ʰ	3ⁿᵏ	2ʰ	2ⁿᵒ	CapalboP¹	HcpO 86 RobertM.Shrt120 PnsionPln 8
13 Sep75 8Bow	6 f :22¹ :44³¹:09⁴ft	7-5	▲116	2²	23½	24	2³	CaplboP²	HcpS 91 Scam 113 Pension Plan 8
6 Sep75 7Bel	6½ f :23³ :46³¹:17³ft	3¾	123	1ʰ	1½	1ʰ	1½	CapalboP⁷	Alw 88 PensionPlan123 FrkieAdams 7
23 Aug75 8Rkm	1₁₆ :46³¹:104¹:424ft	3¾	118	1ʰ	1ʰ	3²	4⁶	CapalboP⁴	HcpS 90 Kiss andRun115 ContinousCt 6
2 Aug75 8Rkm	17⁰ :45³¹:101¹:401ft	4¾	115	2ʰ	1½	1ʰ	1ⁿᵏ	CapalboP⁶	HcpS 95 PensionPlan115 AlmostGrwn 7
19 Jly 75 8Rkm	17⁰ :46 1:102¹:41 ft	5½	115	3ⁿᵏ	1ʰ	1ʰ	21¼	CapalboP⁵	HcpO 90 ContinuousCt123 PensionPln 7
5 Jly 75 8Rkm	6 f :22 :44³¹:09²ft	2½	▲118	2ʰ	2ʰ	1½	1ⁿᵏ	CapalboP³	HcpO 97 PensionPln118 PrceDrlingtn 8

Oct 30 Suf 3f ft :35⅗h   Oct 26 Suf 3f m :36⅘h   Oct 22 Suf 3f ft :35⅘h

In route races pace can influence the final time as well as the final result. A very slow early pace may or may not prejudice the final time depending upon the action that follows, but it will help a front runner to reach the stretch with more gas in the tank. Naturally, a very fast or highly competitive pace will frequently bring about the opposite result. The very best horses, however, are prone to use that fast pace as a springboard to track records.

EIGHTH RACE	1 MILE (chute). (Buckpasser, June 25, 1966, 1:32⅗. 3. 125.)
AP 35688	Forty-first running WASHINGTON PARK HANDICAP. $100,000 added. 3-year-olds and upward. By subscription of $100 each, which shall accompany the nomination, $250 to
August 24. 1968	pass the entry box and $750 additional to start, with $100,000 added, of which $20,000 to second, $15,000 to third and $10,000 to fourth. The winning owner to receive a trophy. Closed with 27 nominations.

Value of race $112,700. Value to winner $67,700; second, $20,000; third, $15,000; fourth, $10,000.
Mutuel Pool, $282,271.

Index	Horses	Eq't A Wt PP St	¼	½	¾	Str	Fin	Jockeys	Cl'g Pr.	Owners	Odds to $1
35524Sar¹	—Dr. Fager	4 134 9 1	6¹	2ʰ	1½	1³	1¹⁰	B Baeza		Tartan Stable	.30
35415AP¹	—Racing Room	4 116 2 7	4½	3²	2³	2¹½	2¹½	J Sellers		Llangollen Farm	10.40
35553AP⁴	—Info	4 112 3 6	8²	6²	3¹	3³	3¹	E Fires		Mrs E J Brisbine	37.00
35580AP¹	—Out the Window	b 4 115 5 8	9⁶	9⁷	7²	5½	4ⁿᵏ	H Moreno		J R Chapman	13.90
35625AP³	—R. Thomas	b 7 118 1 9	5¹	1ʰ	4²	4²	5⁶	J Nichols		Wilson-McDermott	24.80
35553AP⁶	—Cabildo	5 114 8 10	10	10	10	10	6ⁿᵒ	M Sol'mone		Mrs J W Brown	a-13.60
35625AP²	—Angelico	5 111 6 5	1ʰ	4½	5½	7³	7ⁿʰ	L Pincay Jr		Foxcatcher Farm	16.00
35606Atl²	—Hedevar	6 112 10 2	3½	8ʰ	6ʰ	6²	8¹½	T Lee		Mrs Edith W Bancroft	47.60
35625AP¹	—High Tribute	b 4 112 7 3	7½	7¹½	9⁵	9²	9¹¾	D Brumfield		Elmendorf	18.40
35433AP³	—Kentucky Sherry	3 112 4 4	2½	5½	8¹	8ʰ	10	J Combest		Mrs J W Brown	a-13.60

a-Coupled, Cabildo and Kentucky Sherry.

Time, :22⅘, :44, 1:07⅗, 1:32½ (new track and world record). Track fast.

$2 Mutuel Prices:	8—DR. FAGER	2.60	2.20	2.20
	3-RACING ROOM		3.80	3.20
	4-INFO			5.20

B. c, by Rough'n Tumble—Aspidistra, by Better Self. Trainer, J. A. Nerud. Bred by Tartan Farms (Fla.).
IN GATE—5:36. OFF AT 5:36½ CENTRAL DAYLIGHT TIME. Start good. Won easily.
DR. FAGER, away alertly but hard held to be reserved just off the lead, moved with a rush while still under restraint to take command leaving the backstretch, continued slightly wide to shake off RACING ROOM on the final turn, commenced lugging in while drawing off through the stretch run and won with something left.

The reliability of speed figures as a handicapping tool is significantly lower in route races whenever established running styles figure to create a superfast or slow, snail-like pace.

EIGHTH RACE	1⅛ MILES (chute). (1:45⅖). Twentieth running MOTHER GOOSE. SCALE WEIGHTS.
Bel	$75,000 added. Fillies. 3-year-olds. Weight, 121 lbs. By subscription of $150 each, which shall accompany the nomination; $375 to pass the entry box; $375 to start,
June 4. 1976	with $75,000 added. The added money and all fees to be divided: 60% to the winner, 22% to second, 12% to third and 6% to fourth. Trophies will be presented to the winning owner, trainer and jockey. Closed with 14 nominations.

Value of race $80,850. Value to winner $48,510; second, $17,787; third, $9,702; fourth, $4,851. Mutuel Pool, $328,981.
Off-track betting, $129,405.

Last Raced	Horse	EqtAWt	PP	St	¼	½	¾	.Str	Fin	Jockeys	Owners	Odds to $1
22 May76 8Bel4	Girl in Love	3 121	4	5	5	5	5	27	11¼	JCruguet	Elmendorf	4.00
22 May76 8Bel2	Optimistic Gal	3 121	2	2	25	25	12	12	211	BBaeza	Mrs R B Firestone	1.00
29 May76 8GS1	Ancient Fables	b3 121	5	1	410	48	42	3½	36¾	ACorderoJr	Brazil Stable	18.50
22 May76 8Bel5	Artfully	b3 121	3	4	32	34	33	42	43¼	GPIntels'noJr	R N Webster	30.40
22 May76 8Bel1	Dearly Precious	3 121	1	3	1½	1½	23	5	5	JVelasquez	R E Bailey	1.20

OFF AT 5:02½ EDT. Start good. Won driving. Time, :22⅖, :44⅖, 1:08⅘, 1:35⅖, 1:48⅘. Track fast.

$2 **Mutuel Prices:**

4-GIRL IN LOVE	10.00	4.00	4.40
2-OPTIMISTIC GAL		2.60	2.20
5-ANCIENT FABLES			3.80

Ch. f, by Lucky Debonair—Lover's Quarrel, by Battle Joined. Trainer, John P. Campo. Bred by Elmendorf Farm (Ky.).

GIRL IN LOVE, badly outrun on the backstretch, commenced to rally after going five furlongs, raced wide into the stretch, continued to advance under left-handed pressure and proved clearly best after catching OPTIMISTIC GAL. GIRL IN LOVE pulled up lame. OPTIMISTIC GAL, bothered by DEARLY PRECIOUS while racing outside that rival on the backstretch, took over while racing well out in the track on the turn, quickly opened a clear lead but wasn't able to withstand the winner. ANCIENT FABLES failed to be a serious factor. ARTFULLY raced within striking distance to the stretch and flattened out. DEARLY PRECIOUS ducked out into OPTIMISTIC GAL after the start, made the pace while bearing out into that rival throughout the run down the backstretch and was finished soon after going six furlongs.

7. Except for the top speed figure with front-running tendencies mentioned earlier (see point 3 above), the presence of a powerful, one-dimensional track bias of any kind makes speed figures as irrelevant as the times they are based on.

On a stretch runners' track the final quarter-mile time is somewhat helpful, but the dominant handicapping considerations are stamina, class, condition, and post position.

On a front runners' track the early fractions and early position calls in the running line are the best clues to the cashier's window.

If the bias is also to the inside part of the track, post position is the player's best means of separating contenders.

Virtually every racetrack in America provides aberrant conditions like the ones described here sometime during the racing season. The player who can recognize these prevailing situations and then adjust his handicapping will have the best shot at the equivalent of a perfect game. It's possible to sweep the card on days like that.

NOTE: *The early speed in the Schuylerville Stakes, the sample race exhibited in Chapter 4 (pages 41–42), was Our Dancing Girl. This determination was made by noting the first call position of Our Dancing Girl in her race with the great Ruffian. Post number two didn't hurt either. The next best speed in the race seemed to be Secret's Out and the top closer But Exclusive. This was the result.*

SEVENTH RACE
Saratoga
JULY 29, 1974

6 FURLONGS. (1.08) 57TH RUNNING THE SCHUYLERVILLE. $25,000 Added. 1st Division. Fillies, 2-year-olds. By subscription of $50 each, which shall accompany the nomination; $125 to pass the entry box; $125 to start, with $25,000 added. The added money and all fees to be divided 60% to the winner, 22% to second, 12% to third and 6% to fourth. Weights, 119 lbs. Non-winners of a sweepstakes allowed 3 lbs.; maidens, 7 lbs. Starters to be named at the closing time of entries. A trophy will be presented to the owner of the winner. Closed Monday, July 15 with 30 Nominations. Value of race $27,625, value to winner $16,575, second $6,077, third $3,315, fourth $1,658. Mutuel pool $108,621, OTB pool $48,764. Exacta Pool $79,247. OTB Exacta Pool $98,708.

Last Raced	Horse	Eqt.A.Wt PP St	¼	½	Str	Fin	Jockey	Odds $1
10Jly74 8Aqu3	Our Dancing Girl	b 2 116 2 1	1²	12½	1²	1no	Bracciale V Jr	10.20
19Jun74 8@th5	Secret's Out	2 119 5 3	2¹	2²	2³	22½	Vasquez J	4.70
12Jly74 4Aqu2	But Exclusive	2 116 7 7	6½	5⁴	5⁵	3¹	Cordero A Jr	3.60
8Jly74 6Crc1	Some Swinger	b 2 116 4 4	5²	41½	3½	41½	Velasquez J	6.00
20Jly74 3Mth1	My Compliments	2 116 1 5	3²	3½	4hd	56	Venezia M	1.60
14Jly74 6WO2	La Bourrasque	b 2 116 3 6	7	6⁵	6⁵	67½	Turcotte R	5.90
15Jly74 3Aqu2	Precious Elaine	b 2 112 6 2	4hd	7	7	7	Santiago A	15.60

OFF AT 4:42 1/2 EDT. Start Good, Won driving. Time, :22⅖, :45½, 1:11½ Track fast.

$2 Mutuel Prices:	2-(B)-OUR DANCING GIRL	22.40	7.00	4.60
	5-(E)-SECRET'S OUT		5.00	4.00
	7-(H)-BUT EXCLUSIVE			3.20

$2 EXACTA 2-5 PAID $80.40.

B. f, by Solo Landing—Amber Dancer, by Native Dancer. Trainer Rigione J. Bred by Elcee H Stable (Fla).

OUR DANCING GIRL quickly sprinted clear, saved ground while making the pace and, after settling into the stretch with a clear lead, lasted over SECRET'S OUT. The latter prompted the pace throughout, lugged in slightly nearing midstretch and finished strongly, just missing. BUT EXCLUSIVE, off slowly, finished well while racing wide. SOME SWINGER rallied along the inside leaving the turn, eased out for the drive but lacked the needed late response. MY COMPLIMENTS had no excuse. LA BOURRASQUE was always outrun after breaking slowly. PRECIOUS ELAINE broke through before the start and was finished early.

Owners— 1, Elcee-H Stable; 2, Schott Marcia W; 3, Levin W A; 4, Mangurian H T Jr; 5, Reineman R L; 6, Levesque J L; 7, Brodsky A J.

Trainers— 1, Rigione J; 2, Picou J E; 3, Imperio D A; 4, Root T Jr; 5, Freeman W C; 6, Starr J; 7, Conway J P.

Scratched—Elsie Marley (30Apr744Aqu1).

13.
Theory vs. Experience

For each and every piece of information in the past performance profile, there is a popular theory purporting to measure its exact significance. The interesting thing about that is I know of no winning player who subscribes to any such rigid approach to any aspect of the game.

WEIGHT

The old saying that "weight will stop a freight train" is true enough. But except for a few special cases, it is pure conjecture that a fit racehorse can be stopped or slowed by the addition of a few pounds. Weight is simply the most overrated factor in handicapping.

Perhaps 105 pounds will help a horse run a fifth of a second faster than 110 pounds and two-fifths of a second faster than 115. But there is no proof to demonstrate the validity of such a rigid relationship. Indeed between 105 and 115 pounds the amount of weight carried by the horse is demonstrably unimportant.

Beyond 115 pounds, the effect of added weight on performance is an individual thing.

Some horses can't handle 120 pounds; others are able to run just as fast and as far with considerably more. Past performance profiles usually provide sufficient clues to make such determinations; but because the betting public tends to automatically downgrade the chances of a top-weighted horse, the reward for a more flexible attitude is generally generous mutuel prices.

Gallant Bob	126	Dk. b. or br. g (1972), by Gallant Romeo—Wisp O'Will, by New Policy. Breeder, J. L. Homan (Ky.).

Owner, R. Horton. Trainer, J. D. Morquette.

					1975	16	12	1	2	$229,213
					1974	10	3	4	0	$58,118

22 Nov75	8Key	6 f :221 :4511:094gd	3-5 ^119	2½	1½	1½	11½	GalltnoG3	AlwS 93 GallantBob119	BearerBond 8
4 Oct75	8Key	6½ f :22 :4441:163ft	2-5 ^119	3½	2¹	11½	1²	GalltnoG3	AlwS 94 Gallant Bob 119	Talc 6
6 Sep75	8Key	7 f :214 :4411:24 ft	6-5 ^129	3¹	32	2h	1³	GalltnoG7	HcpO 89 Gallant Bob 129	Talc 9
13 Aug75	8Mth	6 f :204 :4341:092ft	2 ^129	27	23½	2½	11½	GalltnoG5	HcpO 93 Gallant Bob 129	Talc 7
5 Jly 75	8Bow	6 f :22³ :4541:102ft	2-5 ^127	2h	11½	1³	13½	GalltnoG5	HcpO 91 GallantBob127 FrchWhistler 6
21 Jun75	8AP	7 f :22 :4431:232ft	4½ 124	1h	1½	12	1¹	GalltnoG5	AlwS 85 Gallant Bob 124	Doug 11
1 Jun75	8Del	1-₁₆ :4621:12 1:461ft	3-2 ^117	1h	1h	56	512	GalltnoG5	AlwS 66 GreyBeret111 Dr'sEnjyDollrs 10
24 May75	8Del	6 f :214 :45 1:111ft	4-5 ^124	2h	2h	2h	1½	GalltnoG4	AlwS 89 Gallant Bob 124	Bold Gun 7
22 Mar75	8Pim	6 f :224 :4611:111ft	1 ^122	3½	2h	11	2h	GalltnoG8	AlwS 90 BombayDuck122 GallantBob 9
15 Mar75	8Aqu	7 f :22³ :4531:234sy	2-5 ^119	2h	2h	1½	3¾	GalltnoG8	AlwS 81 Lefty 113	Tass 8
1 Mar75	8Aqu	6 f :214 :4521:094ft	3 117	1h	11	2½	33½	GalltnoG9	AlwS 90 Singh 114	Laramie Trail 10
22Feb75	8Key	7 f :221 :45 1:253ft	2-5 ^119	13	16	18	110	GalltnoG1	AlwS 81 GallantBob119	WickedPark 11
15 Feb75	8GS	6 f :221 :4541:11 gd	2-5 ^122	1h	13	15	19	GalltnoG6	AlwS 88 GallantBob122	LuckeyLeaf 7
1 Feb75	8Bow	6 f :224 :4631:12 gd	4-5 ^124	13	15	15	14½	GalltnoG8	AlwS 83 GallantBob124 PendulmSam 6
25 Jan75	8Key	6 f :222 :4611:132sy	4-5 ^119	1½	1h	1½	1²	GalltnoG6	AlwS 75 Gallant Bob 119	Sgt. Hunt 7

Nov 29 Key 4f ft :48⅘b

Give me an obviously sharp horse with a proven superiority over the contenders and I'll gladly support him carrying 120, 125, or 128 pounds, providing of course that he has successfully carried that kind of weight before. Give me a horse that is not in shape and I don't care what weight he carries.

A few years ago I remember getting 6–1 on a horse that had beaten the same field of starter handicap horses five straight times. The betting crowd was so afraid of the horse's 134-pound weight assignment that it failed to accept him at face value.

If the fans had bothered to look up his record, they might not have been so apprehensive. The season before the horse won a similar-class event under 136 pounds. To a certain extent the same kind of situation occurs several times a season at every racetrack in America.

Of course, common sense dictates paying some attention to large weight shifts or to heavy weight assignments, especially when two or more closely matched contenders are involved.

1¼ MILES—SUBURBAN HANDICAP, AQUEDUCT, JULY 20, 1974

True Knight ✳   **127**   Dk. b. or br. h (1969), by Chateaugay—Stealaway, by Olympia.
Breeder, J. W. Galbreath (Ky.).   1974.. 8 3 0 $283,638
   1973..12 3 2 2 $200,858

Owner, Darby Dan Farm.   Trainer, T. L. Rondinello.

Jly 13-74	8Mth	1 1-4 2:02	ft 8-5	^124	9¹³ 4³ 11½ 13¾	Riv'aMA⁵	HcpS 92	TrueKnight124 EcoleEtage HeyRube 9
Jun16-74	9Suf	1 1-8 1:48⅗ft 3-5	^121	7¹⁸ 7¹⁹ 58½ 4³	C'd'oAJr⁶	HcpS 95	BillyComeLately109 Forage NorthSea 7
May27-74	8Bel	1 1:34⅖ft	7	125	8²² 8¹³ 79¾ 68¼	Riv'aMA⁵	HcpS 88	ArbeesBoy112 Forego Timel'ssMom'nt 8
Apr 6-74	8GS	1 1-4 2:06 sl 6-5	125	68¾ 4³ 21½ 1¾	C'd'oAJr4	HcpS 70	TrueKnight125 ProveO't PlayTheF'ld 6
Mar23-74	9Hia	1 1-4 2:01⅕ft 9-5	124	7¹⁹ 77¼ 32½ 2¹	C'd'oAJr³	HcpS 91	Forego 129 True Knight Play the Field 7
Mar 7-74	8Bow	1 1-4 2:05⅘ft 3-5	^123	14¹⁵10¹⁰ 54¾ 1½	C'd'oAJr4	HcpS 96	True Knight 123 Delay Ecole Etage 14
Feb23-74	9GP	1 1-4 1:59½ft	1	^123	6¹⁶ 45½ 2h 2½	C'd'oAJr4	HcpS 97	Forego127 TrueKnight GoldenDon 6
Feb 9-74	9GP	1 1-8 1:48⅗ft 2½	123	5¹⁶ 51⁶ 46 2no	C'd'oAJr³	HcpS 91	Forego125 TrueKnight Proud andBold 5
Nov22-73	8Aqu	1⅜ 1:55 ft 4½	126	119¼ 9⁷⅓ 3½ 12	C'd'oAJr⁹	HcpS 87	TrueKnight126 Triangular NorthSea 12
Oct27-73	7Aqu	2 3:20 ft 4½	124	5¹² 3⁸ 3¹⁷ 4¹⁸	C'd'oAJr²	WfaS 78	Prove Out 124 Loud Twice A Prince 6
Oct15-73	8Aqu	1 1-8 1:47 ft 4	122	8¹¹ 55½ 36 34¾	Cast'daM⁷	HcpS 96	Riva Ridge 130 Forage True Knight 9
Sep22-73	8Bow	1 1-8 1:49⅘ft 5½	120	9¹⁴ 8¹⁰ 11 14	C't'daM⁵	HcpS 102	TrueKnight 120 Delay BurningOn 12

July 19 Bel 3f ft :39b   July 12 Bel 4f ft :50b   July 8 Bel 6f ft 1:16b

Forego   **131**   B. g (1970), by Forli—Lady Golconda, by Hasty Road.
Breeder, Lazy F Ranch (Ky.).   1974 7 5 2 0 $322,378
   1973 18 8 3 3 $188,909

Owner, Mrs. Edward F. Gerry.   Trainer, S. W. Ward.

Jly 4-74	8Aqu	1⅜ 1:54½ft 2-5	^129	⊂15 48 2h 1¾	Gust'sH⁶	HcpS 88	Forego129 BillyComeLately ArbeesBoy 7
Jun26-74	8Aqu	7 f 1:21½ft 2-3	^132	6¹² 6¹² 56½ 2¾	G'tinesH²	HcpS 94	Timel'ssM'm'nt112 Forego N'rthSea 8
May27-74	8Bel	1 1:34⅖ft 6-5	^134	6¹¹ 2h 11½ 2²	G'tinesH²	HcpS 94	ArbeesBoy112 Forego Timel'ssMom'nt 8
May18-74	8Bel	7 f 1:22½ft 7-5	^129	8⁹ 63½ 11½ 12½	Gust'sH⁷	HcpS 91	F'r'go129 Mr.Pr'sp'ct'r Tim'l'sM'm'nt 8
Mar23-74	9Hia	1 1-4 2:01⅕ft 4-5	^120	5¹⁰ 1½ 11½ 1¹¹	G'tinesH⁵	HcpS 92	Forego 129 True Knight Play the Field 7
Feb23-74	9GP	1 1-4 1:59½ft 7-5	127	48 2² 1h 1½	G'stinesH²	HcpS 98	Forego127 TrueKnight GoldenDon 6
Feb 9-74	9GP	1 1-8 1:48⅗ft 2½	^125	46 32½ 21 1no	G'tinesH⁷	HcpS 91	Forego125 TrueKnight Proud andBold 5
Dec 8-73	8Aqu	1 1-8 1:47⅘ft 3-5	^127	56 34 11½ 1¾	G'tinesH⁶	HcpS 99	For'go127 MyG'll'nt Key to theK'gd'm 7
Nov24-73	8Aqu	1⅜ 1:54⅗ft 2	^123	45 32½ 13 15	Gust'esH⁹	HcpS 89	Forego123 MyGallant Twice aPrince 10
Nov10-73	6Aqu	7 f 1:22½ft 4-5	^122	35½ 36 34 34	GustinesH²	Alw 84	North Sea 115 Tap The Tree Forego 5

July 19 Bel 3f ft :35⅗b   July 15 Bel 7f ft 1:24h   July 13 Bel 3f ft :36⅗b

Two honest, hard-hitting stakes horses.

The difference between Forego and True Knight was never more than a length or two. In Florida during the winter of 1974 Forego won three straight races over True Knight, each by a narrow margin. In the spring Forego was twice unsuccessful in attempts to carry 130 or more pounds. And he was, in fact, meeting weaker horses than True Knight. Either he had lost some of his edge in condition or as a four-year-old was inhibited by such heavy weight loads. True Knight, on the other hand, was razor sharp; and on July 13, 1974, one week before the Suburban, True Knight put in his best lifetime race.

Given True Knight's obvious edge in condition, the spread in the Suburban weights and Forego's 131-pound impost were plus factors that deserved to be taken into account. Somehow, and I don't believe it yet, True Knight paid $10.60.

There is one special circumstance in which a rigid approach to the weight factor is supported by fact. Few people know about it.

Before the turn of the century the Jockey Club Scale of Weights was created as a concession to the natural maturation rate of horses. It is a common fact that a horse is not as well developed at age three as it is likely to be at age four.

Racing secretaries use the scale of age-linked weight concessions as a guide when carding races for horses of mixed age groups.

7th Arlington Park

1¹⁄₁₆ MILES (inner turf). (1:41⅘). CLAIMING. Purse $5,500. 3-year-olds and upward. 3-year-olds. 113 lbs.: older. 122 lbs. Non-winners of two races since May 20 allowed 2 lbs.; a race, 4 lbs. Claiming price, $13,000; 2 lbs. allowed for each $1,000 to $11,000. (Races where entered for $10,000 or less not considered.)

4th Detroit Race Course

6 FURLONGS (chute). (1:08). CLAIMING. Purse $2,500. 3- and 4-year-olds, non-winners of two races. 3-year-olds. 115 lbs.: 4-year-olds. 120 lbs. Non-winners of a race in 1974 allowed 3 lbs.; a race since Nov. 10, 5 lbs. Claiming price, $2,500.

THE JOCKEY CLUB SCALE OF WEIGHTS

DISTANCE	AGE	JAN. & FEB.	MAR. & APR.	MAY	JUNE	JULY	AUG.	SEP.	OCT.	NOV. & DEC.
½ Mile	2	...	...	...	...	...	105	108	111	114
	3	117	119	121	123	125	126	127	128	129
	4	130	130	130	130	130	130	130	130	130
	5 & up	130	130	130	130	130	130	130	130	130
6 Furlongs	2	...	...	...	...	...	102	105	108	111
	3	114	117	119	121	123	125	126	127	128
	4	129	130	130	130	130	130	130	130	130
	5 & up	130	130	130	130	130	130	130	130	130
1 Mile	2	...	...	...	...	...	...	96	99	102
	3	107	111	113	115	117	119	121	122	123
	4	127	128	127	126	126	126	126	126	126
	5 & up	128	128	127	126	126	126	126	126	126
1¼ Miles	2	...	...	...	...	...	...	...	...	...
	3	101	107	111	113	116	118	120	121	122
	4	125	127	127	126	126	126	126	126	126
	5 & up	127	127	127	126	126	126	126	126	126
1½ Miles	2	...	...	...	...	...	...	...	...	...
	3	98	104	108	111	114	117	119	121	122
	4	124	126	126	126	126	126	126	126	126
	5 & up	126	126	126	126	126	126	126	126	126
2 Miles	3	96	102	106	109	112	114	117	119	120
	4	124	126	126	126	126	125	125	124	124
	5 & up	126	126	126	126	126	125	125	124	124

NOTE: *Fillies are entitled to a five-pound sex allowance in races against colts.*

For reasons I cannot fathom, there is a great deal of controversy in racing circles about the legitimacy of age-linked weight concessions. Every season there is talk of abolishing or amending the scale of weights. Most say that three-year-olds should not get automatic weight concessions in the late summer or fall. Nonsense. It seems to me the old-timers had a pretty good idea. The effectiveness of the scale and the need for the concessions are made abundantly clear in the following remarkable statement, checked out in a research project that included several thousand races.

When a three-year-old is assigned actual top weight in a race for horses three years and up, the three-year-old has little or no chance of winning. I suggest you read that again.

In all stakes and allowance races run at seven of the nation's most popular tracks during 1973 there were only two exceptions to this maxim. In all of 1974 there were only three exceptions. In 1975 and the first half of 1976 there were but five more exceptions to the rule.

All ten horses that defied the scale of age-linked weight concessions were curiously unable to repeat the feat at any other time, and only one was able to win a follow-up race of any kind during the next two months of competition. Ten exceptions and over 400 top-weighted three-year-olds that were unable to give away weight to their elders. That's information worth keeping in mind.

SEX

In Europe fillies race against colts and win with absolute impunity. In America most trainers are reluctant to match the so-called weaker sex against males. Ruffian's tragic demise in the match race against Foolish Pleasure didn't help reverse the trend. But to his credit, it didn't change Frank Whiteley Jr.'s commitment to the experiment. Only two of Honorable Miss's races shown in the p.p.s below were against members of her own sex.

Honorable Miss		120	B. m (1970), by Damascus—Court Circuit, by Royal Vale.							
Owner, Pen-Y-Bryn Farm. Trainer, F. J. Whiteley, Jr.			Breeder, Mrs. T. Bancroft (Ky.).		1976	8	3	2	1	$100,148
					1975	13	7	2	0	$183,857

30 Aug76 8Bel	6 f :22³ :45⁴1:10 ft	7-5 ▲130	97½ 53½ 1h	14½	ShmrW10	HcpS 92	HonorableMiss130	Lachesis 10
25 Jly 76 8Aqu	7 f :23² :47 1:24²ft	1 ▲118	6¹² 6⁹ 4²	31½	VsquezJ2	HcpS 78	El Fitirre 114	Nalee'sKnight 6
12 Jly 76 8Aqu	6 f :22¹ :44⁴1:09 ft	1 ▲119	10¹⁰10¹² 910	5⁶	VsquezJ10	HcpS 91	North Call 115	Our Hero 10
4 Jly 76 8Aqu	6 f :22 :44⁴1:09²ft	1 ▲125	5¹⁴ 4¹¹ 47	51½	VsquezJ5	HcpS 95	Red Cross 118	Shy Dawn 5
27 May76 8Bel	6 f :22³ :45⁴1:10²ft	2-5e▲123	6¹¹ 6⁵ 2¹	13¾	VasquezJ1	Alw 90	Honorable Miss 123	Lachesis 6
15 May76 8Bel	7 f :22² :44²1:21 ft	9-5 ▲121	9¹² 9⁹½ 57½	26¼	VasquezJ1	HcpS 91	LordRebeau115	HonorbleMiss 9
1 May76 8Aqu	7 f :22¹ :44²1:22²sy	4¾ 122	8¹¹ 8¹³ 57	2¾	VasquezJ5	HcpS 88	DueDiligence111	HnrbleMiss 8
23 Apr76 8Aqu	6 f :22² :45⁴1:10³gd	1 ▲123	6¹⁴ 6¹⁰ 33	1¾	VasquezJ3	Alw 90	Ⓟ HonorbleMiss123	FltVictrss 6
1 Nov75 8Bel	7 f :22 :44³1:22⁴ft	7-5e▲125	11¹⁷10¹² 58½	45½	VasqezJ9	HcpS 82	No Bias 116	Step Nicely 11
13 Oct75 8Bel	6 f :22³ :45³1:09⁴ft	9-5e▲133	14¹¹11¹⁶½ 5¹½	1²	VasqzJ15	HcpS 93	Honorable Miss 133	No Bias 15
25 Sep75 8Bel	7 f :22⁴ :45³1:23¹sy	1-2 ▲119	48½ 46 3½	22¾	VasquezJ1	Alw 90	Ⓔ FltVictress112	HnrbleMiss 4

Sept 14 Bel 4f ft :46⅜h	Sept 10 Bel 4f ft :46⅘h	Sept 5 Bel 4f ft :48b

Because of a variety of economic factors, it is true that a filly of $15,000 claiming class will usually run one- or two-fifths of a second slower than a colt of the corresponding claiming class. But if the filly is in a race with colts and is intrinsically the fastest horse in the field, my research shows that there is nothing linked to sex differences that will prevent her from proving her superiority on the track. Simply put, a fast filly will beat a slow colt and a fast colt will beat a slow filly.

One caution: During the late spring and early summer, female horses tend to go into heat. Occasionally that will bring out excessive kidney sweating and other nervous habits. A filly acting in that manner during the post parade is telling you she has other things beside racing on her mind. (This can happen in a race carded exclusively for fillies too.)

WORKOUTS

The racetrack is open for training in the early morning hours, and the *Daily Racing Form* clockers have a tough job. As many as thirty horses can be out on the racetrack at the same time, and there are no names or numbers on the saddlecloths to help identify the horses.

DELAWARE PARK – Track Fast

Three Furlongs		Four Furlongs					
A Long Way	:40 b	Bog Road	:49⅖ b	Amystar	1:01⅖ h	Spanish Dew	1:00⅖ h
Arctic Ability	:36⅖ h	Boldinthepark	:50⅗ bg	Army Hitch	1:04 b	WilmingtonFlask	1:01⅘ hg
Decladation	:38 bg	Chinese Trumpet	:49⅖ b	Black Power	1:01⅘ b	Woulda Coulda	1:03 b
Deep	:38 b	Count Knave	:49 bg	Blackjack Davis	1:03 b	You'reSensationl	1:03⅘ b
Don Miguel	:40 b	Custers LastStand	:48 h	Cold Voyage	1:05 bg	Zasperilla	1:03⅘ b
Fair Toe	:38⅖ bg	Demonic	:48 h	Double Chop	1:03⅗ b		
GlitterandGlmor	:38⅘ b	Demonic	:52 b	Gun Cotton	1:07 b	**Six Furlongs—1:09**	
Grundgy Twerp	:36 h	Dim Royalty	:51⅘ b	Hillybob	1:00 h	Cellini	1:16 b
Long Tall Texan	:37 b	Double Nymph	:51 b	I'm A Lady Pilot	1:03 b	Mickey Solo	1:15 b
Loom's Boy	:37 b	Ercildoun	:51⅘ b	Kintla's Folly	1:01 b	Plant Native	1:18 bg
No No Niki	:38 b	FurtherMoreLdy	:51 b	Las Profesoras	1:02 b	Sinister Knight	1:16⅘ b
Royal Exstasy	:38 b	Grassisgreener	:51 b	Lassie Dear	1:00⅘ h	Tim Lee Lad	1:16 bg
Satan's Speed	:38 bg	Haf Pro	:50 b	Late Spring	1:05 b		
Some Duce	:37 b	Landing Field	:49 b	Mercado II	1:00 h	**Seven Furlongs**	
Summer Secret	:38⅘ b,	LuckyThirtyThre	:49 bg	Over the Stile	1:03⅘ bg	Bee Abe	1:29 b
Sweet Chutney	:38⅘ bg	Lynne Baby	:52 b	Pilgrim's Plight	1:04⅘ b	Better Arbitor	1:27 h
Tiger Castle	:36⅘ h	Norton Priory	:48⅘ b	Pinch Pie	1:03⅘ b	**1 Mile—1:35⅕**	
Two Coats	:38 b	Princess Hairan	:50⅘ b	Prince Berry	1:03 bg		
White Skies	:36 h	Real Terror	:52 b	Prophetic	1:03⅘ b	T. V. Vixen	1:39⅖ h
		Five Furlongs—	:57⅕	Ready Axe	1:03⅘ b	The Eclipser	1:45⅘ b

HILLYBOB & LASSIE DEAR (5) were in company. PINCH PIE (5) was given an easy trial. LAS PROFESORAS (5) was given an easy trial. MERCADO II (5) was impressive. BETTER ARBITOR (7) is being brought to hand in good fashion. T. V. VIXEN (1M) went very smartly. Her fractions were 23, 35, 48.3, 1:01, 1:13, 1:27 & 1:39.2. And was allowed to gallop out one mile. one eighth in 1:53.1.

ITEM: Because of typographical mistakes and omissions, workouts that appear in the daily tabulator listings are frequently more accurate than works appearing below the past performance profile. In addition, these tabular listings often contain the clocker's comments about some of the more noteworthy training drills of the day.

ITEM: When a horse ships from a section of the country serviced by one edition of the *Form* to another serviced by a different edition, the out-of-town workouts will frequently be omitted from the past performances. I have complained about this to the publisher of the *Daily Racing Form*, but aside from a smattering of California workouts that now make their way into the Eastern edition and vice versa, the response has not been satisfactory. Maybe if we all scream about this together we will get better results.

ITEM: The absence of workouts from any past performance profile does not mean the absence of training. Some works are missed, missing, or misidentified. A few trainers have access to private training tracks. Until all states adopt a rule requiring local workouts, the player is simply going to have to keep a record of the trainers who like to sneak their hot horses past the public.

For obvious reasons, this practice is most often attempted with first-time starters in cheap maiden claiming races and is particularly rampant in Maryland, a breeding state where the racing commission is not known for its compassion for the fan, and where there are almost fifty private training tracks within a 100-mile radius of Bowie, Laurel, and Pimlico.

ITEM: The times of workouts are as accurate as the clockers are skillful and honest. Because the vast majority of clockers are honest and skillful but not well paid, the player should expect a few of the best workouts to be misrepresented.

The most accurate clocking crews operate in New York (under the direction of Frenchie Schwartz), in California (where a workout identification system is used), and in Florida during the high-class winter meets. At all but a few racetracks, however, 95 to 99 percent of the workouts accorded to established stakes horses, and 70 to 80 percent of the rest are as accurate as a hand-held stopwatch can report them. In Maryland and Kentucky I would not be willing to stand by that statement.

ITEM: Some tracks offer an auxiliary training track to handle the overflow of horses on the grounds. These training tracks tend to be considerably deeper and slower than the main track, and the following table of times should be adjusted accordingly.

MAJOR-TRACK TABLE OF NOTEWORTHY WORKOUT TIMES

DISTANCE	BREEZING (WITHOUT SERIOUS WHIPPING)	HANDILY	FROM GATE	MUD
3 Furlongs	.35⅘b	.35⅖h	Add ⅖ sec.	Add ⅘ sec.
4 Furlongs	.48b	.47⅗h	Add ⅖	Add 1
5 Furlongs	1:00⅗b	1:00⅕h	Add ⅖	Add 1⅕
6 Furlongs	1:13⅗b	1:13h	Add ⅖	Add 1⅖
7 Furlongs	1:27b	1:26⅖h	Add ⅖	Add 1⅗
1 Mile	1:41b	1:40⅖h	Add ⅖	Add 1⅘
1⅛ Miles	1:56b	1:55⅖h	Add ⅖ sec.	Add 2 sec.

Admittedly, the value of the above chart is limited. It is only a guide. On lightning-fast racetracks the standards should be adjusted by at least one full second, and at minor tracks few horses will ever work fast enough to spark the player's attention.

The value of workouts is not restricted to speed. Indeed, a fast workout is not often conclusive evidence of improved physical condition; nor is a series of short, speedy drills of any special import to a horse that consistently shows high early speed in its races. Instead the player should consider the value of workouts in the light of the following principles; they are the concepts many of the best trainers use, and the ones many of the best players use as well.

1. Pay special note to the frequency of workouts and give a horse extra credit for positive physical condition if it has several good workouts to its credit or has raced well recently and has worked four furlongs or longer at least once in the interim. This is especially true at minor racetracks and for horses that have been out of action sometime during the recent past.

Royal Rhett 115 Ch. g (1973), by Royal Union—Sweet Straw, by Jackstraw.
Breeder, Al Rossi (Ill.). 1976 4 3 0 0 $6,787

Owner, Lepere Stable. Trainer, Ron O. Goodridge.

10 Sep76	10Cka	5 f :22^2 :46^2 :59^{2}ft	13	118	1^h 1^1 1$^1\frac{1}{2}$ 1$^1\frac{1}{2}$	WolfC^5	Alw 90	RoyalRhett118 DarkAvenger 8
28 Jly 76	8FP	5$\frac{1}{2}$ f :23^2 :48^{2}1:07^{4}ft	7-5	^{4}118	2$\frac{1}{2}$ 3^2 4^2 5$^2\frac{1}{2}$	WolfC^4	Alw 80	MeanMr.Green114 SadiesMn 7
19 Jly 76	5FP	6 f :23 :47 1:13^{2}ft	8-5	120	13$\frac{1}{2}$ 13$\frac{1}{2}$ 14$\frac{1}{2}$ 15	WolfC^7	Alw 80	RoyalRhett 120 GreatPeach 8
29 May76	3FP	5$\frac{1}{2}$ f :23 :47^{2}1:07 gd	8-5	^{4}120	11$\frac{1}{4}$ 12$\frac{1}{2}$ 14 1^3	WolfC^1	Mdn 87	RoylRhett120 AbleScrtaryJr. 10

(Sept 9)Cka 4f ft :51$\frac{2}{5}$b   (Sept 2 Cka 5f ft 1:00$\frac{1}{5}$hg)   (Aug 27 Cka 5f ft 1:02$\frac{3}{5}$bg)

---

2. A recent fast workout at three or four furlongs is a positive sign if the horse has shown little early speed in its recent races (or has been racing in a route and is now attempting a sprint). Conversely, if the horse has been showing high early speed in its races or is attempting a significantly longer distance, a longer, slower workout would suggest the trainer's attempt to build staying power. In the

first example below, Princely Song showed high speed in his training drill of July 11 and won a sprint off that work four days later. In the case of Bold Forbes, trainer Laz Barrera had employed several long slow workouts in his strategy to prepare the colt for a maximum effort in the Kentucky Derby. His workout prior to the Preakness, a blazing-fast half-mile, did nothing to advance the horse and may have put him too much on edge. For the Belmont, the workout line shows that trainer Barrera was very conscious of the stamina factor. A masterpiece of horsemanship on display.

Princely Song ✳ **114** Dk. b. or br. c (1972), by Cornish Prince—Songster, by Jester.
Br., Warnerton Farm of Ky., Ltd. (Ky.). 1976 4 1 1 0 $12,150

Owner, A. & Christine Willcox. Trainer, L. Rettele 1975 3 2 0 0 $8,809

3Jly 76	5Hol	⊤ 1 :474¹:113¹:36²fm	3½	114	52	43½	6²¼	7³	OlivaresF⁷	Alw 85 Chindo115	EarlyCotton 7
26Jun76	7Hol	1 :454¹:10 1:35²ft	40	114	32	2h	2½	2½	OlivaresF⁷	Alw 88 HomeJerome114 PrincelySong 7
4Jun76	7Hol	6 f :22 :442¹:08²ft	2⅔	115	64	66½	7¹¹	6¹¹	HawleyS⁷	Alw 86 Maheras116 RestlessRestless 7
20May76	7Hol	6 f :22 :442¹:09³ft	1	▲115	1½	1½	1½	1nk	HawleyS¹	Alw 91 PrincelySng115 Chief'sHolday 7
22Nov75	8Key	6 f :22¹:451¹:09⁴gd	7	114	33½	31½	42	43	TrctteRL⁸	AlwS 90 GallantBob119 BearerBond 8
10Nov75	6Key	7 f :22¹:454¹:23³sy2-3	▲114	1½	11½	16	15	TurctteRL¹	Alw 91 PrincelySong114 Bee aTipper 7
27Oct75	9Key	6½ f :23 :46²¹:17³ft	3	119	1h	11½	13	18	TrctteRL⁸	Mdn 89 PrincelySong119 CourtRportr 10

✳:July 10 Hol 4f ft :46²⅝h June 20 Hol 6f ft 1:16h June 17 Hol 5f ft 1:01h

---

Bold Forbes **126** Dk. b. or br. c (1973), by Irish Castle—Comely Nell, by Commodore M.
Br., Eaton Farms & Red Bull Stable (Ky.). 1975 .. 8 7 0 1 2 $318,890

Owner, E. R. Tizol. Trainer, L. S. Barrera. 1975 .. 8 7 0 1 $62,749

15 May76	8Pim	1⅜ :45 1:09 1:55 ft	1e	126	12	12	2h	34	CoroAJr⁴	ScwS 91 Elocutionist126 Play theRed 6
1 May76	8CD	1¼ :454¹:10²²:01³ft	3	126	15	1½	1½	11	CrdroAJr²	ScwS 89 BoldForbes126 HonestPlesre 9
17 Apr76	8Aqu	1⅛ :46 1:09⁴1:47²ft	2-5	▲126	13	11½	14	14½	CdroAJr⁵	ScwS 98 Bold Forbes 126 On The Sly 7
20 Mar76	8Aqu	7 f :22¹ :44 1:20⁴ft	8-5	119	2h	12	17	17¾	CdroAJr⁷	AlwS 97 Bold Forbes 119 Eustace 8
28 Feb76	8SA	1¼ :453¹:093¹:35 ft	2	117	12	21	14	13	PincyLJr⁵	AlwS 94 BoldForbes117 Grandaries 7
14 Feb76	8SA	7 f :22 :443¹:21⁴ft	8-5	▲119	1h	2½	12½	3½	PincyLJr⁷	AlwS 93 ThrmlEnrgy117 StaindGlass 7
24 Jan76	8SA	6 f :22¹ :45 1:09³ft	6-5	▲120	2½	2²	2½	2no	PincyLJr²	AlwS 91 Sure Fire 114 Bold Forbes 6
31 Dec75	4SA	5½ f :214 :442¹:03 ft	1-3	▲122	1½	2½	2h	35	PincayLJr¹	Alw 94 Sure Fire 114 Beau Talent 5
3 Aug75	8Sar	6 f :214 :441¹:094ft	1-10	▲120	12	18	110	18	V!squezJ⁵	AlwS 91 BoldForbes120 FamilyDoct'r 5
23 Jly 75	8Bel	6 f :222 :452¹:092ft	8-5	120	11½	12	14	15	PincyLJr²	AlwS 96 Bold Forbes 120 Iron Bit 5
15 Jun75	7PR	6 f :222 :443¹:10³ft	1-6	▲118	12	14	15	11³	HiraldoJ²	Stk 10¹Bold Forbes 118 Lovely Jay 4
4 Jun75	4PR	6 f :23 :453¹:112ft	1-4e	▲114	12	13½	15	18	HiraldoJ³	Alw 97 Bold Forbes 1¹4 Lovely Jay 10
25 Apr75	1PR	5 f :22 :453 :591ft	1-6	▲116	14	15	16	18½	HiraldoJ³	Alw 95 Bold Forbes 116 Lovely Jay 5
11 Apr75	1PR	5 f :22 :453 :584ft	1-3	▲115	15	15	15	⁴5	HiraldoJ⁴	Alw 97 Bold Forbes 115 Lovely Jay 5
12 Mar75	1PR	5 f :22 :454 :592ft	35	116	15	16	18	11⁷	HiraldoJ²	Mdn 94 BoldForbes¹16 MyDad'sBrdy 8

June 1 Bel 1m ft 1:50⅖bg May 27 Bel 1¼m ft 2:43⅖b May 13 Pim 4f ft :45⅗h

---

3. A workout of any distance at any reasonable speed one or two days before a race is a useful "blowout" and can often be interpreted as a positive sign of trainer intention. To obtain Sunday workouts, which are not included in the

Monday *Daily Racing Form* (published Saturday evening), check the racing secretary's office on entering the track. Some tracks announce these workouts over the public address system or post them in a designated location in the grandstand.

Speed Burgoo **116** B. f (1972), by Scotland—Queen Corona, by Bernburgoo.
Breeder, K. Blitsch (Ill.).
Owner, S. Wheeler. Trainer, Rex Loney.
$2,500
1976..10 1 0 1 $2,010
1975..12 1 4 1 $3,300

9 Sep76 9Lat	1¹⁄₁₆ :49¹¹:18¹¹:53⁴sy	16	117	10³¹10²²10¹⁷ 8¹⁷	MurchisnJ8	2500		ClassyCanuck109 KennyLeVn 12
2 Sep76 9ElP	6 f :24 :49 1:17 sl	26	120	78½ 88½ 57½ 33	MurchsnJ3	2500 62	J.Artest114	Day ofComfree 8
23 Aug76 9ElP	1 :48 1:13⁴1:40³ft	8e	117	55½ 88½ 91⁹ 8²⁸	MurchsnJ7	2000 51	Quarnos 120	O Song 8
12 Aug76 9ElP	1¼ :49²1:15²2:09²ft	53	120	3½ 67½ 69½ 6¹⁵	MurchsnJ1	2000 59	Phil's Regret 115	Controblss 7
3 Aug76 6ElP	1 :47⁴1:13³1:40³ft	8½	115	35 45½ 6⁹ 6²²	McDowlM7	2000 57	JacCourt120	LilThermo 7
26 Jly 76 2ElP	1 :48³1:14²1:43 ft	5¾	116	41½ 3¹ 3½ 11¼	MurchsnJ1	2000 67	SpeedBurgoo116	HeACrook 10
19 Jly 76 6ElP	6 f :23¹ :46⁴1:12²ft	26	115	54½ 54½ 5⁶ 5½	CrtwrhtN1	3500 78	FairDiamond115	BoxcrBetty 6
13 Jly 76 2ElP	6 f :23 :47 1:14³ft	27	112	5⁷ 66¾ 75¾ 95¼	CwrightN1	2500 72	Go Go Liza 112	Karen Lou 10
7 Jly 76 9ElP	6 f :23 :47 1:13 ft	26	118	53½ 41½ 52½ 5⁵	MurchsnJ4	2000 80	℗Oh Katy 113	Roy's Choice 9
2 Jly 76 2ElP	6 f :23 :46¹1:12 ft	35	112	11¹³12¹⁴11⁹¼11¹⁷	CrtwrghtN6	2500 73	Dr. Mills 114	Bixby Imp 12
8 Nov75 2CD	6 f :23¹ :47³1:15²sl	58	115	97¾ 91⁰ 8⁹ 8¹¹	BeechJJr7	3000 58	Wa Tonka 117	Vent Du Sud 12

July 25 EIP 3f ft :38⅕b

---

4. Most stakes-class horses work fast, and with a well-trained horse every training drill has a purpose. The following past performance profile shows the great Kelso preparing for the Washington, D.C., International, a 1½-mile classic run each fall on Laurel's grass course. In this particular case, Kelso, who was never 100 percent comfortable on the grass, lost by a narrow margin to Mongo, one of the top grass horses of the past twenty-five years. The defeat was surely no disgrace and certainly not the fault of trainer Carl Hanford, who made all the right moves.

Kelso ✕ **126** Dk. b. or br. g (1957), by Your Host—Maid of Flight, by Count Fleet.
Breeder, Mrs. R. C. duPont.
Owner, Bohemia Stable. Trainer, C. H. Hanford.
1963..11 9 1 0 $544,762
1962..12 6 4 0 $289,685

Oct19-63⁷Aqu	2 3:22 ft 1-6 ▲124	41¾ 12 16 1⁴	Val'z'lal1	WfaS 87	Kelso 124	Guadalcanal 124	Garwol 7
Sep28-63⁷Aqu	1 1-4 2:00⅘ft 1-4 ▲126	34 2½ 1½ 13½	Val'z'lal2	WfaS 96	Kelso126	NeverBend120	CrimsonSatan 8
Sep 2-63⁷Aqu	1 1-8 1:49⅘ft 2-3 ▲134	32 3¹ 1² 15½	Val'z'lal7	AlwS 92	Kelso134	CrimsonSatan129	Garwol 8
Aug 3-63⁶Sar	1 1-8 1:50⅘ft 1-3 ▲130	4³ 42½ 1¹ 12½	Val'elal2	SpwS 93	Kelso130	Saidam111	SunriseCounty 7
Jly 4-63⁷Aqu	1 1-4 2:01⅘ft 2-5 ▲133	32 31½ 11½ 11½	Val'z'lal7	HcpS 91	Kelso 133	Saidam 111	Garwol 7
Jun19-63⁷Aqu	1 1-8 1:48⅘ft 1-3 ▲132	33½ 31 1² 11½	Val'uelal3	AlwS 97	Kelso 132	Lanvin 114	Polylad 5
Mar23-63⁸Bow	1¹⁄₁₆ 1:43 ft 4-5 ▲131	55 33 21½ 1¾	Val''z'lal5	HcpS 98	Kelso131	CrimsonSat'n124	G'sh'gWind 6
Mar16-63⁶G.P	1 1-4 2:03⅕ft 1-5 ▲130	2h 12 1² 13½	Val'uelal2	HcpS 83	Kelso 130	Sensitivo 112	Jay Fox 6
Feb23-63⁷Hia	1 1-4 2:01⅘ft 2-5 ▲131	3¹ 42½ 23 22½	Val''z'lal5	HcpS 87	BeauPurple125	Kelso131	Heroshogala 9
Feb 9-63⁷Hia	1 1-8 1:48⅘ft 2½ 128	45 42 1² 12¾	Val'z'lal1	HcpS 128	Kelso 128	Ridan 129	Sensitivo 6
Jan30-63⁸Hia	7 f 1:22⅘ft 2½ 128	2h 32 43½ 45½	Val'z'lal4	HcpS 89	Ridan 127	Jaipur 127	Merry Ruler 5
Dec 1-62⁸G.S	1 1-2 2:30⅕ft 2-5 ▲129	1h 13 13 1⁵	Val'z'lal2	AlwS 105	Kelso 129	Bass Clef 117	Polylad 5

Nov 5 Lrl tc 1 1-8m fm 1:50⅘h | **Nov 4 Lrl tc 3f fm :37⅘b** | **Nov 1 Lrl 7f m 1:27¾b**

5. A horse that races regularly, particularly one in good form, does not necessarily need any workouts to stay in shape. A prior victory without workouts is sufficient proof of this.

Mrs. Herman **119** B. m (1971), by Map Maker—Lana Belle, by To Market.
Breeder, Mrs. R. C. duPont Jr. (Md.). 1976 10 3 1 1 $16,810
Owner. Janet Greenberg.Trainer, H. Jacobson. 1975 9 3 0 1 $15,360

```
15Jly 76  5Aqu   1 :45⁴¹:102¹:36⁴ft 2¾  117 1½ 1³ 1⁶ 11½  VenziaM⁶ 18000 82 (F)Mrs.Herman117 IceStar II.  8
 8Jly 76  2Aqu   7 f :22² :45²1:25 gd 3¾ 113 3² 1½ 1⁴ 13¾  VenezaM² 13000 76 (F)Mrs.Herman113 MagcalLdy  8
 1Jly 76  9Aqu   1 :45⁴¹:094¹:35³ft 3 ⁴117 1½ 1⁵ 1⁸ 1⁹   VeneziaM⁷ 7500 88 (F)Mrs.Hrmn117 T.G.ForEthyl 10
24Jun76  1Bel    6 f :23¹ :46³¹:112ft 4½ 115 1ʰ 1² 1¹ 2ⁿᵏ  VeneziaM⁴ 7000 85 (F)QckPassage113 Mrs.Hermn 10
31May76  9Bel    6 f :22³ :46¹¹:123ft 13 112⁵ 3¹ 3¹ 22½ 52½ MrtinJF¹¹ 9500 77 (F)Form inColor112 Gynarchy 11
19May76  1Bel    7 f :23² :47³¹:25³sy 2½ ⁴110⁵ 2¹ 1ʰ 35½ 5¹⁰ MartinJE⁸ 9500 64 (F)Sarmaletta118 LoudCry  8
16May76  3Bel    6 f :23 :46³¹:124ft 8-5 ⁴118 1½ 1ʰ 2ʰ 3¾ MontyaD⁴ c7500 77 (F)DoubleSkip114 QuietSuzne 9
10May76  3Bel    6 f :22⁴ :46²¹:121¹ft 7½ 113 2³ 2½ 1ʰ 4½  MontoyaD⁷ 8500 80 (F)Sarmaletta115  AuntBud 11
```

NO WORKOUTS SINCE→June 12 Aqu 3f ft :38b

---

6. To better determine the readiness of a first-time starter or an absentee, the player should review the daily tabular workout listings for additional clues. In maiden special-weight (nonclaiming) races at the top-class racetracks, very few first-timers win without showing snappy speed in one or more training trials or drawing at least one rave review from the clockers. Even fewer win without showing at least one very good workout at five furlongs or longer among other trials that stretch back over four, six, or eight weeks of preparation. A good workout from the starting gate is also reassuring.

In cheap maiden races superfast workouts are rarely to be trusted. In fact, the most promising workout line for claiming maidens is the one that contains a few closely spaced workouts of modest speed. A workout line that contains no training drills, however, is a signal to watch the tote board. In sharp hands such a horse can be expected to run a top race.

In either case—in the high-grade maiden race or the low-grade maiden claimer—first-time starters are bad risks if the field contains a lightly raced horse with proven ability. Conversely, the more proven losers in a field, the greater credit one should give to a well-bred, well-trained first-time starter.

Little Riva   118 B. c (1973), by First Landing—Iberia, by Heliopolis.
Breeder, Meadow Stud, Inc. (Va.).   1975 . 0 M 0 0   (—)

Owner, Meadow Stable. Trainer, L. Laurin.

June 3 Bel 3f ft :35h   May 29 Bel 3f ft :59⅗h   May 24 Bel 5f ft 1:00h

---

On the Belmont Stakes day card of 1975 Riva Ridge's half-brother—the horse you see above—was fit and ready to run a top race at first asking. The following workouts predate those included in his past performance profile.

May 20—Bel 4f ft 47⅕b . . .
May 16—Bel 3f ft 35b . . .
May 10—Bel 6f ft 1:13⅕h . . . COMMENT: "Little Riva showed
       good speed."
May 7—Bel 5 f ft 1:02⅖b . . .
May 1—Bel 4f 48b . . . COMMENT: "Little Riva is coming to
       hand."

In California the *Form* not only provides accurate workouts but also includes the latest six workouts in the past performance profile of a first-time starter. This is an excellent idea, and I wish the *Form* would supply such information as a matter of course for all its editions.

The two past performance examples below show the kind of training program necessary to get a claiming-class maiden ready for a winning try. Note the subtle but real difference in workout times between the maiden trying to win a $20,000 claiming event and the more expensive colt.

Hollywood Park is a lightning-fast racetrack. For a top-class maiden event, a first-timer would need to show much faster training trials.

Elroy Braun 118 Dk. b. or br. c (1974), by Old Bag—Marcy Lynx, by Mount Marcy.
Breeder, R. E. Schleicher (Ky.). 1976 0 M 0 0 ——
Owner, R. E. Schleicher. Trainer, S. Martin. $20,000
July 11 Hol (TR) 5f ft 1:01⅕hg   July 7 Hol 4f ft :50h   July 2 Hol 4f ft :49⅖h
June 27 Hol (TR) 5f ft 1:02hg   June 22 Hol 4f ft :48⅗h   June 17 Hol 4f ft :48⅗hg

---

Devil's Bluff 114 Dk. b. or br. c (1974), by Big Bluffer—Witchy Norma, by Crimson Satan.
Breeder, Braugh Ranches (Texas). 1976 0 M 0 0 ——
Owner, Braugh Ranches. Trainer, L. Regula. $30,000
July 22 Hol 4f ft :48⅘h   July 18 Hol 1(TR) 5f ft :59⅗hg   July 14 Hol 4f ft :47⅘h
July 10 Hol 6f ft 1:15⅖h   July 4 Hol 1(TR) 5f ft 1:00⅗h   June 27 Hol (TR) 5f ft 1:02⅕hg

---

It may seem hard to believe, but when Seattle Slew, the unanimous two-year-old champion of 1976, made his debut at Belmont Park on September 20, 1976, he had no published workouts in the Western edition of the *Form*. A few mediocre works were listed in the Eastern *Form* but they were no indication of his true ability. The heavy play he received on the tote board suggested that his subsequent dynamite performance was not a surprise to his trainer. W. H. Turner is nobody's fool.

Seattle Slew 122 Dk. b. or br. c (19794), by Bold Reasoning—My Charmer, by Poker.
Breeder, B. S. Castleman (Ky.). 1976 0 M 0 0 (——)
Owner, Karen L. Taylor. Trainer, William H. Turner, Jr.

---

7. A workout on the turf course is an extremely valuable clue to trainer intention. A good drill on the turf is excellent evidence of the horse's ability to handle such footing. Sometimes the trainer will enter such a horse in a grass race immediately following a good turf work; sometimes he will wait until the workout is no longer listed in the past

performances. As a rule, it makes good sense to keep a special record of all good turf works.

BELMONT PARK –
(Turf) Course Firm (Dogs Up)

Four Furlongs		Thirty Years	:47⅖ h	Hosanna II	1:04⅗ h	Our Doctor	1:15	b
Captain Max	:49⅕ b	Yvetot	:50⅖ b	Ode to Romeo	1:04⅖ b	PoliticalCoverup	1:18	b
Duveen	:48 h	**Five Furlongs**		Spanish Dagger	1:00⅖ h			
Inward Bound	:49⅘ b	Alibhai's Luck	1:02⅕ b	**Six Furlongs**		**Seven Furlongs—1:20⅘**		
Manifest	:48⅘ b	Carlogie	1:02⅘ h	Go Double	1:14⅗ h			
Ruling All	:48⅘ b	Close to Noon	1:01⅗ h	Herculean	1:15 h	**Barcas**	1:32⅖ b	
Run Tara Run	:49⅖ h	Evening Dance	1:02⅕ h	I'm All	1:17 b	I Encircle	1:33	b

SPANISH DAGGER (5) looks good.

The following horse gave ample evidence of her ability to handle turf racing in two workouts prior to her winning turf race on July 13, 1976.

Miss Gallivant 113 B. f (1973), by Gallant Man—Year Around, by Hill Prince.
Breeder, L. R. Miller (Md.). 1976 7 2 1 1 $16,180
Owner, Dr. S. or L. Miller. Trainer, L. Rettele. 1975 0 M 0 0 ——

18Jun76 ⁶Hol	1¹⁄₁₆ :47 1:11¹¹:42²ft	3½	116	1ʰ	1½	14	1⁶	HawleyS²	Alw 83 ⒻMissGallivnt116 Save aLtle	7
11Jun76 ⁶Hol	6 f :22¹ :45¹¹:09²ft	5	114	3½	1½	1½	1³	HawleyS⁵	Mdn 92 ⒻMsGallivant114 Shanagoldn	7
5Jun76 ⁴Hol	6 f :22¹ :45²¹:09⁴ft	7¼	114	5¹³⁄₄	2¾	33½	3⁸	HawleyS⁵	Mdn 82 ⒻMadamGaylady114 Deploy	9
26Mar76 ⁴SA	1 :46²¹:121¹:38⁴ft	3½	116	1½	11	6⁷	9²²	ValdezS³	Mdn 53 ⒻBidBoldly116 Shamara	9
13Mar76 ³SA	1¹⁄₁₆ :46³¹:122¹:46³ft 8-5	*116	1¹½	5³	915	93⁷	ToroF³	Mdn 32 ⒻChavalarious116 BidBoldly	9
22Feb76 ³SA	6 f :21³ :443¹:104ft 6-5	*117	43½	44½	45½	55¾	HawleyS²	Mdn 79 ⒻContingentFee117 Jaunting	10
25Jan76 ³SA	6 f :22 :45 1:10³ft	2	*117	87½	65	54½	22½	PincayLJr⁶ Mdn 83 ⒻWandle117 MissGallivant	11

July 9 Hol (tc) fm 1:28⅕h   *July 2 Hol 6f ft 1:13h   *June 26 Hol (tc) 5f fm 1:00⅖h

8. Improving workouts generally denote improving physical condition. With the workout line below, all that Patriot's Dream needs is a slight drop in class.

Patriot's Dream 113 Ch. c (1973), by Gunflint—Ambitious Lady, by Petare.
Breeder, Ocala Stud, Inc. (Fla.). 1976 7 1 1 2 $10,590
Owner, H. Allen. Trainer, E. Jacobs. 1975 5 1 0 1 $6,769

18July 76 ⁸Aqu	6 f :22¹ :451¹:10³ft	16	112	3³	3³	53½	64½	VelasqzJ² (HcpS)	86 ArabianLaw112 FullOut	7
8July 76 ⁸Aqu	6 f :22² :451¹:09²ft	11	113	4¹½	52½	42½	36½	MontoyaD² Alw 90 SoyNumeroUno111 ArabanLw	6
30Jun76 ⁸Aqu	1 :451¹:084¹:34¹ft	40	114	2½	2¹	56	69½	MontyaD⁴ AlwS 85 DanceSpell 114 Zen	6
22Jun76 ⁵Mth	6 f :22¹ :452¹:114ft 3-5	113	3⁴	3¹½	4³	36½	EdwrdsJW⁴ Alw 74 KindIndeed118 SecondTerm	5	
15Jun76 ⁷Mth	6 f :22¹ :443¹:10 ft	2¾	115	2½	2¹	2³	23½	EdwrdsJW⁶ Alw 86 SunnyClime120 Patriot'sDrm	6
30May76 ⁶Bel	Ⓣ 1 :454¹:10 1:343fm	10	115	3¹	9¹²10²⁰10²⁶ HrnandzR² Alw 72 FifthMarine115 Burundi	10			
21May76 ⁷Bel	6 f :22¹ :452¹:10 ft	2	114	1¹	1¹½	1²	1¾	VeneziaM¹ Alw 92 Patriot'sDrm114 Financl Whiz	7

July 23 Bel (trt) 5f ft :59²⅖h   July 14 Bel (trt) 5f ft 1:00⅕h   July 5 Bel (trt) 4f ft :49b

9. A series of closely spaced workouts or workouts mixed with racing ordinarily points out a horse in sound physical health. Very often the average horseplayer eliminates an active horse with mediocre finishes in his past performance profile without realizing how fit the horse really is. On the other hand, a horse in apparent good form cannot be expected to hold that form if the trainer insists on working the horse hard and fast every few days between starts. Studying the strengths and weaknesses of trainers is the only reliable way to make accurate judgments about this type of training regimen.

This horse is racing fit. She has shown improved speed in her recent starts. Pretty soon she's going to get a field she can lead from wire to wire.

Cameo Girl	**116**	Ch. f (1972), by Dandy K.—Octopus Girl, by Octopus				
		Breeder, J. E. Sowards (Ky.).		1975	9 1 1 0	$2,440
Owner, J. E. Sowards. Trainer, J. E. Sowards.		$3,500		1974..11	1 3 1	$3,774

7 Nov75 ¹CD	6 f :23	:47³¹:153³sy	10	115	1¹	1¹	74¼	9¹⁰	McCllrJW⁶	3500 58 Ⓕ Mark theSpt115 GameFce 12
3 Nov75 ²CD	6 f :22²	:46¹1:123ft	90	116	3¹	63¾	83½	9¹²	McCllrJW⁹	5000 71 Ⓕ ImprsiveMry114 Hln'sMsic 9
25 Oct75 ²Kee	6 f :22³	:46¹1:121ft	20f	109	3½	35½	56½	6¹²	McCllrJW¹	5000 69 Proud Spirit 112 Fuel 10
18 Oct75 ²Kee	6 f :23	:48¹1:142sy	9½	114	11½	11	67¼	9¹⁹	BrmfldD¹¹	5000 51 Ⓕ May'sJwll 115 TooMchCrn 12
11 Oct75 ⁷Beu	6 f :23	:46¹1:113ft	57	119	75¼	11³	11¹⁸	11²²	UrrutiaJ⁶	Alw 66 Darby Dale 114 Scott Man 11
17 Feb75 ⁸Lat	5½ f :24¹	:50²1:103m	5	108	2¹½	2h	1h	1ⁿᵒ	McCulrJW²	Alw 65 Cameo Girl 108 Just Miss 8
8 Feb75 ⁵Lat	6 f :23	:46²1:11¹ft	5½	114	3²	46	41¹	42¹	McCurJW³	Alw 71 Dr.Abs116 Holloway'sMistke 6
18 Jan75 ⁴Cwl	4½ f :22³	:47²:544m	2½	114	5	42½	2²	2⁶	McCurJW⁴	7500 82 Clemstone 122 Cameo Girl 6
Jan 2-75⁸Cwl	6½ f 1:25⅗m	64	117	2½	2½	2h	78½	McCu'rJW⁹		Alw 62 Donda'sMir'e122 CoolltB'e Jan't'sDe't 10

Nov 1 CD 5f ft 1:05b   Oct 24 Kee 3f ft :37b   Oct 22 Kee 5f ft 1:04b

This horse is crying for a rest. Instead, he was entered in a stakes race against For the Moment and other top-class juvenile colts.

Heidee's Pal	**122**	B. c (1974), by Tinajero—Debbys Charm, by Debbysman.				
		Breeder, M. M. Garren (N. Y.).		1976..11	1 2 1	$16,404
Owner, M. M. Garren. Trainer, Gilbert Puentes.						

3 Sep76 ⁶Bel	6 f :22⁴	:46²1:104ft	13	115	63¼	52¾	45¼	47¾	MapleE⁶	Alw 80 HeyHyJ.P.115 Albi'sTrckStp 6
19 Aug76 ⁸Sar	6 f :22²	:46 1:122ft	10	119	12¹⁰	108¾	64¾	2²	MapleE⁶	AlwS 76 FratelloEd115 Heidee'sPal 17
9 Aug76 ³Sar	6 f :22³	:46³1:12 m	6¾	120	2½	3nk	2½	53	MapleE⁵	27500 77 JollyQuill 119 Strtp'sGlitters 8
28 Jly 76 ⁵Aqu	6 f :22³	:46¹1:131ft	20	122	77	99	9¹¹	97	SantgoA⁵	35000 70 Plantaris 119 PrinceNoName 9
17 Jly 76 ⁷Aqu	5½ f :22	:45²1:044ft	13	115	77	79½	6¹²	6¹²	SantiagoA⁶	Alw 77 Bucksaw 115 Hey Hey J. P. 7
10 Jly 76 ³Aqu	5½ f :22³	:47 1:054sy	5½	122	31½	21¼	11	1nk	StgoA⁸	M25000 84 Heidee'sPal 122 PrinceNoNe 8
2 Jly 76 ⁴Aqu	5½ f :23	:47 1:06 ft	2½	122	41¼	43	33	32½	StgoA³	M25000 80 Bucksaw 122 Dobrynin 7
24 Jun76 ⁴Bel	5½ f :23²	:47²1:062ft	20	118	3¹	3nk	2½	22	SngoA⁹	M20000 81 PeppyPeppis122 Heidee'sPal 6
16 Jun76 ³Bel	5½ f :23⁴	:44 1:07 ft	14	118	55	98¾	88¼	79¾	SngoA⁸	M20000 70 Hawaiian Ways120 Dky'sBlrc 6
28 May76 ⁴Bel	5½ f :22⁴	:46³1:053ft	49	1175	87¼	98½	9¹³	9¹⁷	MartinJE⁴	Mdn 70 MedievalMn122 FirstPretse 10
21 May76 ⁴Bel	5½ f :23	:46⁴1:054ft	5¾	122	42	55¼	7¹³	7¹⁶	TrtteR⁵	M35000 70 FlagOfficer122 WincomaLss 10

Sept 9 Bel trt 4f ft :47¾h   Sept 1 Bel 4f ft :50⅖h   Aug 26 Sar trt 5f ft 1:02h

10. Consult the clocker's comments, where available, for special mention of noteworthy training drills, fractional times, workouts in company, and other important clues. Pay particular attention to the tone of the clocker's remarks. If the comment is a positive one, you might well expect improvement from the horse in the next race or two. A good "horses to watch" list can be compiled this way, depending of course on the reliability of the clocker in question.

SAMPLE CLOCKER COMMENTS, BELMONT PARK, SEPTEMBER 1976

SEATTLE SLEW is sharp. WARM FRONT had all his speed. DANCE SPELL acts good. HONORABLE MISS was full of run. ASHMORE AND MAITLAND II were in company. BOLD FORBES is doing well. FIGHTING BILL had jockey Day up.

Most of the horses who drew the comments above were well-known stakes horses. However, there were two strangers who worked in company on even terms, and the player might not have paid attention to the modest comment they received. But the moment Ashmore was exposed as a contender for the $350,000 Jockey Club Gold Cup, the value of Maitland II's stock increased.

Workouts in company are particularly useful to the trainer and the horseplayer. Very often a trainer will not know which of two lightly raced horses is the faster. A workout in company may provide a definitive answer. As you might imagine, one of the most reliable workout clues is a victory by the slower of two horses that worked in company. From that moment onward, the faster worker becomes a four-star entry in my "horses to watch" list. A young maiden working on even terms with a known stakes horse is another key clue provided by workouts in company.

SAMPLE CLOCKER COMMENTS, BOWIE, SEPTEMBER 1976

(4) BACAYE still retains her speed. (4) SILVER FLORIN had a high turn of speed in his trial. (5) INCÁ ROCÁ with jockey Snell in the irons went in fractions of :22.1, :34, :46.1, :59.1 galloping out in 1:12.4. (5) ROYAL DRAFTSMAN is ready for another winning effort. (6) MUM BOLD had a useful trial. Additional Workout on Oct 6, 75, ALTO REBOT (4F) :50 B.

Most of the above comments are quite helpful and to the point, but I would tend to downgrade the clocker's note on Royal Draftsman unless prior results demonstrated the particular clocker's reliability as a tout.

RUNNING STYLE AND THE DISTANCE FACTOR

While most racehorses tend to have a preferred racing distance and some horses are incapable of winning a race when out of their element, there is great power in the training regimen to alter the distance capability of the horse. In addition, there is a most intriguing and predictable relationship between each different distance and running style.

A good trainer can increase or decrease the distance potential of a horse through workouts, special equipment, and actual races at longer and shorter distances. Allen Jerkens does it all the time; so do hundreds of other trainers of lesser talent. The following two principles illustrate the manner in which the vast majority of horses react to distance manipulations:

1. A horse that has been sprinting will most often race closer to the lead or will even set the pace in a longer, slower-paced route event.
2. A horse that has been on the pace in a longer, slower route may be unable to cope with the faster pace of a sprint but is nevertheless likely to show improved stretch punch.

The past performance profiles below demonstrate both principles at work.

Operating ✳   **112**   Ch. m (1971), by Dr. Fager—Cutting, by Bold Ruler.
Breeder, O. Phipps (Ky.).   1976 . 6 1 0 0 $6,440
Owner, Shinrone Farm, Inc.   Trainer, Frank Kirby.   1975 . . 1 0 0 0   (—)

```
 3 Aug76  7Aks    6 f :221 :4541:111ft     4  112  361 351  22  111  LivelyJL5     Alw 81 Operating112   CordialPrince 8
28 Jly 76  7Aks   170 :4541:1221:45 gd    51e 114  14  14  21  68   HarmonB2      Alw 65 BrotherSasa112   GunChoke 8
16 Jly 76  7Aks   170 :4641:11 1:413ft    41  114  111 1h  551 681  WhtdDW3       HcpS 84 ⑤Roger'sChce115 RockyTrip 8
23 Jun76  7Aks    170 :4811:1141:422ft    21  114  741 55  912 911  McBdeB10      Alw 75 ⑤Baygo 120       Quivira 11
 9 Jun76  7Aks    51 f :214 :4531:051ft   14e 114  961 1083 981 751 McBdeB12      Alw 79 ⑤FashionNews114  TruxTop 12
20 May76  6Aks    6 f :222 :4541:111ft    33  114  551 54  79  791  McBrideB2     Alw 72 ⑤Mk andWne120    FashnNws 10
26 Jly 75  7A.P   6 f :222 :4541:103ft    11  114  983 810 811 915  RubbiccoP4    Alw 75 ⑤Mary Dugan 114      Salus 9
```

Midnight Tattoo   **122**   Dk. b. or br. g (1970), by Blue Tattoo—Dainty Joy, by Johns Joy.
Breeder, D. E. Breshears, S. F.   1976 . 19 2 1 3 $9,296
Cheesman & J. H. Cole (Ark.).   1975 22 5 3 3 $17,980
Owner, W. A. Morris.   Trainer, Roy Landis. $7,500

```
 8 Sep76  7Det   170 :4821:14 1:454ft   21 ▲122  2h  1h  2h 1nk GarciaJR6   6250 68 MidnightTattoo119 FltMkna  8
30 Aug76  6Det     1 :48 1:1341:41 ft   2 ▲114  52  2h  21 1nk GarciaJR6   6500 74 MidnightTattoo114    Rabish  7
 7 Aug76  3Det   1 1/16 :4721:1241:463ft  6  109  311 431 431 511 HrreraA7   H2500 59 DepndbleMel 110 QckDiscvry 7
16 Jly 76  6Aks   6 f :221 :4531:112ft  16  116  991 812 541 3nk StageJL2   c6500 80 Nu I Shud 119      Nobby Dod 11
 3 Jly 76  6Aks   6 f :23  :4621:112ft  87  116  108 1081 910 871 SntgeJL10  7500 72 Terms 122       Sturdy Money 10
23 Jun76  6Aks    6 f :22  :4441:104ft  54  116  1213 1212 14111111193 SangeJL7  8500 73 Amerix 119      Proud State 12
28 May76  6Aks    6 f :223 :4621:124sy  20  117  1015 812 89  691 HreraA12  c6500 64 Twiddley De 112      Tin Horn 12
25 May76  6Aks    6 f :221 :4541:122ft  26  117  11121114 87  421 HerreraA4  7000 73 Shoeshiner 117       Kenya A. 12
21 May76  4Aks    6 f :22  :4441:11 ft  21  112  11151021 813 511 HereraA11  7000 71 Solid Mix 112      City Visitor 11
```

Kind Tom   **113**   Ch. g (1970), by Pinnacle—Kindness, by Stymie.
Breeder, Mrs. T. Thompson (Tex.).   1976 20 2 2 5 $5,901
Owner, J. C. Farley.   Trainer, Lonnie Abshire. $2,500   1975 26 3 3 3 $11,703

```
27 Aug76  2RD   170 :49 1:1441:462gd  21 ▲122  2h  1h  32  461 BrynMW10  2500 61 BigBdGrgry116 SouthnGuest 10
23 Aug76  7RD   1 1/4 :4841:13 1:46 ft  13  114  641 44  451 412 BryanMW5  3250 67 SecondFrost116 TiffanyFair  8
26 Jly 76  2RD   1 1/4 :48 1:1321:48 ft  21 ▲122  13  111 1h  311 MelndzJH7  2500 67 Busy King 116     Perry's Boy 10
18 Jly 76 10RD    ⑦1    1:393fm   22  112  431 46  510 812 CostaAJ4  4500 11 Akaroa 116       I'm Baffled 11
 4 Jly 76 10RD   170 :4741:1241:443ft  31  114  12  12  121 313 CostaAJ10  3250 75 Regal Fox 122    Fleet Court 10
18 Jun76  2RD   1 1/4 :4831:1241:473ft  61  116  1h  12  311 361 SolomonG4  2500 64 Lancer'sImge122 Paddy'sKn  7
11 Jun76  9RD   170 :4811:1341:453ft  71  117  12  12  21  481 WelchH4   2500 63 Mr. Cad 122   Lancer's Image  7
 7 Jun76  1RD   6 f :221 :4541:123ft  41  119  851 773 812 88  SolmonG11  2500 72 TexasToy111   ShamrockTim 12
22 May76  3RD   6 f :221 :4621:123ft   8  116  54  311 64  711 ClinchW12  2500 79 Liberal Man 116   Hesourpet 12
15 May76  3RD   6 f :222 :4611:123ft  15  116  321 221 221 261 ClinchW4  2500 74 PennamtRaiser122 KindTom  8
```

Aug 17 RD 5f ft 1:04b

Kirby Lane   **115**   Gr. c (1973), by Native Charger—Dancing Puppet, by Northern Dancer.
Breeder, Albert & Stantely (Fla.).   1976 3 2 0 1 $14,520
Owner, Gedney Farm.   Trainer, L. S. Barrera.   1975 . . 5 1 2 0 $10,420

```
21 May76  5Bel   6 f :22  :4441:084ft  33  113  331 32  1h  12  CordroAJr2 Alw 98 Kirby Lane 113    Sunny Clime  7
12 May76  6Bel   6 f :233 :4631:103ft 9-5e 113  53  621 513 311 VasquezJ6  Alw 88 PrlessMcGth106  DeltaLegcy  7
 1 Jan76  9SA   1 1/16 :4631:1121:44 ft  6-5 ▲120  66  31  111 131 PincyLJr10 Alw 82 Kirby Lane 120      Tregillick 11
24 Nov75  4Aqu   1 :48 1:13 1:374ft  8-5 ▲122  12  11  121 131 BaezaB8    Mdn 77 KirbyLane122  FingerPaints 14
13 Nov75  5Aqu   1 :4741:1341:382sy  3  122  521 521 31  21  BaezaB3    Mdn 73 L'Heureux 122    Kirby Lane  9
 5 Nov75  4Bel   1 :4731:1221:373ft  51  122  11  1h  1h  211 BaezaB2    Mdn 79 Play the Red 122 Kirby Lane  8
25 Oct75  1Bel   6 f :223 :46 1:113sy  10  122  87  871 77  751 VelasqzJ3  Mdn 78 Just a Dandy 122 QuickCard  9
18 Oct75  3Bel   6 f :231 :4621:112sy  15  122  711 812 711 471 BaezaB4    Mdn 78 PrivateThghts122 LrdHnrbee  8
```

June 3 Bel trt 3f ft :35⅗h   **May 26 Bel trt 1m ft 1:40½h**   **May 19 Bel trt 4f sy :49b**

Charleston 114

Ch. c (1973), by Graustark—Jitterbug, by Northern Dancer.
Breeder, Greentree Stud, Inc. (Ky.).

| | | | | | | | | | | 1976 | 10 | 2 | 3 | 0 | $20,050 |
| | | | | | | | | | | 1975 | 1 | M | 0 | 0 | $540 |

Owner, Greentree Stable. Trainer, John M. Gaver.

2 Aug76	6Sar	7 f :45³¹	:45³¹:234ft	5½	114	1½	4½	2½	2½	GustinesH¹	Alw 85	Rich asCroesus114	Charlestn	6
26 Jly76	6Aqu	6 f :22²	:45²¹:094ft	12	1·13	5⁹	5¹⁰	5¹²	5¹³	VelezRl⁴	Alw 81	SoyNumeroUno113	WatrFwr	5
26 May76	6Bel	1½ :46	1:10³¹:49¹ft	1-3e^1075	14	1¹½	2ʰ	2ⁿᵏ	VelezRl³	Alw 81	QuietLittleTable112	Chrlstn	5
29 Apr76	7Aqu	1 :46⁴¹	1:11¹¹:36 ft	2½	112	1²	1½	2ʰ	4²½	GustinesH⁵	Alw 84	House of Lords 120	Malign	6
21 Apr76	6Aqu	7 f :22⁴	:45⁴¹:22 ft	7½e	111	45½	35½	58½	56½	GustinesH³	Alw 84	DanceSpll 110	GabeBnzur	7
10 Mar76	9GP	7 f :22	:44¹ 1:21 ft	9	114	68½	56½	7⁸	6¹⁰	GustinsH²	AlwS 89	Sonkisser116	GayJitterbug	7
26 Feb76	8Hia	1½ :46⁴¹	1:12¹:49³sy	3-2 ^115	1ʰ	1ʰ	1½	14	GustinesH⁶	Alw 84	Charleston115	ChateauRyale	8
20 Feb76	7Hia	7 f :22⁴	:46¹¹:24 ft	2½ ^122	98¾	87½	5⁶	56½	GustinesH²	Alw 79	Sonkisser 122	Legendaire	11
4 Feb76	5Hia	7 f :23¹	:46¹¹:234ft	2-3 ^115	54½	3³	2ʰ	1½	GustinesH⁸	Alw 86	Charleston 115	GaitorRatten	9
23 Jan76	8Hia	6 f :22²	:45²¹:10 ft	2½	115	54½	3⁴	32½	2²	GustinesH²	Alw 91	LoadedOrBsted 122	Charlstn	11
20 Sep75	4Bel	6½ f :22⁴	:45³¹:172sy	6-5e^120	52½	41¹	4⁹	4¹⁰	GustinesH⁴	Mdn 79	Meritable 120	Azirae	9

July 25 Bel 3f ft :34⅗h   July 21 Bel 6 ft 1:11⅘h   July 17 Bel 5f ft 1:03⅖b

Sensitize 119

B. h (1971), by Sensitivo—Ye-Cats, by Mr. Busher.
Breeder, W. J. Fowler &
Mr. & Mrs. A. N. Winick (Fla.).

| | | | | | | | | | | 1976 | 16 | 2 | 2 | 4 | $7,377 |
| | | | | | | | | | | 1975 | 7 | 0 | 1 | 1 | $1,693 |

Owner, J. Chaffee. Trainer, Roy Houghton. $2,500

2 Sep76	1Det	6 f :22⁴	:46⁴¹:133ft	10	119	31½	11½	1¹	2½	MapleS⁴	2500 71	Rod N Reel 119	Sensitize	11
26 Aug76	1Det	6 f :22²	:45⁴¹:114ft	5½	119	3⁴	3⁴	5⁶	6¹²	JonesK³	2500 69	Anaconda122	TheCommissar	10
19 Aug76	4Det	1 :48¹¹	1:34¹:40¹ft	3½	119	1³	3ⁿᵏ	35½	7¹⁶	JonesK³	2500 62	Larb;Hills119	RomanTudor	9
4 Aug76	9Aks	1¹⁄₁₆ :47²¹	1:32¹:464ft	6½	122	18	15	1ʰ	26	JonesK¹¹	2500 66	Quatre Blanc 122	Sensitize	12
29 Jly76	1Aks	6 f :21⁴	:46 1:12¹ft	3½	122	41½	1¹	1⁴	14	JonesK¹	2500 76	Sensitize 122	Lori's Jet	12
23 Jly76	1Aks	6 f :23¹	:47 1:133ft	2½	^122	76½	6⁵	4⁵	77½	JonesK⁷	2500 61	ThunderMug117	Mac'sPrize	11
15 Jly76	1Aks	6 f :22³	:46 1:12²ft	3½	119	65½	56½	55½	32	JonesK⁴	2500 73	Hasty'sPlsre116	Mac'sPrize	12
2 Jly76	2Aks	6 f :22⁴	:46²¹:124ft	3½	120	67	53¾	43½	3⁴	JonesK⁷	2500 71	Hooki Lau 116	C. B's Beau	11
23 Jun76	2Aks	6 f :22³	:45³¹:123ft	4½	120	45½	34½	2⁹	3²	JonesK¹²	2500 72	CharmingK. 113	JamSession	12
9 Jun76	1Aks	1¹⁄₁₆ :47²¹	1:31¹:484ft	11	117	2½	2¹	4⁶	11¹⁷	JonesK⁶	2500 45	Dandy Tiz 115	Sab's History	12

BREEDING

I am not what you might call a student of breeding. Over the years I have found that it makes better sense to study the horse's racing record and pay attention to the trainer's techniques. Nevertheless, I learned rather early in my handicapping adventures to pay more than a little attention to the bloodlines of horses in certain clear-cut situations. So I forced myself and learned to recognize the top two-year-old sires, the top mud sires, and of course the top turf sires. I did that because it was impossible to handicap certain races without knowing which newcomer to the turf or which first-time starter would be more likely to cope with a five-furlong race in April, a muddy track, or a grass race. I now find that there are fewer and fewer cases where breeding knowledge is the significant factor. Consider turf racing.

For the first sixty years of this century turf racing was

not very popular in the United States. Few racetracks had turf courses and those that did scheduled perhaps one grass race every two or three days. Those were the good old days for a student of turf breeding, days when a few European-born sires produced virtually every turf race winner this side of the Atlantic.

During the 1960s American racetrack owners built dozens of turf courses. Belmont Park has two turf courses, as do Arlington Park and a few other tracks. Indeed three out of every five racetracks now card an average of six turf races a week, weather permitting. That's change number one. Change number two is the influence of breeding itself. Fifteen years ago there were only a handful of established turf sires; at present the number is well past 200 and counting.

As more and more horses are imported from Europe and as more and more horses are trained over turf courses, the signal importance of breeding will continue to be diluted and diminished. In the meantime, I have lifted forty of the world's most potent turf course sires. Secretariat is included in anticipation of what I think he will sire; he was the greatest turf racer I ever saw. Asterisks denote extraordinary turf potency. Get them while they last. (*See page 143*)

Mud

Although previous form in the mud (including strong workouts) is the best indication of ability to handle an off-track, a few sires and sire families tend to transmit the trait to nearly all their offspring. The most prominent of these are Bagdad, Better Bee, and the entire Bold Ruler line (especially What a Pleasure and the Bold Commander–Dust Commander wing of that line).

Cinteelo, a son of Jacinto, who in turn was a son of

THE NEARCO FAMILY	THE RIBOT FAMILY
*Amerigo	Arts and Letters
Bold Bidder	Graustark
Hail to Reason	Ribocco
Indian Hemp	Sir Ribot
Nasrullah	*Tom Rolfe
Neartic	
Northern Dancer	THE HYPERION FAMILY
Royal Charger	Alibhai
Secretariat	Assagai
Sir Gaylord	Khaled
*Sir Ivor	Swaps
Turn To	Vaguely Noble
T.V. Lark	
What a Pleasure	THE PRINCEQUILLO FAMILY
	*Advocator
OTHER DOMINANT	*Jean Pierre
TURF SIRES FROM	*Prince John
ASSORTED FAMILIES	*Round Table
Bagdad	*Speak John
Bolero	*Stagedoor Johnny
Dr. Fager	*Tambourine
Gallant Man	
Herbeger	
Intentionally	
Mongo	
Sea Bird	
The Axe II	

NOTE: *The very best turf sire in the country is Stagedoor Johnny. That's particularly interesting because Stagedoor Johnny never raced on a grass course in his life.*

Bold Ruler, is a case in point. In 1976 he was the number-one mud runner in America.

Cinteelo		**119**	B. c (1973), by Jacinto—Teela, by Cockrullah.					
Owner, J. M. Schiff. Trainer, T. J. Kelly.			Breeder, J. M. Schiff (Ky.).	1976	6	2	0	2	$24,600
				1975	7	2	0	1	$13,260

19 May76	8Bel	1¹⁄₁₆ :46²1:131:43¹sy	2-3 ▲106⁵	1²	11½	1⁵	17½	VelezRI³	Alw 86	Cinteelo106 BabyFaceBeau	8
1 May76	6Aqu	1 :45 1:09 1:34⁴sy	6-5e▲104⁵	2h	11	1⁵	18½	VelezRI⁴	Alw 93	Cinteelo 104 El Portugues	7
17 Apr76	6Aqu	1 :45²1:09⁴1:35¹ft	2 ▲104⁵	2h	2h	1½	32¾	VelezRI¹	Alw 87	RoughPunch112 BrownCat	7
27 Mar76	6Aqu	1 :46 1:09⁴1:35²ft	14 112⁵	1h	1h	2h	3⁴	VelezRI⁴	Alw 85	MountSterlng119 NwCollctn	9
3 Mar76	6Aqu	7 f :23¹ :46³1:23⁴ft	3 115	32½	3³	7¹¹	8¹⁴	VelasquzJ⁵	Alw 68	GabeBenzur117 PlayTheRed	8
24 Jan76	5Hia ⊤	1¹⁄₁₆ 1:43²fm	4½ 119	4²	3⁴	35½	57¼	CruguetJ¹	Alw 74	ControllerIke122 GrstarkLad	8
21 Nov75	7Aqu	1 :44⁴1:08⁴1:34⁴sy	12 117	1³	1⁵	1⁴	1⁶	CruguetJ⁴	Alw 92	Cinteelo 117 Play the Red	9
15 Nov75	5Aqu	7 f :23 :46 1:23²ft	37 115	41½	51½	3nk	42¾	CruguetJ²	Alw 81	JumpOvr theMn122 Wn'tYld	8
28 Aug.75	4Bel	7 f :23¹ :47 1:25¹ft	3-2 ▲120	53¼	2½	11½	1¹	CrugtJ⁶	M35000 76	Cinteelo 120 Ahoy John	9

| June 3 Bel 3f ft :35b | May 30 Bel trt 5f ft 1:01¾h | May 26 Bel trt 4f ft :52b |

Speed Sires

In early season two-year-old races at three, four, and five furlongs the emphasis is on speed and precocious physical development. If the get of Loom, Mito, Mr. Washington, and other one-dimensional sprint specialists are going to win any top-grade races, they will usually do so in these abbreviated dashes. Many win at first asking. Few hold their form beyond six furlongs.

Stamina Sires

Generally speaking, the staying power of a horse is linked more to its training regimen than to its breeding, but there are a few sires and a few female families that tend to produce long-distance runners. The get of many European sires—Sea Bird, Ribot, and Nijinsky II among others—and the male and female descendents of Princequillo are rarely interested in racing until the distances stretch out to a mile and beyond. However, most top-class American-bred sires, particularly the many sons and grandsons of Bold Ruler, are capable of getting fast, precocious horses that carry their speed as far as their trainers let them. If breeding is your bag, consult the Appendix for a recommended reading list.

OPTIONAL EQUIPMENT

BLINKERS: There is nothing like a pair of blinkers (eye cups) to help keep a horse's mind on its business, particularly a young horse that has had a difficult time running a straight course. Blinkers also tend to improve a horse's gate-breaking ability or early speed; and as a tool of last resort blinkers sometimes help the quitter type—the kind that stops in its tracks the moment another horse challenges it for the lead. If the quitter can't see the competition, it just might hold on long enough to get a piece of the purse.

Although more than half of the 70,000 horses racing in America go to the post with blinkers, "blinkers on" for the first time is generally a very positive sign of trainer intention. "Blinkers off" is not so easy to interpret.

In the case of a speedball, or perhaps a quitter type, the removal of blinkers may help the horse relax a bit and conserve some of its energy for the stretch. A few horses also run better when they can see the competition. For obvious reasons, some trainers remove blinkers when they send a sprinter into a longer race or, conversely, put them on when a router is seriously meant in a sprint.

In the East the oversized edition of the *Daily Racing Form* carries blinker information in the past performance profile, but elsewhere players must rely on result charts to learn about this important piece of equipment.

MUD CAULKS: If the track is muddy, heavy, or slow or the turf course is anything but firm or hard, the addition of mud caulks is a sign of trainer intent; it is also often helpful to the horse itself.

Mud caulks are horseshoes with small prongs for better traction. On fast or hard racing surfaces these shoes can do damage to the horse's ankle or hoof, but on a soggy surface, especially a soggy turf course, mud caulks are a distinct advantage.

The trainer is a cheapskate or a fool if he consistently avoids spending the extra few dollars for mud-caulked horseshoes when conditions are bad enough to warrant them. And the player is taking a big risk if he pays no attention to this information when it is available.

STEEL SHOES AND BAR SHOES: The player takes a bigger risk investing money on horses equipped with steel shoes or bar shoes, unless the horse in question has won with that kind of equipment before. Both types are danger signals. The horse usually has foot problems, and the shoe is an attempt to give more secure footing at the cost of extra, unfamiliar weight.

I am sorry to report that at present there are a number of racetracks that do not care about the fan sufficiently to provide a working shoe board on the grounds. Please yell at the general manager of any such racetrack for me too.

BANDAGES: Many trainers apply bandages on the rear legs as a matter of course to keep a horse from hitting itself in close quarters. But the presence of front leg bandages may have distinctly negative implications: a minor injury or a weak ankle or a sore muscle. Front leg bandages are chiefly used for extra support, and unless the player knows that the horse has raced well with them before (Forego, for example) or is expert at evaluating the horse in motion during the post parade, it is wise to be suspicious.

On muddy racetracks I will not bet a horse with front leg bandages because of the extra weight that is bound to adhere to these wrappings. Try running 100 yards yourself with an ounce of bandages taped to each ankle if you doubt my point. This act of temperance has cost me only four otherwise qualified winners in seventeen years.

PHYSICAL APPEARANCE

It takes a trained eye and many years of experience to reach valid conclusions about physical fitness on sight. A few basics should help; but I caution you to pay close attention to the clues in the *Racing Form* until you have mastered the art.

NEGATIVE SIGNS: Excessive kidney sweat between the flanks. And on cool days, heavy sweating of any kind in the paddock or post parade. Fractious, uncontrollable behavior during the post parade and warm-up period. Unusual swelling at the knee joints. Stiff-leggedness. A gimpy stride, favoring one leg. Cantankerous or listless behavior. A dull coat.

POSITIVE SIGNS: Aggressive but controllable behavior in the post parade and warm-up. A fluid transition from a walking gait to the gallop to the run. Attentive, alert behavior nearing the gate (watch the ears and head). A well-groomed, shiny coat.

JOCKEYS

Most trainers have alliances with one or more jockeys. Some jockeys ride every race for the trainer; others ride only when the trainer is serious. The player should learn who the top jockeys are, who rides for what stable, and who can't ride worth a damn.

Some trainers like to use apprentice jockeys because of the three, five, seven, or ten pounds of weight concession permitted during their apprenticeship.

My standards for jockeys may not meet your standards, but I will play a well-qualified contender ridden by a hot three- or five-pound apprentice, by an established veteran or star, by a rider who has won with the horse before, or by a stable favorite. But under no circumstances will I play a horse ridden by a ten-pound apprentice or a proven incompetent. I do not discriminate against women jockeys, but there are few I am presently impressed with. And there is one more point to be made about jockeys. At one time or another, all of them hit slumps. Terrible slumps. Like zero for thirty-five or two for sixty. Not only should the player avoid these jockeys when they are losing, but he should expect improvement from the horses they rode when a switch is made.

A few years ago Johnny Rotz, a solid twenty-year veteran, was riding so atrociously that the "Rotz off" angle produced six longshot winners in two weeks and a dozen more during the next two months. Mr. Rotz apparently got the message and retired the following winter.

14.
The Drug Factor

SEVENTH RACE
CD 34634
May 4. 1968

1 1-4 MILES. (Northern Dancer, May 2. 1964, 2:00, 3, 126.) Ninety-fourth running KENTUCKY DERBY. Scale weights. $125,000 added. 3-year-olds By subscription of $100 each in cash which covers nomination for both the Kentucky Derby and Derby Trial. All nomination fees to Derby winner, $500 to pass the entry box, $1,000 additional to start, $125,000 added, of which $25,000 to second, $12,500 to third, $5,000 to fourth. $100,000 guaranteed to winner (to be divided equally in event of a dead heat). Weight, 126 lbs. The owner of the winner to receive a gold trophy. A nomination may be withdrawn before time of closing nominations. Closed Thursday, Feb. 15, 1968, with 191 nominations.
Value of race $165,100. Value to winner $122,600; second, $25,000; third, $12,500; fourth, $5,000.
Mutuel Pool, $2,350,470.

Inde::	Horses	Eq't A Wt	PP	1/4	1/2	3/4	1	Str	Fin	Jockeys	Owners	Odds to $1
34451Aqu1	Dancer's Image	3 126	12	14	14	10½	8h	11	11½	R Ussery	Peter Fuller	3.60
34402Kee1	Forward Pass	b 3 126	13	32	44	34	22	2½	2nk	I Valenz'ela	Calumet Farm	2.20
34402Kee3	Francie's Hat	3 126	10	113112	72	72	42	32½	E Fires	Saddle Rock Farm	23.50
34402Kee2	T. V. C'mercial	b 3 126	2	9½	81	91	6½	5h	41	H Grant	Bwamazon Farm	24.00
34307CD4	Kentucky Sherry	3 126	4	1½	12	12	1h	32	51	J Combest	Mrs Joe W Brown	f-14.70
34325CD2	Jig Time	b 3 126	3	7½6½	6½	4h	6h	6½	R Brouss'rd	Cragwood Stable	36.30
34425GG2	Don B.	3 126	7	52 52	51	51½	74	75	D Pierce	D B Wood	35.50
34307CD2	Trouble Brewing	b 3 126	5	12½ 91	112	134 124	8nk	B Thornb'rg	Coventry Rock Farm	f-14.70
34325CD1	Proper Proof	3 126	11	133121	122	112	81½	94	J Sellers	Mrs Montgomery Fisher	9.90
34325CD4	Te Vega	b 3 126	6	8h13h	131	122	92 10¾	M Mang'llo	F C Sullivan	f-14.70
34307CD1	Captain's Gig	3 126	9	2h 2h	21	32	102	11½	M Ycaza	Cain Hoy Stable	6.10
34451Aqu2	Iron Ruler	3 126	1	10½ 7½	8½	9h	111	123	B Baeza	October House Farm	5.70
34325CD3	Verbatim	b 3 126	8	6h10h	14	14	13no	A Cord'o Jr	Elmendorf	37.40
34402Kee5	Gl'ming Sword	b 3 126	14	4½ 3½	4h	102	131 14	E Belmonte	C V Whitney	31.20

f-Mutuel field.

Time, :22⅕, :45⅘, 1:09⅘, 1:36⅕, 2:02⅕. Track fast.

$2 Mutuel Prices:

9-DANCER'S IMAGE	9.20	4.40	4.00
10-FORWARD PASS		4.20	3.20
7-FRANCIE'S HAT			6.40

Gr. c, by Native Dancer—Noors Image, by Noor. Trainer, L. C. Cavalaris, Jr. Bred by P. Fuller (Md.).

IN GATE—4:40. OFF AT 4:40½ EASTERN DAYLIGHT TIME. Start good. Won driving.

DANCER'S IMAGE, void of speed through the early stages after being bumped at the start, commenced a rally after three-quarters to advance between horses on the second turn, cut back to the inside when clear entering the stretch at which point his rider dropped his whip. Responding to a vigorous hand ride the colt continued to save ground to take command nearing the furlong marker and was hard pressed to edge FORWARD PASS. The latter broke alertly only to be bumped and knocked into the winner, continued gamely while maintaining a forward position along the outside. moved boldly to take command between calls in the upper stretch and held on stubbornly in a prolonged drive. FRANCIE'S HAT, allowed to settle in stride, commenced a rally after three-quarters and finished full of run. T. V. COMMERCIAL closed some ground in his late rally but could not seriously menace. KENTUCKY SHERRY broke in stride to make the pace under good rating, saved ground to the stretch where he drifted out while tiring. JIG TIME faltered after making a menacing bid on the second turn. PROPER PROOF was always outrun. CAPTAIN'S GIG tired badly after prompting the issue for three-quarters. IRON RULER failed to enter contention. GLEAMING SWORD broke alertly but sharply to the inside to bump with FORWARD PASS, continued in a forward position for five furlongs and commenced dropping back steadily.

NOTE: DANCER'S IMAGE DISQUALIFIED FROM PURSE MONEY BY ORDER OF CHURCHILL DOWNS STEWARDS, MAY 15, 1968 AND RULING SUSTAINED BY THE KENTUCKY STATE RACING COMMISSION

On the first Sunday in May 1968 the ninety-fourth running of the Kentucky Derby was decided in the laboratory of the state chemist. A small trace of the prohibited painkilling drug phenylbutazone was found in the urine sample of Dancer's Image, the winner of the world's most famous horserace. Thoroughbred racing in America hasn't been the same since.

Today phenylbutazone ("Bute") and the contoversial diuretic furosemide (Lasix) are legal in a dozen racing states (including Kentucky) and are used promiscuously nearly everywhere else. What this means to the future of racing I can only guess, but in the late 1970s there are serious questions about the sport's willingness to adopt an open, well-defined policy on this explosive issue.

Bute tends to reduce swelling in the joints and dulls the horse's sensory apparatus. Lasix, an effective treatment to curb bleeding in the nasal passages, flushes out watery substances with amazing efficiency. The sudden widespread use of these and other drugs, detectable and undetectable, is more than a little bit suspicious.

I have personally conducted studies on horse performance where drug information was made available to the player, and in 1974 and 1975 I published reports in *Turf and Sport Digest* and in *The New York Times*. A special research commission working at the request of the New York State Racing and Wagering Board agreed with my conclusions and offered a few of its own in a 1976 midsummer report. The key facts about drugs as they affect the horseplayer are as follows.

1. Because drugs interfere with the horse's warning system (pain), more horses are breaking down with drugs than without them.

2. Administering Lasix for the first time can and often does create a wake-up effect.

3. Although the regular use of Bute is widespread, it is impossible to measure its value as a handicapping factor.

4. In some cases either or both drugs can act as a screen to the detection of other drugs.

5. The public disclosure of drug information is inadequate in most states and nonexistent in some others. It is

hard to believe, but Kentucky, the blue-blooded breeding state, the home of the Kentucky Derby, is one of the many states that refuse to provide the racegoing public with race-day drug information. I think that is scandalous.

6. The testing procedures used to protect against drug abuse are not sufficient to cope with the variety of sophisticated drugs currently on the market. A multimillion dollar, nationwide, industry-run testing laboratory is the only realistic answer to this problem, but there is presently little interest in that proposal.

7. It is not possible to tell whether trainers who persistently put over dramatic form reversals are in fact training their horses from the bottle. But the player should keep a record of all such horsemen for future reference.

8. If the player is suspicious of the drug factor to the extent that he begins to blame defeats on it, he is probably overstating the case. Nevertheless, he owes it to the sport to take the time to save the past performance profiles of all such defeats. Draft a resume of the circumstances and forward this information to the stewards or the racing commission. Contrary to typical racetrack cynicism, most racing officials are becoming more sensitive to the drug problem. A little fan pressure is the best way to keep these folks on the ball. If all else fails, write to me care of the publisher. I'm no crusader, but this is one issue that's worth fighting about.

15.
To Bet or Not To Bet, and How Much?

When a gambler goes to Las Vegas for a weekend of roulette, craps, or blackjack, he should know in advance that the percentages constantly favor the house. Before the payoff odds are calculated, approximately 3 to 6 cents is raked off the top of every dollar wagered and the payoff odds are always lower than the actual mathematical odds.

This of course is the house take, and except for the one-in-a-million blackjack memory expert, no amount of skill will change the odds to the player's favor. I'm sorry folks, but the only way to beat the house is through unabashed luck—the longer one plays craps or roulette, the greater the probability for a wipeout.

A good casino gambler, then, is simply one who knows to quit if he's lucky enough to be ahead.

In betting on pro football and other team sports, the point spread theoretically balances out the action between supporters of two competing teams, and the player usually pays a 10 percent charge, or "vigorish," for the privilege of betting with a bookie. I won't go into the theories of proper football betting strategy in this book other than to say that racetrack bettors should only have it so easy. Consider the following:

By flipping a coin to determine which team should be played, anyone can expect approximately 50 percent winners. With any degree of skill at all 60 to 70 percent of spot-play winners is not only possible, but anyone calling himself a professional should be ashamed if he can't do that well. (Are you there Jimmy the Greek?)

At the racetrack the average field has nine horses, most of which have never faced each other before and never will again. The best horse in the race may get into trouble, step on a pebble, lose its jockey, jump a puddle, or decide to go for a swim in the infield lake. The jockey may have a toothache or commit a terrible mistake, or the stewards may have or do the same.

Meanwhile, for all his trouble in researching the complexities of racing, the horseplayer is told that the state and the track will take away some 20 cents per dollar on straight win bets and that much and more on most combination bets like the exacta or big triple. That's a tough nut to overcome. Good handicapping and thorough research help, but sound money management is just as important.

Whether you are a four-time-a-year novice or a once-a-week regular, the way you play your money at the track will determine whether you win or lose and how much you win or lose. Through skill, the odds can be turned to the player's favor, but it takes intelligent handling of betting capital to be in a position to take advantage. At 20 cents on the dollar, you can get wiped out pretty fast if you do not have a healthy respect for your money.

If you know something about two-year-old sprint racing but lack an understanding of stakes, claimers, or routes, it would be smart to concentrate your strongest bets on your specialty. If you use speed figures and know how to recognize a speed-figure standout, it would be foolish to bet the same amounts on races when you have no reason to be so confident. And if you do not know *what* you know, you should spend some time finding out.

Keep a record of your bets. Be honest with yourself.

Do you know how to spot a track bias when you see one? Do you have a feel for turf racing or stakes? Are claiming-class sprints easier than allowance-class routes? Do you have special insights about the winning and losing tendencies of the top trainers in your area? Perhaps you find it easy to narrow the field to live contenders but very difficult to separate the winner from the second- or third-best horse. Can you pass up a race or an entire card, or must you have a bet every half-hour?

Asking questions like those above will do wonders for your profit-and-loss statement. They will also bring to light the strengths and weaknesses in your game.

When I go unprepared to a strange racetrack, I do not

bring very much money. Without the necessary insights about the track, the trainers, and all the other fundamentals that influence results, I am no more likely to win than thousands of other players in the crowd. I have my winning days at such racetracks—I do pay attention—but I have to be lucky and extremely cautious with my money.

When I do prepare for a serious assault on a track, I do the research necessary to uncover any prevailing track bias and learn as much as I can about the trainers, jockeys, and horses I will be asked to compare. At most racetracks that kind of preparation takes about thirty to fifty hours of advance work, requires two hours of daily follow-up, and yields approximately one to three good bets a day; but that is not enough action for me and I know it.

Most racing fans, myself included, like something to root for in almost every race. It's tough to sit through a whole card waiting around for the ninth-race goodie. So most of the time I don't.

Instead, and as a concession to my personality, I separate my money into serious *prime* bets and *action* bets. Nothing would upset my concentration more than a $40 winner that I liked well enough to think about but didn't bet a dime on. Perhaps you feel the same way.

I have two very stiff requirements for a serious prime bet. Bitter experience has taught me that holding to these requirements is the safest way to guard my capital and maximize my skill.

When I think the horse deserves a 50 percent or better chance to win the race, I expect to be right at least 50 percent of the time. That's my first requirement. The second is a payoff price of 8–5 ($1.60–$1.00) or higher.

Fifty percent may seem to be an outrageously high win percentage to achieve, but with the tools and insights I have been detailing in this book it really isn't all that difficult.

King Leatherbury dropdowns coming back after a

month's rest win 60 percent of the time. Front runners on the rail in $1\frac{1}{16}$-mile races at Pimlico win almost as often. Other high-percentage strategies and tools include Van Berg repeaters going up in class, fast Calder front runners shipping into Gulfstream, Tony Basile–trained first-time starters at Keeneland, fit Jerkens–trained horses right back or stretching out in distance, minor track classification codes, hidden class dropdowns in allowance races, speed horses ready to get the lead for the first time, post position studies, Key Races, trainer patterns, clocker's comments, result charts, class pars, speed figures, track bias, and so on. Anyone willing to put in the necessary research time can pick 50 percent spot-play winners with these tools and insights. And the prices will astound you.

I have personally taught much of this material to nine of my friends, including two absolute novices. Within one year all were able to approach or exceed 50 percent results. Nothing is stopping you from achieving as much. If, however, you find your winning average is lower—35 percent, for example—you must adjust your minimum-odds requirement to compensate.

Logically, 35 percent winners would require payoff odds of 5–2 or better, but frankly I am not at all sure it is possible to win at the races without being able to pick a higher percentage of winners. A lower win percentage is an invitation to long losing streaks. I further believe my criteria help create enough selectivity to provide safe but profitable betting opportunities. By these standards an odds-on favorite can never be a prime bet, unless I am playing it to place and getting a bargain minimum of 80 cents on the dollar.

An exacta or daily double can never be a prime bet unless the total investment needed to cover the selected combinations yields a 50 percent chance of cashing a winning ticket at an expected 8–5 or better. To fulfill the two requirements in the case of a key horse wheel, it is sometimes

necessary to buy extra combinations on the lowest antici-
pated payoffs. And in those cases where I am confident to
play one horse as a key with two, three, or four others, I
reduce my total investment in the exotic bet and place at
least some money in the win pool to protect myself. I may
also be inclined to use my key horse underneath the three
contenders for additional protection. For solid crisscross
plays using three or four live contenders, I will rarely invest
more than half of my typical prime betting unit. Exactas
often present inflated payoff possibilities, but the risk is
usually increased as well.

I repeat, a prime bet is an estimated 50 percent chance
to cash a winning ticket at 8–5 or better. All other bets are
action bets and I separate the two categories in the following manner:

PRIME BETS: A maximum of 5 to 8 percent of total betting
capital for the meet per play; 8 percent reserved for
superconfident plays. Maximum of three prime bets allowed in one day, unless first two out of three win.

ACTION BETS: A maximum of 2 to 3 percent of total betting
capital for the meet per day. On a day with three prime
bets, no action bets are permitted beyond a token $2 to
$5 per race.

EXPENSES: Deduct 1 percent per day.

For example, if my total available betting capital for
the meet is $2,000, a prime bet would be $100 to $160,
depending on how well I have been doing at the meet and
how much more than a 50 percent edge the horse really has.
On that scale I would feel free to play the rest of the card
with $40 to $60 on contenders lacking prime betting qualifi-
cations, on wild stabs, daily doubles, or exactas.

As capital increases (or decreases) the amount of the
bet changes, but not the percentages.

I expect to lose money with my action bets and I do. But I have a lot of fun with them; I watch races more carefully because of them, and they help keep my equilibrium. A small price to pay for peace of mind.

I realize of course that not many racing fans can afford to put aside $2,000 to bet on horseraces. Not many should either. But the truth is many horseplayers lose that much and more in a season, and if you go to the racetrack regularly and want to improve your chances of success, you must take care to plan your betting activity along similar guidelines.

Whether your typical daily capital is $100 or you bring considerably more to the track, the point is to consolidate the power of your money on the races in which you have some insight.

Betting odds-on favorites is taking the worst of it. Betting a large percentage of your capital in the daily double or big triple is a sure-fire way to put yourself in the hole to stay. Betting a disproportionate amount of your money on any one race places too much emphasis on the luck factor. Doubling up your bet to "get even" on the last race is a way to triple your losses in track record time.

Every horseplayer has losing streaks. But there is no reason why a player should lose serious money during such streaks.

Losing three or four prime bets in a row is a warning sign, a sign to cut down all serious play until the problem is solved. Maybe you have lost touch with the track or have failed to note the presence of a hot trainer. Maybe you are bothered by personal problems, or a tough defeat has upset you more than you thought.

Take a day or two off. Go to a ballgame. Rediscover your family and friends. Watch TV, and if that doesn't work, try a few exercises in fundamentals.

Rather than trying to pick the race winner, try instead

to pick the worst horse in the race or the horse most likely to be in front ten strides out of the gate. Check the past three days of racing. Has there been a subtle change in the bias? Has the bias disappeared? It happens.

These exercises can be fun, and like a baseball player who needs to take extra batting practice, you will find they help straighten out many a weakness. Try some of them, or invent others to suit your fancy. Lighten up. It's only a game.

16.
La Prevoyante to Win, My Wife to Place

With the advent of the big triple and other popular, exotic forms of wagering, very few racing fans have been schooled in the finer points of place and show betting. While no argument will be presented here to suggest an emphasis on the minor payoff spots, there are times at the track when it pays handsomely to think second best.

In the early 1960s I remember being at a New York racetrack when so much money was bet on the mighty Kelso to win and so little was bet on him to place that he paid $2.40–$3.60–$2.40 across the board. By thinking win, and win only, the crowd in attendance that day offered one of the safest bets of modern times, an overlay of gigantic proportions. If Kelso was worth 20 cents on the dollar to win the race, which I will not debate, he was surely worth 80 cents on the dollar to finish second or better. It's doubtful Lloyds of London could have offered a better deal.

Of course, most racetrack crowds do not let such absurd situations occur every day, but I've seen enough $3.60 win, $4.00 place payoffs in my lifetime to give the tote board a close look before parting with my money. And if in truth I wasn't always careful to do that, my wife, Laurie, gave me ample cause to do so a few years ago.

At Saratoga during the 1972 racing season Laurie thought it would be a good idea if she came out to the track to see Robyn Smith, a pretty tough cookie and one of the best female jockeys in America. My friend Andy Beyer and I traded in our two reserved seats plus a dollar for three seats together. Andy and I were enjoying a spectacular meeting but didn't know we were about to miss out on the easiest bet of the year.

During the first six races on the card Robyn won one and lost one; so did Laurie. Andy and I had won the one Robyn and Laurie lost and had lost the one they both had won. Not that we were prejudiced against female jockeys or anything; we just figured one race *right* and one race *wrong*.

So the day went. Andy and I had shoved almost half a thousand through the windows to be plus $40 apiece. Laurie had bet maybe $8 and was ahead $50.

I wasn't depressed, far from it, but was glad to see her winning; maybe she would get hooked or something. After all, it would be nice to talk about horses with someone besides Andy. In any case, the point of this setting was the race on deck: the $50,000-added Spinaway Stakes.

La Prevoyante, undefeated and on her way to a two-year-old championship, was the odds-on favorite. Yet in spite of her unblemished record, neither of us thought she was very much horse. She had never run a truly fast race, and she had been beating up on the worst bunch of stakes-class juvenile fillies we had ever seen. She had beaten them pretty badly, though, and she figured to do so again; but there was a new challenger in the field—Princess Double-day—a shipper from Chicago.

Although Princess Doubleday had finished last in her most recent race in the slop, she had raced strongly in Chicago throughout the summer, winning two races and finishing a close third in a stakes. After checking some out-of-town result charts to determine the quality of the Mid-western juvenile fillies and after one last review of the *Form,* Andy and I concluded independently that Princess Doubleday had a great chance to win the Spinaway at 40–1.

Now it isn't too often that a sound piece of handicapping turns up a 40–1 shot that should really be a solid second choice in the betting, and naturally we were excited. We didn't want to go overboard; we still knew that we had to beat an undefeated 1–5 shot. We each decided to make a maximum-limit action bet—$60—and with just five minutes to post Laurie returned from the saddling area to share in the good news. I was surprised by her response. "It all sounds great," she said, "but shouldn't you bet your money to place?" Almost instinctively my stomach grumbled its reply to this heresy. I agreed that it would certainly be safer to bet to place but patiently explained to her that since the money bet to place on a heavy favorite like La Prevoyante would be returned to her supporters in the place pool, she would deflate the place prices on every other horse in the race. I argued that the value of this longshot was only in the win pool.

"As it is," I said, "we have to beat a filly that has slaughtered her opposition half a dozen times just to win our bet. For us to get a big place price on Princess Doubleday, La Prevoyante would have to run third or worse. Besides," I added, "40–1 on this filly is a tremendous overlay." Convinced by my own logic, my stomach relaxed. Laurie said she understood my position but insisted we would be better off if we followed her advice.

By that time I began to feel that Laurie should have stayed out by the trees or gone to talk to Robyn. Shaking our heads in unison, Andy and I gave up on the talking and headed for the win windows. He went upstairs and I went downstairs.

At the windows, after I had traded serious money for pasteboard, a sudden impulse crossed my brain. I ran as fast as I could to the place line and just did get in a small bet before the bell rang. "And they're off," the PA system said. But I knew exactly what was going to happen.

La Prevoyante breezed to victory as Princess Doubleday rallied to get second money.

Back at the seats, we watched the prices go up on the board. La Prevoyante paid $2.80 to win, $3.00 to place, $2.60 to show. Princess Doubleday paid $15.20 in the middle—at least $6 more than an early reading of the tote board had indicated. Laurie didn't say a word, but just counted her money and smiled. Andy, I found out, had made the same play I had, and our impulsive saver wagers to place gave us each a slight profit on the race. But some fifteen minutes later, while scooping some of Saratoga's great homemade ice cream, I nearly choked on the reality of what had happened.

"We're both idiots," I screamed abruptly, causing Andy to spill his sundae on the floor. "Supposing we had been told La Prevoyante was a late scratch and wouldn't be in the Spinaway. What price would we then have made Princess Doubleday to beat the rest of that weak field? Even money? Seven to five? Well, by ignoring the place pool, by being so longshot conscious, we just passed up the sweetest 6–1 prime bet of the year." We could have made an action bet on her to win and quadrupled the place bet with absolute confidence.

Strangely, my stomach never bothers me anymore when I talk horses with Laurie, and ever since that eye-opening experience I have had no trouble remembering to check the place and show pools very carefully. You just never know when the track is going to give it away.

17.
More on Betting

There are many lessons to be learned about betting, many traps that await the reckless, overconfident player. What follows in this chapter are some additional facts of life that every handicapper should find profitable to recognize.

Above all other repetitive mistakes, the average race-track crowd will seriously overbet the chances of horses whose records resemble the past performances below. I can't stress enough the folly of playing horses to win when everything in their records says they don't want to do that. Experienced horseplayers have a pet name for horses like these. They call them "sucker" horses. The term applies just as well to the players who bet on them.

Advising Jean ✳   **116** Ch. f (1971), by Noble Jay—Fleet Rhymer, by Flaming Fleet
Breeder, E. Mull (Md.).   1975   22   0 (12   2) $35,405
Owner, Mrs. W. A. Kelley.   Trainer, W. A. Kelley. $12,500   1974   23   3   5   2 $30,531

25 Nov75	3Aqu	1⅛ :47²1:12 1:51¹ft	3½	114	2⁵	2⁴	2³	2¾	CruguetJ5 13000 78 Ⓕ Czarevna111 AdvisingJean 7
10 Nov75	7Key	7 f :23³ :45¹1:24³sy	9-5	114	8⁴	46½	2⁵	2⁴	LukasM4 13000 82 Ⓕ SlwBeat116 AdvisingJean 8
9 Oct75	2Bel	1₁₆ :48¹1:12⁴1:46 ft	6-5 ▲116	3½	2¹	1½	2³	CruguetJ1 13000 71 Ⓕ WittyWays113 AdvisingJn 8
18 Sep75	5Bel	1⅛ :47²1:111:51¹ft	2	116	2²	2³	2½	2ⁿᵒ	CruguetJ8 14000 71 Ⓕ MssTaubl118 AdvisingJean 8
31 Aug75	9Bel	1₁₆ :46³1:111:45²ft	4	114	2ʰ	1²	1ʰ	2ʰ	CruguetJ4 15000 75 Ⓕ LaVikina116 AdvisingJean 11
15 Aug75	6Sar	7 f :22³ :46 1:25 ft	3	116	3⁷	35½	42½	42¾	CruguetJ4 15000 77 Ⓕ Alla Va 116 La Vikina 8
8 Aug75	1Sar	6 f :22¹ :46²1:24⁴sy	2¾	116	7¹⁴	49½	3⁶	2¾	CrugutJ1 15000 75 Ⓕ WiseHeart114 AdvisingJn 7
25 Jly 75	7Bel	6½ f :22³ :46³1:17⁴sy	17	116	2⁴	64½	55½	46½	VenziaM6 22500 80 Ⓕ Brta'sDandy112 PrcsM.L. 9

Geoffery Vernon   **113** Dk. b. or br. g (1973), by Gameus—Dusty Nancy, by Penaction.
Breeder, J. E. Harman (Fla.).   1976   17   1 (5   4) $8,833
Owner, Sharon Maker & B. Hessling.   Trainer, George Maker. $6,250   1975   3   M   0   0 $170

15 Sep76	7Det	6 f :22² :46¹1:12¹ft	10	118	45¼	47	45	44½	GabrielR10 6250 74 Bhagalphur113 SteamingHot 11
8 Sep76	5Det	6 f :22² :46¹1:22²ft	5½	118	55½	31	2¹	21½	MorgnMR2 6250 76 Mr.Brtolini116 GeoffryVrnn 9
2 Sep76	3Det	6 f :22⁴ :47¹1:13³ft	4½	117	3³	3²	2²	2½	GabrielR5 6250 71 MyFthr'sPde115 GffryVrnon 9
26 Aug76	4Det	6 f :22⁴ :46²1:13³ft	3½	117	2¹	1²	1³	33¹	CamiloJF7 5000 69 Boogie Band 115 Son Jay 9
	†Disqualified.								
16 Aug76	6Det	6 f :22⁴ :46²1:22¾ft	4	117	2½	2²	21½	32½	GabrielR8 6250 75 Chester V. 117 Right Audit 8
11 Aug76	7Det	6 f :22³ :46¹1:24¹ft	16	117	42½	42½	54½	56½	CamiloJF2 6500 70 Tin 120 Esha Brown 9
17 Jly 76	7HP	6 f :23¹ :47¹1:14 ft	12	114	57½	65½	77½	65¾	CamiloJF4 8000 76 SpeedyKlu121 RojaBandera 8
9 Jly 76	8HP	6½ f :23² :47²1:20 ft	23	120	2ʰ	1¹	3⁴	7¹¹	CamiloJF7 Alw 70 SpindleTop115 Baker'sSyrup 7
30 Jun76	5HP	6 f :23⁴ :48²1:16²m	9¾	120	42½	1½	13	2¹	CamiloJF6 8000 69 Bhagalphur110 GeofferyVrnn 7
17 Jun76	2HP	6½ f :22² :47 1:21¹ft	3-2 ▲114	2³	1³	15	1⁸	CmiloJF5 M6250 75 GeofferyVernon114 MistySnt 10
	July 30 Det 4f sl :50b								

Our Kid Dreams   **114** B. g (1971), by Crasher—Five Hundred, by Swiv.
Breeder, Trine Stables, Inc. (Mich.).   1976   22   1 (6   5) $9,771
Owner, Jack C. Van Berg.   Trainer, Jack C. Van Berg. $2,500   1975   14   0   4   6 $3,556

15 Sep76	5Det	6 f :22² :46⁴1:13 ft	3½	119	7¹⁴	66½	43½	2ⁿᵏ	CatalnoW8 2500 75 AlAckerman117 OurKidDrms 11
6 Sep76	10Det	1₁₆ :49¹1:15²1:50 ft	9-5 ▲114	5¹¹	57½	68½	7¹⁴	PerezR5 2500 39 Bucket O'Suds 111 Ludship 8
25 Aug76	5Det	6 f :22 :47 1:24¹ft	2½ ▲119	86½	95¾	65½	43½	PerezR3 2500 72 NativeDory122 AlAckerman 9
17 Aug76	1Det	6 f :23¹ :47¹1:13¹ft	4¾	122	108¾	99	7⁸	3½	PerezR8 2500 73 O'RileyHimself122 TwtyFrKt 12
11 Aug76	4Det	1 :49¹1:42¹1:42¹ft	9-5 ▲117	2²	31½	3½	2ⁿᵒ	CatalnoW4 2500 68 Adml'sCmnd122 OurKdDrms 9
2 Aug76	2Det	6 f :23 :47¹1:13⁴ft	2¾ ▲117	56½	46	35	2½	MapleS5 2500 70 Abreast 119 Our Kid Dreams 9
24 Jly 76	2Det	1 :49²1:54¹1:43²ft	8-5 ▲117	53½	32	35	3⁷	CatalnoW9 2500 55 Timetolight114 SirraGrande 10
7 Jly 76	6HP	6 f :23² :47³1:14³ft	3¾	116	6⁹	66	43	2¹	CatalnoW4 2500 78 ChoctawRidge121 OrKdDrms 10
2 Jly 76	3HP	6½ f :23¹ :48¹1:22³sl	7-5 ▲116	6⁶	55	34½	53½	PerezR7 2500 64 ChoctawRidge116 L.O.Davis 9
25 Jun76	4HP	6½ f :24¹ :49²1:23⁴sl	2 ▲116	64½	42½	11	12½	PerezR8 2500 62 OurKidDreams116 LordSutn 9
17 Jun76	3HP	6½ f :23² :48 1:21 ft	3½	116	56½	45½	23	2ⁿᵏ	PerezR5 2500 76 BroncoBilly121 OurKdDreams 10
2 Jun76	3HP	1 :50¹1:16⁴1:44⁴ft	5½	115	33½	2ʰ	2ʰ	2½	BaconJ1 2500 58 ManOfSummr115 OrKdDrms 10

Sometimes the act of wagering on a horse is more than a simple process of translating one's own opinion into cash. At times it becomes a test of will power. Tipsters, touts, and the blinking lights of the tote board can exert an amazing influence on the rational decision-making process, and any player who doesn't have a basic knowledge of the reliability of these enticing sources of information will be busted out of the game every time.

There is such a thing as "smart money," but it is not likely to be aligned with the tipsters and touts who advertise their "expertise" and sell it for a buck. Nor is it likely to be represented by the wildest spenders in the crowd.

Although most players get caught up in the tidal wave of enthusiasm generated by strong late play on the tote, very few moves of that kind are worth any consideration. Let's take the exceptions:

1. A shipper.
2. A first-time starter or absentee with no positive workouts.
3. A stable that has a history of such doings.

Generally speaking, the winning potential of a horse that gets excessive play is logically limited to the winning capacity of the people behind it. Most often there will be ample clues in the past performance profile to suggest an all-out performance. However, certain trainers—people like Kaye Belle in Kentucky and M. C. Preger in New York—rarely win a race unless the tote board says tilt.

On the other hand, the lack of convincing betting action on a seemingly superior, apparently sharp horse, except in stakes races, is a powerful tote board clue to a probable subpar performance. If the horse has won a few recent races or has been in excellent form and is now dropping to a seemingly easy spot, he should attract heavy play. If he does not, if he flirts with 2–1 or 5–2 odds when he should be 4–5, the player would do well to examine the rest of the field closely. Tepidly played standouts seldom run to their prior good form.

According to long-standing tradition, the morning line—the odds posted on the tote board before the betting begins—is supposed to provide an estimate of the probable post-time odds for each horse in the race. The theoretical value of this line is to enable the player to spot overlays as well as to isolate those horses getting excessive betting action. I'm afraid it rarely does that.

In the days before pari-mutuel betting the morning line was a matter of professional pride. If an operating bookmaker in the track's betting ring didn't make a first-class morning line, the best bettors in the crowd would pounce on his mistakes. In those days a good morning line had to have value. It had to reflect a balanced book of percentages and reflect the realities of the race at hand. Frankly, I envy the players who had a chance to play the game in the age of the trackside bookmaker. It must have been great fun.

Today at the racetrack, in the age of pari-mutuel betting, the morning line is usually put together by a member of the mutuel department. Rarely does it do any more than suggest the probable betting favorites, although in "blind" betting situations—the daily double and exacta—it does exert an influence on the betting habits of uninformed bettors. Almost automatically the average horseplayer will include the top two or three morning-line choices in his double and exacta combinations. This has three predictable effects: (1) it tends to create lower double and exacta payoffs on morning-line choices regardless of their merits; (2) it forces higher payoffs on overlooked longshots; and (3) it sometimes helps to single out a betting stable's serious intentions with an otherwise lightly regarded horse.

Considering the reliability of low payoff possibilities for all morning-line choices in daily doubles and exactas, the player can conclude with reasonable certainty that a horse getting substantially greater play than his morning-line odds in these "blind" betting pools is getting play from informed sources. I know several professional handicappers who pay careful attention to the flow of money in daily doubles and exactas, and all of them say that the morning-line angle is fundamental to their calculations. Naturally, these players put their own money on the line only when a stable with a good winning history is involved.

One of the things that separates professional horse-players from the rest of the crowd is the ability to assign approximate yet realistic odds values to the horses in the race. This has nothing to do with post-time odds.

For example, when Riva Ridge, winner of the 1972 Kentucky Derby, went to Pimlico two weeks later for the Preakness Stakes, it was a foregone conclusion that his overall record and TV popularity would make him a prohibitive odds-on favorite. A good morning line would have surely pegged him at 1–2. A good value line might have been willing to accept 4–5 as a fair estimate of his winning chances—that is, until the rains began to fall on the eve of the Preakness.

Riva Ridge was no mud runner, by any stretch of the term. He had already been beaten in the Everglades Stakes by a common sort named Head of the River and had always worked below par on sloppy tracks. A professional handicapper who knew that about Riva Ridge could hardly have made him anything but third choice in the Preakness to No Le Hace and Key to the Mint, two horses that eventually did finish in front of him (Bee Bee Bee won).

Three weeks later Riva Ridge tackled most of these horses again on a fast racetrack in the 1½-mile Belmont

Stakes. A good value line on the race would have established the horse at even money or 4–5. There was nothing wrong with Riva Ridge. He was still in top form, far and away the best three-year-old in America. And he had trained brilliantly for the race. The only potential danger was Key to the Mint, who was on the comeback trail. With or without some fine-line handicapping of Key to the Mint's credentials (he worked much too fast for the race and, in a rare mistake for Elliott Burch, was somewhat short on distance preparation), the 8–5 post-time odds on Riva Ridge were a gift presented by national TV coverage of the Derby winner's horrible Preakness performance. Although horses are not robots, and it is dangerous to think that every race on paper will be run exactly to specifications in the flesh, there is money to be made betting the best horse in the race at generous odds. That is, in fact, the heart and soul of the game.

"If they ran this race 100 times, how many times would Riva Ridge win?" That's the kind of question that helps to establish the value line. On Belmont's fast racetrack Riva Ridge seemed strong enough and fit enough to have at least 50 percent of the race all to himself. That's the kind of answer that sets up prime betting possibilities, and it happens every day.

Had Andy Beyer and I been thinking in terms of the value line, Princess Doubleday to place would certainly have qualified as a value-line prime bet. And there are several other instances when the value-line concept works to the advantage of players who are capable of thinking second best.

The setting is an exacta event and there is an overwhelming odds-on favorite, a horse that deserves its lofty ranking, a horse that has every advantage over the competition. Although there are some players in the crowd who bet huge amounts of money on such "stickouts," only the very best handicappers among them will avoid betting the occasional phony that will break a bankroll in one shot. Those who have the skill to back 90 percent or more short-priced winners would do far better in the long run betting less money on good horses going to the post at good odds. But that's their problem. When I see a standout odds-on favorite in an exacta event, I will commit myself to a small action bet on it or perhaps bet another horse that I think might have a chance to spring an upset. There are two extremely important exceptions.

In some exacta races the betting public has trouble evaluating the contenders for second money. If sound handicapping turns up two, three, or four logical contenders for second place, a check of the exacta payoff possibilities on the closed-circuit TV system will sometimes open up the door to a maximum bet.

On the other hand, the public sometimes bets most of its exacta money on the dominant race favorite linked with one other apparently fit horse. In such circumstances it pays to take a close look at this "second best" horse. If it lacks convincing credentials, if there are sound reasons to bet against it, a wheel on the rest of the field could produce exciting payoffs. Indeed, this phenomenon occurs many times over in a season and produces a betting pattern that is extraordinarily predictable. Hundreds of illustrations could be given here, none more dramatic than the one facing the player lucky enough to have been at Belmont Park for the greatest performance in the history of Thoroughbred racing, Secretariat's 1973 Belmont Stakes.

Going into the Belmont, Secretariat was lord and master of the three-year-old division, a solid 1–10 shot to become the first Triple Crown winner in twenty-five years. Unlike Carry Back, Northern Dancer, Kauai King, Canonero II, and Majestic Prince—the five horses that

failed to complete the Derby-Preakness-Belmont sweep—
Secretariat came up to the 1973 Belmont at the peak of his
powers, working faster and more energetically for the race
than for any other race in his life. The same could not be
said for Sham, the second-best three-year-old of 1973.

Sham had tried Secretariat twice and had failed both
times. In the Derby Secretariat went very wide on both
turns and with power in reserve outdrove Sham from the top
of the stretch to the wire.

In the Preakness, while under no special urging, Secretariat made a spectacular move around the clubhouse turn—
from last to first—passing Sham in the backstretch. For the
final half of the race Pincay slashed his whip into Sham
with wild fury. Turcotte, aboard Secretariat, never moved a
muscle. But Sham never gained an inch. At the wire he was
a tired horse.

Coming up to the 1973 Belmont, Sham had begun to
show signs of wear and tear. He showed fewer workouts and
they were not as brisk; this horse had been through a rough
campaign. Nine route races in top company in less than
eight weeks. Trips to California, Kentucky, Maryland, and
New York. Actually, the only thing keeping Sham in the
Triple Crown chase was trainer Frank Martin's stubborn-
ness. A more objective view of his chances in the Belmont
said that he would never beat Secretariat and could even go
severely off form.

These were the win odds quoted on the race:

```
Secretariat  ---------- $   .10–$1.00
Sham - - - - - - - - - - - - - - $  5.10–$1.00
Private Smiles - - - - - - - - $14.30–$1.00
My Gallant  - - - - - - - - - - $12.40–$1.00
Twice a Prince - - - - - - - $17.30–$1.00
```

These were the exacta payoff possibilities as they were
flashed on the closed-circuit TV system prior to post time:

Secretariat with Sham - - - - - - - - - - - - - -	$ 3.40
Secretariat with Private Smiles - - - - - - -	$24.60
Secretariat with My Gallant - - - - - - - - - -	$19.80
Secretariat with Twice a Prince - - - - - - -	$35.20

Eliminating Sham from the exacta play meant an investment of $6 (three combinations) and a minimum payoff of $19.80 (My Gallant). What all this means is that the track was offering three horses and excellent payoffs to beat a tired Sham for second place. In fact, the payoffs were almost identical to the odds in the win pool, the odds being offered on each of these three horses to beat Sham *and* Secretariat. By conceding the race to Secretariat, the player had a chance to collect the same odds merely by beating Sham. Now that's what I call value.

Through the weakness of the second betting favorite and the availability of exacta wagering, an exciting but seemingly unplayable race was turned into a very logical, very promising prime bet. In a very real sense, it was like being offered a bonus dividend for understanding the subtleties of a great moment in racing history. It's times like that when a horseplayer knows he is playing the greatest game in the world.

105TH RUNNING—1973—SECRETARIAT

EIGHTH RACE

Belmont

JUNE 9, 1973

1 ½ MILES. (2.26⅘) 105th Running THE BELMONT $125,000 added. 3-year-olds. By subscription of $100 each to accompany the nomination; $250 to pass the entry box; $1,000 to start. A supplementary nomination may be made of $2,500 at the closing time of entries plus an additional $10,000 to start, with $125,000 added, of which 60% to the winner, 22% to second, 12% to third and 6% to fourth. Weights, Colts and Geldings 126 lbs. Fillies 121 lbs. Starters to be named at the closing time of entries. The winning owner will be presented with the August Belmont Memorial Cup to be retained for one year, as well as a trophy for permanent possession and trophies will be presented to the winning trainer and jockey. Closed Thursday, February 15, 1973 with 187 Nominations.

Value of race $150,200, value to winner $90,120, second $33,044, third $18,024, fourth $9,012. Mutuel pool $519,689, OTB pool $688,460.

Last Raced	Horse	Eqt.A Wt	PP	¼	½	1	1¼	Str	Fin	Jockey	Odds $1
19May73 ⁸Pim¹	Secretariat	b	3 126	1	1hd	1hd	1⁷	1²⁰	1²⁸	1³¹	Turcotte R	10
2Jun73 ⁶Bel⁴	Twice A Prince		3 126	5	4⁵	4¹⁰	3hd	2hd	3¹²	2½	Baeza B	17 30
31May73 ⁶Bel¹	My Gallant	b	3 126	3	3³	3hd	4⁷	3²	2hd	3¹³	Cordero A Jr	12 40
28May73 ⁸GS²	Pvt. Smiles	b	3 126	2	5	5	5	5	5	4¾	Gargan D	14 30
19May73 ⁸Pim²	Sham	b	3 126	6	2⁵	2¹⁰	2⁷	4⁸	4¹½	5	Pincay L Jr	5 10

Time, :23⅗, :46⅕, 1:09⅘, 1:34⅕, 1:59, 2:24, (Against wind in backstretch.). Track fast.

New Track Record.

$2 Mutuel Prices:

2-(A)-SECRETARIAT	2.20	2.40	—
5-(E)-TWICE A PRINCE		4.60	—

(No Show Wagering)

Ch. c, by Bold Ruler—Somethingroyal, by Princequillo. Trainer Laurin L. Bred by Meadow Stud Inc (Va).

IN GATE AT 5:38; OFF AT 5:38, EDT. Start Good. Won Ridden out.

SECRETARIAT sent up along the inside to vie for the early lead with SHAM to the backstretch, disposed of that one after going three-quarters, drew off at will rounding the far turn and was under a hand ride from Turcotte to establish a record in a tremendous performance. TWICE A PRINCE, unable to stay with the leader early, moved through along the rail approaching the stretch and outfinished MY GALLANT for the place. The latter, void of early foot, moved with TWICE A PRINCE rounding the far turn and fought it out gamely with that one through the drive. PVT. SMILES snowed nothing. SHAM alternated for the lead with SECRETARIAT to the backstretch, wasn't able to match stride with that rival after going three-quarters and stopped badly.

$2.00 EXACTA (2-5) PAID $35.00

18.
The Winning
Horseplayer

Ideally, the most instructive way to illustrate the practical applications of the material in this book would be to present thousands of actual races, playable and nonplayable.

We would select several different racetracks, do post position studies for each, save and read result charts, compare the past performance records of all the important trainers, and be careful to note and measure the relative power of the racing surface as it influences the action on the track.

To get a fix on the local horses, we could construct classification codes, keep a record of purses, pay attention to the daily tabular workout listings, generate class pars, compute speed figures, hunt for Key Races, and watch whatever races we are privileged to see with eyes geared to detect the unusual as it happens.

Not all professional-class players do all of that.

Some rely strictly on speed figures or generally broad insights to uncover sound betting propositions. Some watch races with such skill that they are able to build a catalogue of live horses for future play. And some concentrate all serious play on one specific type of race—turf events, claiming races, sprints, routes, maidens, or stakes.

Frankly, I have no argument with players who are able to solve more than their share of racetrack riddles through a single window or two. Indeed, specialization according to individual strength makes excellent sense. Different strokes for different folks. On one level that is precisely what this book has been about. But on another level that is not the case at all.

I have been very fortunate. During my years around the racetrack I have been continuously exposed to the varied menu only an extensive itinerary can bring. Five years at Rutgers University, Garden State Park division. Two years of handicapping upward of fifty races a day at five or more tracks for the *Daily Racing Form*. Triple Crown coverage for the Mutual Radio Network. Five hundred daily five-minute seminars on handicapping for WLMD radio in Maryland. The editorship of *Turf and Sport Digest.* Trips to forty-two different racetracks. Serious assaults on eighteen. Summers at Saratoga. And conversations with some of the best thinkers and players in the game. People like Andy Beyer and Clem Florio in Maryland, Jules Schanzer and Saul Rosen at the *Form,* John Pricci of *Newsday* in New York, and Tom Ainslie, the man who gave me the most encouragement to commit to print all the insights I have thus far gained.

It has taken me almost 200 pages to do that. But I think it would help your focus if I reduced the essence of it all to a few key principles and a few key examples.

There are only two kinds of playable prime betting situations: easy ones and hard ones. The easy ones practically leap off the pages of the *Racing Form;* the hard ones require a bit of digging.

To the student of track bias, an easy one may come any time the bias is strong enough to prejudice the outcome of the race. The Travers Stakes on page 37 is a classic illustration of that. So is the Schuylerville Stakes on page 120.

To students of class, easy ones come in many forms. A hidden class dropdown like Caspar Milquetoast on page 98. A Key Race standout like Gay Gambler on page 89. A Shredder, a Secretariat, a Laplander, or a horse with significantly faster speed figures. (Yes, that too is an edge in class.)

Likewise, for those who pay attention to trainers and their methods, there is nothing very complicated about spotting a Mack Miller first-timer on the grass; much the same can be said for dozens of other horses whose past performance records signal the confidence of a winning horseman's best work.

Upsets? Of course. They happen every day. Horses and

the humans who handle them are always capable of throwing in a clunker or improving beyond previous limits of performance. Mistakes? Certainly. The player is no less governed by the same laws of nature. But to win at the racetrack, the player must not only learn from his own mistakes but avoid the trap of punishing himself for having made them. Usually, that kind of genuine confidence comes only from knowing that other straightforward opportunities will not be long in coming.

With no hesitation I can assure you that the tools, concepts, and research techniques contained in this book will isolate the probable race winner with minimum difficulty in hundreds of races each and every season. And two of the most frequently encountered betting situations will bear a striking resemblance to the following pair of examples.

There are many reasons why most players would not want to touch the above race with a ten-foot pole. Despite the grossly inflated purse—put up to encourage the New York State breeding industry—it would be difficult to find a weaker field of nonwinners at any major-class track. Nevertheless, there is a standout, maximum-limit prime bet in this race—the filly Flylet, a horse that embodies a classic winning pattern (see page 117).

In each of her prior races Flylet has shown considerably more early speed than any of her rivals has ever shown. Twice she even took a narrow lead at the first quarter call. On August 11 she met every member of today's field with the exception of No Empty Pocket and First Proof, and she was no less than half a dozen lengths in front of them all for much of the race. I'm sure you can imagine the ease with which she will therefore be able to sail to the front in today's race. And therein lies the heart and power of the pattern.

Except on a stretch-running track, whenever a horse figures to get a clear, uncontested lead on the field for the first time, the player should expect dramatic improvement

1st Saratoga

6 FURLONGS
SARATOGA

▼Start
▲Finish

AUGUST 26, 1976

6 FURLONGS. (i:08). MAIDENS. CLAIMING. Purse $10,000. 2-year-olds, foaled in New York State and approved by the New York State-bred registry. (All purse money from New York Breeders' Fund). Weight, 122 lbs. Claiming price, $20,000; for each $1,000 to $18,000, allowed 2 lbs.

COUPLED: JOSH GOLDNER, RANDY'S CIL and NO EMPTY POCKET.

Listed According to Post Positions

Heidee's Cousin
118 B. c (1974), by Flaneur II.—Buccanette, by Black Beard.
Breeder, Murray M. Garren (N. Y.). 1976 9 M 1 0 $3,080
Owner, Murray M. Garren. Trainer, Gilbert Puentes. **$18,000**

11 Aug76 1Sar	5½ f :22³ :46³1:05⁴m	6½	122	10¹¹ 86½ 8¹⁰ 9¹⁶	VelezRI²	Mdn 72	RedSam 122	RagT meBelle 12
3 Aug76 3Sar	5½ f :22³ :46³1:05³ft	6½	122	8⁸ 7¹⁰ 8¹⁵ 7²⁶	MapleE⁹	Mdn 63	VandySue119	TakeItAlong 9
25 Jly 76 9Aqu	5½ f :24 :49 1:08³ft	3	120	6²½ 5³½ 55½ 45½	MpleE¹	M22500 64	Tacitus 122	Mad Jack 9
18 Jly 76 4Aqu	5½ f :23² :47⁴1:06³ft	6½	122	9⁵ 95¾ 7⁹ 58¼	StgoA⁸	M25000 72	PrinceNoNme117	PictreShw 10
12 Jly 76 4Aqu	5½ f :23² :48 1:07⁴ft	4½	122	4⁴ 3² 32½ 2nk	MapleE⁶	Mdn 74	Ducky'sBolero122	Hdee'sCsn 8
30 Jun76 3Aqu	5½ f :22³ :46³1:06 ft	4	8	5³ 42¹ 5⁴ 53½	StgoA²	M20000 79	HasAFuture120	ChairmanOx 8
27 Jun76 4Bel	5½ f :23² :46²1:04⁴ft	19	1135	4½ 58 68½ 68	MtnJE⁴	M40000 83	Peak Top 122	Proud Arion 9
11 Jun76 4Bel	5½ f :234 :48 1:06⁴ft	30	118	75¾ 7¹¹ 7¹¹ 7¹⁴	StgoA³	M 0000 67	Lancer'sPride122	PrizeNtive 9
31 May76 4Bel	5½ f :22⁴ :46⁴1:05²ft	49	¹175	98¾ 9¹¹ 9²⁰ 9²³	MartinJE⁹	Mdn 65	DukeWayne122	Turn ofCoin 9

Aug 24 Sar trt 4f ft :49¾h Aung 19 Sar trt 5f ft 1:03b July 17 Bel trt 3f sy :36h

Ruddy Duck
118 Ch. c (1974), by High Rank—Meadow Mole, by Egotistical.
Breeder, Mrs. Ann K. Morse (N. Y.). 1976 2 M 0 0 (—)
Owner, Ann K. Morse. Trainer, Thomas M. Waller. **$18,000**

11 Aug76 1Sar	5½ f :22³ :46³1:05⁴m	2e⁴	122	1111118½ 9¹¹ 8¹⁵	TurcotteR⁵	Mdn 73	RedSam 122	RagT meB le 12
12 Jly 76 4Aqu	5½ f :23² :48 1:07⁴ft	4½e	122	5⁶ 5⁹ 5⁸ 5⁷	TurctteR⁵	Mdn 67	Ducky'sBolero122	Hdee'sCsn 8

Aug 21 Sar 5f ft 1:05b Aug 4 Sar 4f ft :54b Aug 9 Sar 4f sy :48¾h

First Proof
122 Dk. b. or br. c (1974), by Only Once—Flora Bonda, by Auditing.
Breeder, Maxion Farms (N. Y.). 1976 2 M 0 0 (—)
Owner, William J. Maxion. Trainer, Everett F. Schoenborn. **$20,000**

19 Aug76 8Sar	6 f :22² :46 1:12²ft	93	115	16¹⁷13¹⁵11¹⁰10⁹	TurcteR¹³	AlwS 69	FratelloEd115	Heidee'sPal 17
12 Jly 76 4Aqu	5½ f :23² :48 1:07⁴ft	35	122	8²³ 8³⁰ 8²⁵ 8¹⁹	VeneziaM²	Mdn 59	Ducky'sBolero122	Hdee'sCsn 8

Aug 2 LD 3f ft :38bg July 23 LD 49f ft :50¾bg July 9 FL 4f ft :50¾bg

Flylet
117 B. f (1974), by Flying Error—Whiglet, by Whig.
Breeder, Saverio Cardile (N. Y.). 1976 6 M 0 1 $1,440
Owner, Saverio Cardile. Trainer, Saverio Cardile. **$19,000**

19 Aug76 8Sar	6 f :22² :46 1:12²ft	38	112	3³ 98½12¹³11¹²	SmithRC⁴	AlwS 66	FratelloEd115	Heidee'sPal 17
11 Aug76 1Sar	5½ f :22³ :46³1:05⁴m	8½	119	3³ 33 66½ 69½	BaezaB¹¹	Mdn 78	RedSam 122	RagT meB e 12
3 Aug76 3Sar	5½ f :22³ :46³1:05³ft	28	119	1½ 3² 4⁸ 6²⁰	RujanoM¹	Mdn 69	VandySue119	TakeItAlong 9
19 Jly 76 4Aqu	5½ f :22³ :47 1:06²ft	20	115	52¼ 86½ 9¹³10¹⁶	RjnoM⁵	M35000 65	ⒻRegal Jay119	Vandy Sue 10
12 Jly 76 4Aqu	5½ f :23² :48 1:07⁴ft	16	119	1¹ 2h 21½ 33¾	RujanoM⁴	Mdn 70	Ducky'sBolero122	Hdee'sCsn 8
6 May76 4Bel	5½ f :23¹ :47³1:07³ft	11	115	2h 6⁴ 7¹⁶ 8²²	DayP⁷	M45000 59	ⒻSly Grin 119	Rethread 8

July 18 Bel trt 3f ft :38⅘b July 10 Bel trt 3f m :40b July 3 Bel 5f ft 1:01hg

Randy's Cil
119 B. f (1974), by Thomasville—Brimstar, by Mielleux.
Breeder, Dr. L. D. Star (N. Y.). 1976 3 M 0 1 $1,440
Owner, Winifred Star. Trainer, Adrien Gauthier. **$20,000**

19 Aug76 8Sar	6 f :22² :46 1:12²ft	5½e	112	17¹⁷12¹⁴10⁹¾ 98¾	VelqezJ¹⁵	AlwS 69	FratelloEd115	Heidee'sPal 17
11 Aug76 1Sar	5½ f :22³ :46³1:05⁴m	4e	119	99¾ 9⁷ 4⁶ 3⁶	VelasqezJ⁹	Mdn 82	RedSam 122	RagT meBelle 12
3 Aug76 3Sar	5½ f :22³ :46³1:05³ft	15	119	9¹¹ 8¹¹ 69¾ 5¹⁷	VelasqzJ³	Mdn 72	VandySue119	TakeItAlong 9

July 24 Bel 4f sy :49¾h July 18 Bel trt 3f ft :36¾h

Big Albert
118 Ch. c (1974), by O'Hara—Lisl's Favor, by Noholme II.
Breeder, Dr. D. J. DeLuke (N. Y.). 1976 2 M 0 0 (—)
Owner, Assunta Louis Farm. Trainer, Ramon M. Hernandez. **$18,000**

11 Aug76 1Sar	5½ f :22³ :46³1:05⁴m	7½	122	12¹³12⁹½10¹¹10¹⁶	HerndzR⁷	Mdn 72	RedSam 122	RagT meBe e 12
15 Jly 76 4Aqu	5½ f :22⁴ :47¹1:05³ft	36	122	11¹⁴11¹⁴11¹³10¹³	HerndezR²	Mdn 71	Turn of Coin 122	Red Rolfe 12

Aug 21 Sar 4f ft :48¾hg Aug 7 Sar 3f ft :38h Aug 5 Sar 5f ft 1:03¾b

No Empty Pocket
118 B. c (1974), by Zip Pocket—May Boss, by Boss.
Breeder, Dr. L. D. Star (N. Y.). 1976 7 M 1 0 $976
Owner, L. D. Star. Trainer, Adrien Gauthier. **$18,000**

19 Aug76 1Key	5½ f :22⁴ :47 1:06³ft	9¼	118	76¾ 7⁸ 5¹⁰ 57½	LogioA⁴	M¹0000 79	LimestoneCowby120	Lry'sLk 7
11 Aug76 4Mth	5½ f :23 :46³1:05⁴ft	5	114	42½ 55 55 5⁷	MiceliM⁴	M8000 81	Night Games 118	Stangley 8
23 Jly 76 3Key	5½ f :22⁴ :47²1:07¹ft	4¾	120	42½ 34½ 33½ 22½	LogcioA³	M5000 81	Manza117	NoEmptyPocket 6
18 Jly 76 4Aqu	5½ f :23² :47⁴1:05³ft	23e	118	10¹⁰10⁸½10¹⁵10¹⁷	RhdsC¹	M20000 63	PrinceNoNme117	PictreShw 10
11 Jly 76 4Aqu	5½ f :22² :47 1:07 ft	10e	122	9¹¹ 9¹¹ 87½ 86½	RchdsC⁴	M18000 71	BrghtJade122	HI tothePrnce 10
21 May76 4Bel	5½ f :23 :46³1:05⁴ft	34	116	10⁸ 99¾ 9¹⁵ 8¹⁶	RdsCH⁷	M30000 70	FlagOfficer122	WincomaLss 10
27 Apr76 4Aqu	5 f :23⁴ :4⁻² :59¹ft	11	118	6⁸ 6¹⁰ 7¹⁸ 7²²	RodrzJA⁴	20000 67	I Got Em 122	Translation 7

June 30 Bel trt 4f sy :50b

over recent performances. If the horse already rates close to the competition, as Flylet certainly does, the expected improvement is odds-on to result in victory. Odds-on is what I said and odds-on is what I meant. Give a horse like that a slow-breaking field or a front-running racetrack, and the only thing that will beat it is an act of god or war.

In the actual race Flylet went wire to wire, scoring a handy three-length victory, and paid a juicy $15.60.

9th Churchill Downs

MAY 3, 1975

1 1-16 MILES
CHURCHILL DOWNS
START & 4 FINISH

1 1/16 MILES. (1:41⅗). ALLOWANCES. Purse $25,000. 3-year-olds. Weight, 122 lbs. Non-winners of a race of $9,775 at a mile or over allowed 3 lbs.; a race of $6,000 at any distance, 5 lbs.; a race of $4,875 at any distance, 7 lbs.; a race of $3,900 at a mile or over in 1975, 9 lbs. (Maiden, claiming and starter races not considered.)

Jim Dan Bob 113 B. c (1972), by Wa–Wa Cy—Legayle, by Bar Le Duc.
Breeder, G. Begley (Ky.).
Owner, G. Begley. Trainer, A. Montano.
| | | 1975 | 10 | 0 | 3 | 3 | $7,754 |
| | | 1974 | 11 | 4 | 2 | 2 | $9,265 |

26 Apr75	7CD	7 f :23⁴ :47¹¹:25 ft	52	117	77¼ 7¹⁴ 6¹⁵ 5¹²	ArroyoH¹	Alw 70	Greek Answer122	Gatch 7
17 Apr75	7Kee	7 f :23 :46 1:23⁴ft	92	1075	9¹³ 99¾ 9¹⁰ 96¾	TrsclairAJ⁷	Alw 80	HoneyMark114	Brent'sPrnce 11
3 Apr75	7Lat	1 :47¹¹1:12¹1:40²ft	8-5e	114	78¾ 4¹⁰ 2¹⁰ 37¼	McKnghtJ⁹	Alw 69	Some Dude 115	Count Paco 9
29 Mar75	7Lat	1 :48 1:13²1:40 gd	7½	112	5²¼ 34½ 34½ 3⁸	McKnhtJ²	AlwS 71	NaughtyJke119	PromndeLft 8
18 Mar75	8Lat	1 :48³1:441:43³gd	3¾	113	35 44½ 3⁷ 2²	McKnghtJ⁶	Alw 59	ClarenceHenry120	JimDan 9
7 Mar75	7Lat	6 f :24 :48¹1:15¹gd	8-5	▲116	2h 1⁵ 11½ 2no	VasqzG¹	A—— 72	MowingJoe113	JimDanBob 5
21 Feb75	7Lat	1⅟₁₆:48⁴1:441:49⁴ft	2½	113	3³ 2h 2¹ 2¹½	VasquezG³	Alw 59	ClarenceHnry116	JmDanBob 6
1 Feb75	6Key	1⁷⁰:47¹¹1:441:47 gd	11	119	5⁹ 4¹² 58½ 5¹¹	Ortizl3	Alw 54	Go Go Treniers 119	Prfct Gn 6
25 Jan75	8Key	6 f :22² :46¹¹1:13²sy	11	112	58¼ 4⁸ 5¹¹ 6¹⁹	Ortizl4	AlwS 56	Gallant Bob 119	Sgt. Hunt 7
17 Jan75	8Key	6 f :22² :46¹¹:12 ft	17	117	66½ 5¹¾ 3¹½ 3¾	Ortizl3	Alw 81	SneakyWin 117	Dr.FrankB. 8
Dec28-74	7Cwl	6½ f 1:23⅗sy	1	▲119	1² 1² 1¹ 1¹	VasquezG²	Alw 79	JimDanBob119	Clar'nceH'ry B.J.King 6

April 24 CD 4f sy :52b   March 27 Lat 3f ft :39b   March 5 Lat 3f ft :37h

Ruggles Ferry 117 Gr. c (1972), by Drone—Trotta Sue, by Promised Land.
Breeder, F. Preston (Ky.).
Owner, Mrs. F. Preston. Trainer, H. Trotsek.
| | | 1975 | 5 | 2 | 1 | 0 | $12,075 |
| | | 1974 | 13 | 2 | 2 | 6 | $26,884 |

24 Apr75	7Kee	1⅛:47¹¹1:12 1:49 sy	53	117	5⁹ 4⁴ 3⁷ 57¾	ArroyoH⁸	AlwS 84	MasterDerby123	HoneyMark 6
15 Apr75	7Kee	1⅟₁₆:47 1:11 1:42³gd	6	115	5⁶ 5⁴ 2³ 2⁵	ArroyoH⁵	Alw 88	MasterDerby123	RugglsFrry 6
22 Mar75	9FG	1⅟₁₆:46¹¹1:10²1:49³ft	14	115	10²⁰ 9¹⁴ 9¹¹ 98¼	BarrowT²	AlwS 88	MasterDrby123	ColonelPowr 11
14 Mar75	9FG	6 f :22¹ :46 1:10⁴ft	1-2	▲120	67½ 54½ 2² 1¹	BarrowT⁴	Alw 94	RugglesFerry117	BravestRman 11
15 Feb75	6Hia	7 f :23 :45²1:23²ft	7	117	108½ 79¾ 3² 1h	BarrowT⁷	Alw 88	RgglsFerry117	BravestRman 11
Nov16-74	8CD	1 1:36 ft	15	75	52½ 35¼	HcpS 84	CircleHome116	MasterD'rby R'gl'sF'ry 9
Nov 6-74	8CD	7 f 1:25⅖sy	9	115	11¹⁸10¹⁴ 5⁵ 3²½	BarrowT⁹	Alw 77	MasterD'rby122	W'yw'rdR'd R'gl'sF'ry 11
Oct19-74	7Kee	1⅟₁₆1:25⅘ft	8½	122	10⁹¾ 88½ 3⁵ 35¼	BarrowT⁹	ScwS 88	Pack'rC'pt'n122	M'st'rD'by R'gl'sF'ry 11
Oct 9-74	7Kee	6 f 1:09³⁄₅ft	5½	115	65¾ 66½ 4½ 1¹½	BarrowT⁵	Alw 94	RugglesFerry115	Ga'ntBob Pack'rCa'n 6
Aug28-74	7AP	6 f 1:11⅗gd	9	▲119	7⁷ 43¼ 22½ 2¹½	BarrowT⁶	Alw 84	CraftyD'ne119	R'gglesFerry DonOman 7

April 30 CD 5f ft 1:03⅖b   April 23 Kee 3f ft :36b   April 20 Kee 5f 1:04b

Dixmart 122 B. g (1972), by Swoon's Son—Liz Piet, by Piet.
Breeder, Copelan & Thornbury (Ky.).
Owner, C. O. Viar & R. Holthus. Trainer, R. Holthus.
| | | 1975 | 7 | 2 | 3 | 2 | $29,800 |
| | | 1974 | 13 | 2 | 2 | 3 | $11,085 |

22 Apr75	6Kee	7 f :23 :45⁴1:23 ft	6½	122	7⁸ 66½ 2⁴ 2²	CampbllRJ¹	Alw 89	Paris Dust 116	Dixmart 9
5 Apr75	7OP	1⁷⁰:46¹¹1:141:414ft	8	113	7⁹ 63¾ 2½ 1⅔	CampbllRJ³	Alw 87	Dixmart 113	Doug 6
31 Mar75	9FG	6 f :22 :45⁴1:112ft	6-5	▲118	41¾ 5² 4¹ 3²	CampbllRJ³	Alw 86	Jay'sGig114	BourrePadnah 9
26 Mar75	6OP	6 f :22 :45¹1:10⁴ft	5¾	113	3² 2³½ 22¼ 2no	CmpblRJ¹⁰	Alw 91	Pleasure Prize 113	Dixmart 10
11 Mar75	6OP	6 f :22¹ :46⅟₁₃1:13sl	4½	112	86¾ 7⁷¼ 4³ 11½	CmpblRJ³	22500 79	Dixmart 112	Kayjo 11
4 Mar75	6OP	6 f :21⁴ :45¹1:12 ft	3½	114	5⁴ 54½ 3nk 2nk	RiniA⁹	15000 85	Warrior Knight 112	Dixmart 10
18 Feb75	6OP	5½ f :22² :46¹1:05³ft	4½	116	8⁴ 53½ 4¹½ 36½	RiniA⁹	15000 83	BourrePadnh111	GrtRhythm 12
Oct19-74	5Haw	6½ f 1:16½ft	8-5e	▲114	87½ 8¹⁴ 7¹⁴ 7¹¹	LivelyJ¹	Alw 81	Str'teMiss114	J'dgeBol'm'r Hon'yM'rk 9

April 29 CD 6f ft 1:18b   Mar 25 OP 3f ft :37⅖b   Mar 20 OP 5f ft 1:02⅗b

Marauding

119 Gr. c (1972), by Warfare—Juliet, by Nearctic.
Breeder, Barrett M. Morris & Virginia M. Morris (Ky.).

Owner, Bromagen Cattle Co. Trainer, G. P. Bernis.

						1975 . 8 2 2 2	$32,450
						1974 10 1 3 0	$7,955

2 Apr75	6Kee	7 f :23 :4541:23 ft	3½ 122	3² 5⁴½ 34½ 33	LouvereGE⁷	Alw 88 Paris Dust 116	Dixmart 9
5 Apr75	9OP	1½ :4641:10²1:51⁴ft	17 123	5³½ 9⁴½ 85½ 85½	McHrgeD⁷	AlwS 79 PrmisedCity126 BldChapeau 14
5 Mar75	9OP	170 :47²1:131¹:44²gd	2e 119	3¹ 2ʰ 4¹½ 54½	MelncnL²	Hcp0 69 PromisedCity120 Me n'Mine 12
8 Mar75	7OP	170 :23 :47²1:42 ft	4½ 117	1½ 1ʰ 1ʰ 1ʰ	MelanconL¹	Alw 86 Maraudng117 CountryByJim 7
8 Feb75	8OP	6 f :21³ :4511:11¹ft	4½ 122	5¹½ 44 5³½ 2²½	MelnconL⁸	Alw 86 PoorOldJoe 114 Marauding 8
4 Feb75	8OP	6 f :214 :4431:10²ft	2½e⁴120	5³½ 47 3¹ 3¹	MelnconL⁴	Hcp0 92 King Jody 112 Untwine 11
5 Feb75	8OP	5½ f :221 :4621:06 gd	27 117	5²½ 4²½ 3¹½ 1½	MelnconL⁴	Alw 88 Marauding 117 Peto'sFellow 12
4 Jan75	8LaD	6 f :231 :4821:14²m	9-5 ^115⁵	1¹½ 16 1³ 2½	WolfCG⁶	Alw Hot Paque 111 Marauding 6
Nov30-74⁹FG		6 f 1:³³½gd 68 112	4²½ 33 5⁸½ 5¹¹	Mel'onL⁶	Hcp0 70 HoneyM'k117 RusticRuler MidniteR'o 14

April 28 CD 1m ft 1:45⅗b   April 21 Kee 3f ft :37⅜b   April 16 Kee 5f ft :59h

Naughty Jake

122 Dk. b. or br. c (1972), by Gallant Romeo—Matrona, by Terra Firma.
Breeder, S. Turner (Ky.).

Owner, Mildred Bachelor. Trainer, J. Bachelor.

						1975 . 8 2 0 1	$25,650
						1974 . 3 1 1 0	$17,675

29 Apr75	8CD	1 :4641:11 1:36²ft	4½ 122	2¹½ 2½ 31½ 33½	VasqzG⁴	AlwS 94 RoundStake122 RushingMan 5
15 Apr75	7Kee	1¹ₘ :47 1:11 1:43²gd	9½ 123	33½ 43½ 55½ 4¹²	VasquezG¹	Alw 81 MasterDerby123 RugglsFrry 6
29 Mar75	7Lat	1 :48 1:13²1:40 gd	1-3 ^119	1½ 1³ 1½	VasqzG³	AlwS 79 NaughtyJke119 PromndeLft 9
22 Mar75	7Lat	6 f :23 :47¹1:12⁴sy	2-3 ^122	2⁶ 23 1¹ 1⁴	VasquezG⁷	Alw 84 NaughtyJake122 ColonialPnt 7
20 Feb75	3Hia	1¹ₘ :46³1:11 1:42⁴sy	5½ 117	7¹¹ 5¹¹ 48 49½	ValdizanF¹	Alw 79 CircleHome119 Administratr 7
29 Jan75	9Hia	7 f :22² :4441:22½ft	30 115	6⁸ 5⁸ 65½ 65½	ValdiznF⁵	AlwS 89 Ascetic 115 Ellora 11
18 Jan75	9Hia	6 f :22 :4431:10¹sy	74 115	75³ 56½ 45 41½	ValdiznF⁶	AlwS 90 Ricks Jet 114 Prevailer 11
Jan 9-75⁹Crc		6½ f 1:19¾ft 15 122	6⁷ 6⁸½ 67 45½	ValdiznF⁴	Alw 87 Strateaway113 Prevailer IrishRing 6

April 27 CD 3f ft :35h

Mr. Snow Cap

113 B. g (1972), by One More Chorus—Orange Ice, by Iceberg II.
Breeder, H. G. Tilson (Ky.).

Owner, Audley Farm Stable. Trainer, D. Smith.

						1975 . 6 2 2 1	$9,210

24 Apr75	4Kee	6 f :22 :45 1:10¹sy	4 114	6⁸ 56½ 49 5¹⁴	DelahyeE¹⁰	Alw 77 BearerBond112 CmmrclPilot 11
18 Apr75	6Kee	7 f :23³ :4631:24²ft	6-5 ^112	2¹½ 2½ 2½ 12½	DelahsyeE²	Alw 84 Mr. Snow Cap 112 Easabaya 10
9 Apr75	7Kee	6 f :22² :4541:03ft	8-5 ^114	43 21 2½	DelahsyeE³	Alw 88 RushingMan118 Mr.SnwCap 9
22 Mar75	7FG	6 f :22² :4441:12²ft	3-2 120	54½ 44 31½ 2ⁿᵒ	DelahsyeE¹	Alw 86 FlwlssFinish120 Mr.SnwCap 7
26 Feb75	8FG	6 f :214 :4531:11¹ft	1-2e⁴120	4½ 1½ 2¹ 34½	AndersnJR⁸	Alw 87 Tailor'sTack120 BoldChapau 9
16 Feb75	2FG	6 f :224 :4811:14¹sl	3-2 ^120	1½ 11 12 15	DsyeE¹¹	M10000 77 Mr.SnwCap120 BrtherBadBy 12

April 17 Kee 3f ft :35⅜b   April 7 Kee 3f ft :36b   March 28 FG 3f ft :37b

Victory Judge

113 B. c (1972), by Traffic Judge—Choiseul, by Victory Morn.
Breeder, R. C. Kyle (Can.).

Owner, Sacred Stable. Trainer, A. Battaglia.

						1975 . 8 1 0 0	$1,452
						1974 4 M 1 1	$1,050

17 Apr75	9GP	⊕a 1 1:39²fm	90 114	8¹³ 8¹¹ 8¹³ 8²³	RamosR⁶	Alw 61 TooCordial 114 StepForward 8
10 Mar75	9GP	7 f :22 :4411:21³ft	239 110	55½10¹⁶10²³11²⁸	DennieD¹⁰	AlwS 68 GreekAnswer122 FashinSale 11
1 Mar75	6Hia	6 f :22² :4541:10²ft	54 119	97½ 810 914 9¹³	ArroyoH⁷	Alw 78 SwingLbrSwing117 ZingIng 10
5 Feb75	8Hia	7 f :231 :4531:24⁴ft	66 122	32½ 54½ 9¹7¹1¹⁸	BrumfelcD⁹	Alw 73 Directory 117 Jimbosanin 11
29 Jan75	9Hia	7 f :22² :4441:22 ft	299 112	9⁷ 9¹⁵12011¹⁷	ArroyoH¹¹	AlwS 78 Ascetic 115 Ellora 11
18 Jan75	3Cwl	6½ :24² :4831:23⁴m	2 ^120	15 16 15 19	SaylerB⁵	Mdn 79 VictoryJudge120 ZperGgette 8
Jan10-75⁸Cwl		5½ f 1:08⅘sy 5 105	6¹⁴ 5¹¹ 54½ 41½	ClinchT¹	Alw 81 Mike'sPal 116 PrinceArc NoDate 7
Jan 2-75⁸Cwl		6½ f 1:25⅖m 13 116	6³½ 31½ 31½ 8¹⁸	GastonR⁶	Alw 53 Donda'sMir'e122 CoolItB'e Jan't'sDe't 10
Dec21-74³Cwl		a1 1:42⅖gd 2-3 ^120	14 1¹ 2ʰ 35½	SaylerB¹	Mdn 61 Cool ItBabe117 BrightM'ch V't'ryJ'ge 10
Dec 7-74⁸Cwl		1¹ₘ 1:54⅕sy 29 111	2¹½ 1ʰ 1ʰ 2¹½	SaylerB⁴	Alw 65 Clar'ceH'ry113 Vict'yJ'ge JimDanBob 6

April 21 GP 7f ft 1:28⅜h

Greek Answer

122 B. c (1972), by Northern Answer—Greek Victress, by Victoria Park.
Breeder, E. P. Taylor (Can.).

Ownr, W P. Gilbride. Trainer, F. H. Merrill.

						1975 5 3 0 1	$57,707
						1974 .11 5 2 2	$187,261

26 Apr75	7CD	7 f :23⁴ :4711:25 ft	1-3 ^122	1½ 12½ 12 1¾	SolomneM⁷	Alw 82 Greek Answer122 Gatch 7
19 Mar75	9GP	1¹ₘ :46 1:10¹1:42⁴ft	6-5 ^122	15 16 13 14	SolmneM⁶	AlwS 87 Greek Answer 122 Decipher 8
10 Mar75	9GP	7 f :22 :4411:21³ft	3-5 ^122	1½ 1½ 14 15	CstdaM¹¹	AlwS 96 GreekAnswer122 FashinSale 11
29 Jan75	9Hia	7 f :22² :4441:22 ft	3½ 122	1½ 11½ 22 44½	CastaM¹⁰	AlwS 90 Ascetic 115 Ellora 11
18 Jan75	6Hia	6 f :22 :4431:10¹sy	3-5 ^122	1ʰ 1ʰ 2ʰ 3¹	CstndaM⁴	AlwS 91 Ricks Jet 114 Prevailer 11
Oct19-74⁸Bow		7 f 1:24⅖ft 2-3 ^119	22½ 22 1ʰ 2¾	Hin'j'saH⁶	AlwS 80 Gall'tBob113 Gr'kAnswer ParvaHasta 10
Sep15-74⁸WO		1-70 1:42⅕ft 7-5 122	11½ 11 22½ 36½	C'st'daM⁷	HcpS 85 L'Enjol'r122 N'r t'eHigh'Sa G'kAnsw'r 11
Sep 2-74⁸AP		6½ f 1:17⅘ft 3½ 122	12½ 11 11½ 1½	C'st'daM²	ScwS 86 Gr'kAnsw'r122 Col'lP'w'r TheB'g'lPr'e 7
Au 24-74⁸Sar		6½ f 1:13 ft 13 121	12½ 12 1½ 2⁴½	Cas'daM⁸	ScwS 92 F'lishPl's're121 G'kAnsw'r OurT'lism'n 8
Aug 5-74⁴FE		6½ f 1:21⅕sl 2-5 ^120	1ʰ 2ʰ 1ʰ 4⁸	GreenW²	AlwS 65 Col'sCl'rion115 OnaP'dSt'l'g P'sleyPal 8
Jly21-74⁴FE		6½ f 1:17 ft 1-3 ^122	1½ 12 1³ 14	GreenW⁴	AlwS 94 Greek Answer 122 L'Enjoleur Hagelin 5
Jun28-74⁶WO		6 f 1:10⅗ft 4-5 ^120	2ʰ 1½ 1³ 17	GreenW⁴	AlwS 94 Gr'kAnswer120 N'r t.HighSea R'lS'ari 6
Jun 9-74⁶WO		6 f 1:10⅖ft 1-2 ^114	1ʰ 1² 13½ 15½	GreenW⁷	AlwS 91 GreekAnswer114 Sgt.Hunt RunJay 7

April 21 CD 1m ft 1:41h

As I explained in Chapter 4, the position of the starting gate relative to the first turn is very important in middle-distance route races at most racetracks. Churchill Downs is one of those tracks.

The favorite in this race—the Twin Spires Purse, an annual fixture on the Derby Day program—is Greek Answer at 3–5. There are several reasons why this choice is out-rageously out of line with reality.

One of those reasons is named Ruggles Ferry, who has run only one subpar race (March 22) while meeting some of the best three-year-old routers in America (Master Derby, Colonel Power, Honey Mark, Circle Home). He has also shown enough speed in several of his races to suggest he can take advantage of his inner post position.

The other reasons lie with Greek Answer himself. This is a colt that has shown a tendency to tire in the late stages at 6½ furlongs and beyond; a colt whose lone win around two turns was scored on Gulfstream Park's notorious front-running track; a colt that will have to use much of his early speed to get clear of this field in the short run to the first turn. These are serious problems for a 3–5 shot to overcome. I make him 6–1.

The crowd made Ruggles Ferry 5–2. I make him even money, a 250 percent overlay. The key to this betting situation is more subtle than that of a Flylet-type front runner, but it is nevertheless there for all to see. The favorite is breaking from a disadvantageous post position, and his past performance history suggests he can ill afford to race under a handicap. The chief competition is easily identified and is set to race from a favorable post.

In the race Greek Answer raced four wide in the run to and through the clubhouse turn, struggled to get the lead on the backstretch, and tired steadily thereafter to finish fourth. Ruggles Ferry saved ground, held a striking position to the far turn, and rallied in the upper stretch to win by seven widening lengths. Had the post positions been reversed, I am sure Greek Answer would have given a much better account of himself.

Learning to recognize the straightforward betting opportunity is fundamental to the player's ambitions for profit. There will be countless other times, however, when the player will have to use all the tools in his bag to uncover the probable race winner. As often as 80 percent of the time, the only conclusion to be drawn from the effort is that no single horse in the field deserves a significant edge. There is great joy, however, in the exception.

SEPTEMBER 24, 1976

th Tdn

$3 PERFECTA WAGERING ON THIS RACE

6 FURLONGS (chute). (1:09⅘). CLAIMING. Purse $2,300. Fillies and mares. 3-year-olds and upward. 3-year-olds, 115 lbs.; older, 121 lbs. Non-winners of three races since June 30 allowed 2 lbs.; two races since then. 4 lbs.; a race since then. 6 lbs. Claiming price. $2,500; if for $2,250. allowed 2 lbs.

Sultan Sue Sis 112 Ro. f (1972) by Venetian Jester—Sultan s Sue, by Strokkr.
Br. Edward & J. Armstrong. Jr (Okla.) 1976 15 5 3 1 $8,642

Owner, R. F. Zupanc. Trainer. Ida Zupanc. $2.500 1975 6 M 3 2 $1,680

1 Sep76 4Tdn	6 f :23³ :48²1:14²sl	2½	108⁵	4² 4¹	3ⁿᵏ 11½	BordenD²	c2000 77	SultanSueSis108 TurningShy	8
3 Sep76 7Tdn	6 f :23 :48¹1:151ft	6-5	▲1115	86¼ 41¼	31½ 21½	BordenD4	2000 71	⑤AmberComt116 S:tnSeSis	8
9 Aug76 6Tdn	6 f :23 :47 1:124ft	2½	▲1115	3⁴ 2³	33½ 36	BordenD²	2500 79	⑤AprilFrost120 MissJeerful	7
5 Aug76 3Tdn	5½ f :22³ :4741:08 m	7½	1125	86½ 86¼	74 64½	BordenD²	2500 74	JazzDancer111 BridgePatrl	8
4 Jly 7610Tdn	6 f :22⁴ :4711:14²ft	6½	117	51½ 3¹	41½ 2ⁿᵏ	GraeIIA³	2500 77	WrkAndTrn120 SltanSueSis	10
5 Jly 7610Tdn	6 f :22² :4611:13 ft	5½	117	86¼ 65½	53½ 45½	FelinoBR⁸	2500 78	ClayPigeon122 GreekWhiz	12
7 Jun76 2Tdn	6 f :22⁴ :4721:144sl	3½	117	74½ 5⁷	41½ 24	FelicoBR¹	2500 75	OverlandWay120 SltnSueSis	10
1 Jun76 6Tdn	6 f :23² :4741:134gd	12	117	96¾ 8⁷	5⁵ 57½	KelleyBA⁴	3500 *2	B'ock!amur 122 Count Adam	9
3 Jun76 5Tdn	6 f :22² :4611:131ft	3	117	3² 21½	1ʰ 12	FelicoBR²	2500 83	SultanSueSis117 HevnlyRosa	9
6 May76 5Tdn	6 f :22³ :4721:133ft	5	120	4³ 2²	15 110	FelicoBR¹	2000 91	⑤SultanSueSis120 HwieToo 11	

Shad Pac 110 B. m (1971), by Clem Pac—Star Shadow, by Stella Aurata.
Breeder. C. P. Blake & S. Laser (Ark.). 1976 15 3 1 1 $6,141

Owner, Lela Mellinger. Trainer, Edward H. Mellinger III. $2.500 1975 21 2 1 2 $4.28/

9 Sep76 1Tdn	5½ f :22⁴ :4731:071⁵ft	18	108⁵	83½ 63½	66 57½	FranscoD⁸	2500 75	GallowayBay116 ShrLove!ins	8
5 Sep76 8Com	4½ f :23³ :47³ :54 ft	10	114	4 53½	67½ 44½	AntusLJ5	2500 89	Hollie'sPaxton115 HenryH.	7
9 Jun76 6Com	6½ f :23 :47 1:19³ft	2½	114	61⁴ 51³	41¹ 47½	LydaR²	2500 84	EasyMission117 G.J.Frmlwy	6
6 Jun76 5RD	170 :48 1:1341:46⁴ft	3	109	45½ 42½	3½ 31½	NewkirkT⁷	2500 64	Humbjo 116 Make Me Gone	8
1 May76 3RD	6 f :22¹ :4631:133m	3	107⁷	31⁰ 3⁷½	31½ 11½	TalricoM¹	2500 75	Shad Pac 107 Althen	7
2 May76 3RD	6 f :22¹ :4621:123ft	17	108⁷	88½ 87½	74½ 61½	TalaricoM¹	2500 79	Liberal Man 116 Hesourpet	12
4 May76 2RD	6 f :22² :4621:114ft	41	1·⁹	65½ 98½	97½ 81¹	WingoR⁹	3500 73	⑤AntherPluck116 Buxomby	10
3 Apr76 5HP	1 :49²1:15²1:42⁴ft	30	11⁵	98½109	91⁶ 91⁵	GilbtCJJr⁵	3200 54	HotShotDor1'5 AkepotSask '0	
5 Apr76 6HP	6½ f :23 :48 1:20²ft	9½	110⁵	57½ 58	69½ 67	RodgzJD³	3200 *2	CocntRow1'5 Kg of theOzks '0	
2C Mar76 5Lat	1 :4741:15 1:44 m	*0	112⁷	4⁵ 22½	11½ 15	NewkirkT⁴	2500 58	⑤ShadPac1'2 Queer Vasht·	8

Crafty Vodelia 115 Dk. b. or br. f (1972), by Noble Commander—Crafty Love, by Crafty
Admiral. Breeder, F. Wiercioch (Fla.). 1976 24 3 2 2 $5,954

Owner, L. R.Benshoff, lessee. Trainer, L. R. Benshoff. $2.500 1975 22 0 0 1 $2,529

18 Sep76 3Tdn	6 f :23¹ :4741:141m	31	114	4³ 33½	21½ 22	RiniA³	2000 76	Rick'sBuckeye120 CrftyVdlia	8
11 Sep76 4Tdn	6 f :23³ :4821:142sl	67	114	83½ 7⁷	53½ 45½	RiniA³	2000 71	SultanSueSis108 TurningShy	8
14 Aug76 5Tdn	6 f :22⁴ :4711:141sl	63	114	4² 75½	66½ 69½	RiniA³	2000 69	King's Levy 122 Fast Arab	8
4a Aug76 7Tdn	6 f :23² :4731:144ft	93	118	52½ 45	66 6⁷	InfanteF⁸	2000 67	⑤Touch O'Ri113 April Silvrs	8
28 Jly 76 5Tdn	5½ f :22¹ :48 1:083ft	21	1117	74½ 8⁷	71⁰ 68	StaffordA⁷	2000 68	⑤Confetti 118 Lady's Hat	8
8 Jly 76 7Tdn	140 :4911:1541:47 sl	25	115	21½ 44½	86½ 81³	RiniA⁴	2000 47	EarlyLady117 CertnlyMntrip	9
30 Jun76 4Tdn	6 f :24 :49 1:16³sy	2½	115	21 1ʰ	11 12	RiniA³	2000 66	Crafty/Vodelia115 FirstBurst	7
24 Jun76 5Tdn	140 :4811:1541:48²sy	5½	117	1² 21	53 61⁰	CooperG³	2000 43	PrceBravos122 StlTheRoses	8
17 Jun76 7Tdn	6 f :22² :4621:142sl	39	117	87¼ 76½	64½ 48½	CooperG²	2500 68	Greek Whiz 118 Our Pirate	8

Sept j Tdn 5f ft 1:03⅘b

Kin O Mine
115 Ch. m (1969), by Mighty Mine—Kimeo, by Ozbeg.
Breeder, J. A. Davis (Cal.).   1976 12 4 1 1 $6,3
Owner, Bunny Coatney. Trainer, Bunny Coatney. $2,250   1975 14 2 3 2 $5,0

4 Aug76	7Tdn	6 f :232 :4731:144ft	4½	120	42½ 65½ 43	44½	MunsterL3	2000 70	ⒻTouchO'Ri113	April Silvrs
24 Jly 76	2Tdn	6 f :224 :4721:142ft	2½	117	32½ 31 42	78½	MunsterL5	2000 68	Part Western 120	Fleet Pac
8 Jly 76	6Tdn	6 f :231 :4731:142sl	8-5 ⁴118	2¹ 1h 1h	1¹	SosaR8	2000 77	ⒻKin O Mine 118	Tiz A Joy
23 Jun76	7Tdn	6 f :223 :4641:14 ft	8-5 ⁴116	73½ 41½ 3½	1¹	SosaR9	2000 79	ⒻKinOMine 116	MissJeerful
5 Jun76	5Tdn	6 f :232 :4711:131ft	8	115	3½ 2½ 2¹	14	SosaR1	2000 83	Kin O Mine 115	Extinguisher
26 Mar76	6Tdn	⊡ a 5 f :234 :4841:014ft	2¾	118	1h 2h 2½	43½	CooperG6	2000 82	ⒻIndianCojo120	AtollsMiss
20 Mar76	7Tdn	⊡ a 5 f :224 :48 1:01¹ft	3¾	118	54½ 53½ 3⁵	24½	GraellA5	2500 84	ⒻTrafficGun113	KinOMine
13 Mar76	10Tdn	⊡ a 5 f :24 :49 1:02 gd	9-5	113	85½ 34½ 32½	1¹	GraellA5	2000 85	Kin O Mine 113	Alfie O
6 Mar76	3Tdn	⊡ a 5 f :242 :4831:01²ft	5	115	22½ 31½ 33½	34	PlackeD9	2000 84	Hub 118	Smart David

Sheer Loveliness
112 B. m (1971), by Molino—Mischief Miss, by Don Mike.
Breeder, Mrs. J. P. Strain (Ohio).   1976 13 3 1 1 $3,4
Owner, J. P. Strain, Jr. Trainer, J. P. Strain, Jr. $2.500   1975 5 M 0 0 $1

19 Sep76	1Tdn	5½ f :224 :4731:07¹ft	28	108⁷	1¹ 1¹ 1²	2²	ShewellJ1	2500 81	GallowayBay116	ShrLovelins
29 Aug76	2Tdn	6 f :231:4721:124gd	19	115	62½ 56½ 47	6¹⁶	D'AmicoA9	2500 69	Angl'sPlsre118	Freemn'sMn
12 Aug76	9Tdn	6 f :224 :4641:13¹ft	54	117	1½ 2¹ 66½	6¹⁵	VaughnJ5	6000 68	ⒻBaryVible115	VincesDr'm
31 Jly 76	5Com	6½ f :243 :4841:214ft	16	117	1h 22½ 1³	11½	PhillipsD10	2000 80	SheerLoveliness117	MsPnRn
22 Jly 76	5Com	4¼ f :232 :471 :534ft	2½	117	1 2¹½ 24	36½†HussrMW9	2000 88	Time ofEmprrs122	MissLrgrs
	†Disqualified and placed seventh.										
15 Jly 76	4Com	6½ f :234 :4731:21¹ft	4½	117	2¹ 1¹ 1½	45	HussrMW2	2000 78	JolliPassage114	MissPanRun
1 Jly 76	10Tdn	6 f :231 :4821:16 m	39	118	11½ 1h 1h	45½	HussrMW4	2500-63	SandyLathe102	CrftyDestino
1 Jly 76	10Tdn	6 f :231 :4821:16 m	39	118	11½ 1h 1h	45½†HussrMW4	2500-63	SandyLathe102	CrftyDestino
	†Placed third through disqualification.										
21 Jun76	2Com	6 f :233 :4731:01¹ft	2¾	116	11½ 12 11	1⁴1½	HussrMW1	1500 82	ShrLovelinss118	GenrlMateo

Bibi Mine
115 Ch. m (1971), by O'Bibi—Condamine, by Deliberator.
Breeder, J. W. Mecom (Tex.).   1976 16 3 4 1 $10,5
Owner, Miller Farm. Trainer, Edward Collins. $2.500   1975 14 1 2 3 $4,2

11 Sep76	6Lat	6½ f :24 :48 1:21¹ft	6½	116	41½ 42½ 54½	6⁵	TennbmM8	5000 70	Tosoro 113	Circus Act 1
5 Sep76	10RD	6 f :221 :4541:113ft	8½	111	42 42 35	45½	TnnbmM5	05000 79	ResJudicada113	MmySowrd
28 Aug76	6Tdn	14o :4711:1341:45 sl	6¾	113	22 23 86	8¹¹	MunsterL8	6000 59	Reasontodare113	BritishRed
12 Aug76	9Tdn	6 f :224 :4641:13¹ft	3	116	4¹ 3¹ 3²	31½	MunsterL6	6000 82	ⒻBaryVible115	VincesDr'm
1 Aug76	7Tdn	6 f :223 :4631:13 ft	27	115	3¹ 52½ 42	53½	MunsterL1	7000 81	Dad'sReflction116	BrlyVsble
24 Jly 76	7RD	5½ f :223 :4621:063sy	7½	117	87½ 91² 68½	68½	SorezW5	A2500 73	Triptique 116	Shaded Silver
27 Jun76	8Tdn	6 f :23 :4621:12 ft	19	116	42½ 54 55½	5¹⁰	MunsterL2	Alw 79	ⒻGoOnDrmng116	Mrge'sPck
9 Jun76	9Tdn	6 f :24 :46 1:12²ft	8½	114	42 22 2½	24	MunsterL2	Alw 87	ⒻBibi Mine 114	Lark Star
1 Jun76	5CD	6 f :223 :4541:12²ft	3¹	117	3¹½ 1½ 1¹½	2nk	SoirezW8	5000 84	ⒻHelen'sMusic117	BibiMine
2⁴ May76	8Tdn	6 f :231 :47 1:13¹ft	3½	116	1h 1h 1h	1¹	MunsterL3	3500 83	ⒻBibiMine116	GoDancerGo

Pajone's Hostess
115 Ch. f (1972), by Pajone—Anchorette, by My Host.
Breeder, W. J. Kosterman (Wash...   1976 13 0 0 1 $55
Owner, W. Kosterman. Trainer, John Myers. $

15 Sep76	10Tdn	6 f :23 :47 1:13²ft	33	115	62½ 43	98³10¹⁴	PlackeD5	3500 68	SkyLock111	Work and Turn
5 Sep76	3Tdn	14o :4741:1331:43 ft	42	108⁵	43½ 6⁹	8¹⁷ 8³⁶	BordenD8	3500 44	LookWho'sHere 122	DuroT
26 Aug76	6Tdn	6 f :23 :4631:13 ft	5	109⁵	51½ 22	54½ 6¹²	KelleyBA9	3500 72	ⒻGrandElm116	April Frost
19 Aug76	9Tdn	6 f :222 :4541:124ft	19	108⁵	33½ 2¹	4¾ 65½	KelleyBA9	3500 80	infieldHomer117	AbilityPls
6 Aug76	7Tdn	6 f :223 :4611:123ft	23	113	32½ 34	67 71⁵	SackettR3	4500 71	LookWho'sHere118	BlyVsble
2⁴ Jly 76	9Tdn	6 f :23 :4621:131ft	15	108⁵	63½ 43½	43½ 78	KelleyBA5	4500 75	Urticante116	Whatawaytogo
22 Jly 76	9Tdn	6 f :231 :4631:133ft	18	109⁵	42 1h	1h 34½	KelleyBA8	4500 76	ⒻMillennum115	Wally'sSisr
15 Jly 76	9Tdn	6 f :224 :4831:121ft	26	115	31½ 2h	75 71⁴	GraellA5	5000 74	IndianSpeed 120	EarlsMeldy
19 Jun76	7Tdn	6 f :224 :4711:14 m	22	117	71½ 31½	52½ 6¹⁰	FelicnoBR6	Alw 69	BoldTom122	Great...bridge
	Aug 2 Tdn 3f ft :37⅖bg										

Foolish Lola
117 Ch. m (1970), by Venetian Jester—Lassa Gal, by Gallahadion.
Breeder, C. Sawyer (Okla.).   1976 10 2 1 1 $2,68
Owner, G. Mancuso. Trainer, Joseph Mazur. $2,500   1975 25 6 4 5 $10,4

10 Sep76	5Tdn	6 f :233 :4641:123ft	2	⁴114	1h 11½ 13	14½	D'AmicoA1	2000 72	ⒻFoolishLola114	IndianLil
27 Aug76	7Tdn	6 f :231 :47 1:141sl	28	113	2½ 73½ 55	55½	D'AmicoA4	2500 72	DriveJoy122	LadofPrtsmuth
31 Jly 76	6Com	5 f :232 :4731:00²ft	4½	117	31½ 33 35	35½	RamosW5	2500 84	Sharpsville 115	Base Fiddle
17 Jly 76	6Com	5 f :23 :4831:00¹ft	3	117	54½ 68 67	65½	RamosW7	2500 82	OpenWind122	KamsinWind
26 Jun76	8Com	6½ f :233 :4731:212ft	2½	⁴112	1½ 1½ 21	22½	RamosW4	2500 79	Wild Boss 117	Foolish Lola
18 Jun76	9Com	6½ f :241 :4821:22 ft	3½	⁴115	1² 1² 15	11²	RamosW1	2000 79	FoolishLola115	RennieBee

Confetti
112 Dk. b. or br. f (1972), by Roman Line—Starstruck, by Dark Star.
Breeder W. H. May (Ky.).   1976 16 4 0 4 $6,1
Owner, K. E. Strickler. Trainer, Homer Dewey. $2,500   1975 16 0 2 3 $2,1

2⁹ Aug76	7RD	6 f :22 :4611:121ft	21	110⁷	87 8¹¹ 8¹³	8¹⁹	MysJRJr8	02500 63	TriplicateCopy 111	BushHoc
28 Jly 76	5Tdn	5½ f :221 :48 1:083ft	9½	118	54½ 34 32	13	InfanteF6	2000 76	ⒻConfetti 118	Lady's Hat
9 Jly 76	zFL	5½ f :233 :48 1:08¹ft	6	114	31½ 3½ 13	13½	VedilgoW4	2000 81	Confetti 114	Northen Proof
3 Jly 76	7FL	5½ f :224 :4641:08¹ft	7	115	63½ 65½ 66½	54½	VedilgoW6	2000 74	Tisha Bell 115	Grossecat
26 Jun76	5FL	6 f :223 :4641:142ft	4	114	42½ 2h 2h	44	VedilgoW1	2000 78	Prove It Su 106	Easy Mike
15 Jun76	6FL	6 f :23 :4611:122ft	13	112	67 57½ 67	76½	WingoR5	A1750 85	Barborian 112	Petit Homme
5 Jun76	6FL	5½ f :222 :4631:061ft	29	111	74½ 76½ 76	65½	WingoR7	3000 85	Misget 111	Anar Kali
22 May76	6FL	5½ f :223 :47 1:071ft	18	111	77½ 67 65	78	RinconR7	3500 78	RuthlessCount116	ShoeTax

Using only the past performance records above, the handicapper would have a hard time justifying a confident selection. Several horses in the field appear to be in good form, while a few others are ostensibly dropping in class. Yet the past performance records do not contain sufficient clues to make conclusive comparisons. The same is true for the majority of claiming races run throughout the country.

There is no track bias, no known trainer pattern, and no unusual betting activity to consider. But there are result charts, and classification codes, and speed figures.

Using speed figures or result-chart time comparisons, we would begin our detective work by determining that Sultan Sue Sis ran the fastest recent race.

On September 11, in an open-grade $2,000 claiming race, Sultan Sue Sis completed six furlongs in 1:14⅖, not very impressive time on first glance. But compared with several other races that day, the time was extraordinary. These were some of the other six-furlong times posted:

$5,000 claiming - - - - - - 1:14⅕
$4,500 claiming - - - - - - 1:14⅘
$3,500 claiming - - - - - - 1:14⅖
$3,000 claiming - - - - - - 1:14⅗

Obviously, Sultan Sue Sis ran a big race last time out and is ready to step up sharply in class. But what about the rest of the field? What about 4–5 favorite Bibi Mine, who is getting play mostly on the basis of her sharp drop in claiming price?

In my judgment, this is not a negative class drop in the classic sense. Considering Bibi Mine's inability to win at the higher claiming level, the drop in class may be what she needs to get back on the winning track. In order to make a clearer determination of that judgment we need to discover more information about the caliber of horses she faced at Latonia. Again, result charts and comparative race times will prove very useful to this end.

The first race on the September 11 Latonia card was a $3,500 maiden claiming race. The fractions and final time were identical to Bibi Mine's $5,000 claiming race, a race for proven winners: .24 . . . .48 . . . 1:14⅕ . . . 1:21⅕. Two conclusions are possible: Either the maiden race was run very fast or Bibi Mine's race was run very slow.

Two other races run that day say Bibi Mine was in a slow field:

$3,500 claiming - - - - - - 1:14⅖
$3,500 claiming - - - - - - 1:14 . . . 1:20⅘

Indeed, Bibi Mine may once have been a much better horse and will probably appreciate the drop in class today, but at present she is not faster than Sultan Sue Sis and has no right to be favored over her.

Crafty Vodelia was recently trounced by Sultan Sue Sis and then came back to race very creditably in an open-grade $2,000 claimer. Another meeting with Sultan Sue Sis will not be what the doctor ordered.

Shad Pac recently returned to competition but gave no indication that she is fit enough to catch these horses in a six-furlong race.

Kin O' Mine has been absent from competition for seven weeks and is stepping up in claiming price. A good performance is likely, considering the interval that preceded her win over a weak field on June 5; but it would be asking too much to have her step into this field of multiple winners to win first crack out of the box.

Sheer Loveliness has shown good early speed on several occasions, but she couldn't hold onto a clear lead in a shorter race last time out. A time-comparison study of the races run that day will also show that Sheer Loveliness was in a slow $2,500 race.

Pajone's Hostess is winless this year and desperately needs a drop in class. Signs of early lick in her recent past performances are valid indicators of improving physical condition; but a win seems unlikely.

Foolish Lola won her last race the same way she scored her only other victory this season: wire to wire. A review of the Thistledown charts for September 10 will make light of her chances to repeat that today. Although she had the rail from start to finish on a track that was extremely biased toward the inside, her fractional times were slower than those for most of the other races on the card. Moreover, she is stepping up sharply in company from a C-class $2,000 claimer to an open-class $2,500 race.

Confetti was in top form at the tail end of July but spent a month in the barn before making her next start. That's a clear sign of physical problems, fully confirmed by her August 29 performance, the worst race on her chart. She now returns with another four-week vacation behind her. If this horse wins, the knowledgeable horseplayers in the crowd should give trainer Homer Dewey a standing ovation; but few if any of them will wager on her chances. Short of clear-cut evidence in the post parade, there is no logical reason to conclude that this horse is back in top competitive form.

EXACTA PAYOFF FOR SULTAN SUE SIS WITH	
Bibi Mine	$ 52
Shad Pac	$ 96
Foolish Lola	$158
Pajone's Hostess	$190
Crafty Vodelia	$210
Sheer Loveliness	$275
Kin O'Mine	$275
Confetti	$390

On the basis of the material that our detective work has uncovered, we may now conclude that Sultan Sue Sis has a decided edge over every horse in the race. Indeed, she need only run within two lengths of her most recent race to win in a walk. For added confidence, her honest record, including five prior wins, suggests that she is likely to do that and more. Given 7–2 odds on Sultan Sue Sis, we should forgive the player who is now making a mad dash to the win windows, but anyone contemplating a wager larger than $30 would be better off investing in the exacta pool.

At $3 per ticket, a straight wheel would cost $24, but it would also leave the player open to two less profitable results (Bibi Mine or Shad Pac). However, there are other alternatives to consider, and the following is only the simplest.

By purchasing two *extra* combinations with Bibi Mine and one with Shad Pac, the player would automatically increase the minimum odds on Sultan Sue Sis to 4–1 ($33 invested, $156 minimum possible payoff) and give himself a chance for considerably greater rewards without additional risk. In a game that taxes the player 20 cents for every dollar wagered, 50 cents extra profit on the dollar is nothing to sneeze at.

SEVENTH RACE
Tdn
Sept'ber 24, 1976

6 FURLONGS (chute). (1:09⅘). CLAIMING. Purse $2,300. Fillies and mares. 3-year-olds and upward. 3-year-olds, 115 lbs.; older, 121 lbs. Non-winners of three races since June 30 allowed 2 lbs.; two races since then, 4 lbs.; a race since then, 6 lbs. Claiming price. $2,500; if for $2,250, allowed 2 lbs.

Value to winner $1,380: second, $460; third, $230; fourth, $115; fifth, $69; sixth, $46. Mutuel Pool, $14,296.
Perfecta Pool, $32,082.

Last Raced	Horse	EqtAWt	PP	St	¼	½	Str	Fin	Jockeys	Owners	Odds to $1
11 Sep76 4Tdn1	Sultan Sue Sis	b4 117	1	7	2h	2h	11	13	RSackett	R F Zuanc	3.60
11 Sep76 6Lat6	Bibi Mine	b5 115	6	8	6½	3½	21	21	LMunster	Miller Farm	.80
15 Sep76 10Tdn10	Jajone's Hostess	b4 115	7	2	4h	4½	41	3no	DPlacke	W Kosterman	16.80
4 Aug76 7Tdn4	Kin O Mine	7 115	4	4	7h	51	3½	4½	BMWilson	Bunny Coatney	21.30
18 Sep76 3Tdn2	Crafty Vodelia	b4 115	3	9	8h	9	5h	51	ARini	L R Benshoff lessee	12.70
19 Sep76 1Tdn5	Shad Pac	b5 110	2	5	31	61	61	61	BAKelley5	Mrs L Mellinger	5.60
10 Sep76 5Tdn1	Foolish Lola	6 117	8	3	51	7h	8½	71	AD'Amico	G Mancuso	12.50
19 Sep76 1Tdn2	Sheer Loveliness	b5 112	5	6	9	82	9	82	JShewell7	J P Strain Jr	23.30
29 Aug76 7RD8	Confetti	b4 112	9	1	13	1h	7½	9	RJMyres7	K E Strickley	82.40

OFF AT 4:08 EDT. Start good. Won driving. Time, :23, :47⅖, 1:14. Track slow.

$2 Mutuel Prices:

1-SULTAN SUE SIS	9.20	3.60	2.80
6-BIBI MINE		3.40	2.80
7-PAJONE'S HOSTESS			6.00

$3 PERFECTA (1-6) PAID $52.80.

Ro. f, by Venetian Jester—Sultan's Sue, by Strokkr. Trainer, Ida Zupanc. Bred by Edward and J. Armstrong, Jr. (Okla.).

SULTAN SUE SIS, with the pace all the way while saving ground along the rail, had to be steadied at the five-sixteenths pole while waiting for an opening, got through along the rail to make the lead and won under steady pressure. BIBI MINE circled horses on the middle of the turn to go up to challenge for the lead, then finished evenly. PAJONE'S HOSTESS lacked the needed response KIN O' MINE closed some ground late. SHAD PAC was through early. FOOLISH LOLA had brief speed CONFETTI set the pace for a half and stopped to a walk.

Before we leave this step-by-step illustration—indeed, before we part company altogether—I would like to point out that Sultan Sue Sis was not preordained to win the above race. There was, in fact, one major clue that could well have destroyed all our expectations. The little *c* next to Sultan Sue Sis' claiming price on the September 11 past performance line indicates she was claimed by the trainer of record—Ida Zupanc.

Considering the extraordinary impact trainers have on the performance potential of all horses, it would be a mistake to bet serious money on a horse whose trainer had given any evidence of incompetence. In the case of Ida Zupanc, no such evidence is revealed in a review of recent result charts. Moreover, her excellent judgment in claiming this improving racehorse ten or fifteen minutes prior to the September 11 race is reason enough to give her the benefit of the doubt. I am not that conservative to pass up 4–1 odds on a 50–50 proposition. But I am also not that foolish to forget that 50 percent winners means 50 percent losers as well. To win at the racetrack the player has to be alert, flexible, and fully in touch with his own limitations. The future may be predictable, but it is never predetermined.

Appendix

*Guide to past performance profiles and the
DAILY RACING FORM—List of North American
tracks—"Points of call" in charts—How to
set up a post position survey—Percentage table
for morning line—How to compute place and
show payoffs—Parallel time chart—Class pars—
Speed figures and track variants—
Recommended reading list*

Guide to

PAST PERFORMANCES

WITH FRACTIONAL TIMES

Position in Race and Margin Behind Leading Horse

27 Jun 74² AP   6f   :22⁴ :46 1:11³ ft 9-5 ▲117⁵ 5³ 4² 2ʰ 1¹½ Jones,¹⁶   c5000 87 ⊕Donnie 117 Lovely Day 8

Note: In past performances the position in the race for "first call" is as follows: In races less than 5 furlongs the first call is the start; at 5 furlongs the first call is the three-sixteenths; from 5½ to 7½ furlongs the first call is the quarter mile; at 1 mile or more the first call is the half.

Distance of Race		1st Call	2nd Call	3rd Call	4th Call	Fractional Times Given At These Points of Call		
2	Furlongs	Start	— —	Stretch	Finish	— —	— —	Finish
5/16	Mile	Start	— —	Stretch	Finish	— —	— —	Finish
3	Furlongs	Start	— —	Stretch	Finish	1/4	— —	Finish
3 1/2	Furlongs	Start	1/4	Stretch	Finish	1/4	— —	Finish
4	Furlongs	Start	1/4	Stretch	Finish	1/4	3/8	Finish
4 1/2	Furlongs	Start	1/4	Stretch	Finish	1/4	— —	Finish
5	Furlongs	3/16	3/8	Stretch	Finish	1/4	1/2	Finish
5 1/2	Furlongs	1/4	3/8	Stretch	Finish	1/4	1/2	Finish
6	Furlongs	1/4	1/2	Stretch	Finish	1/4	1/2	Finish
6 1/2	Furlongs	1/4	1/2	Stretch	Finish	1/4	1/2	Finish
7	Furlongs	1/4	1/2	Stretch	Finish	1/4	1/2	Finish
1	Mile	1/2	3/4	Stretch	Finish	1/2	3/4	Finish
1	Mile, 70 yards	1/2	3/4	Stretch	Finish	1/2	3/4	Finish
1 1/16	Miles	1/2	3/4	Stretch	Finish	1/2	3/4	Finish
1/8	Miles	1/2	3/4	Stretch	Finish	1/2	3/4	Finish
1 3/16	Miles	1/2	3/4	Stretch	Finish	1/2	3/4	Finish
1 1/4	Miles	1/2	1 mile	Stretch	Finish	1/2	3/4	Finish
1 5/16	Miles	1/2	1 mile	Stretch	Finish	1/2	3/4	Finish
1 3/8	Miles	1/2	1 mile	Stretch	Finish	1/2	3/4	Finish
1 1/2	Miles	1/2	1 1/4	Stretch	Finish	1/2	3/4	Finish
1 5/8	Miles	1/2	1 3/8	Stretch	Finish	1/2	3/4	Finish
1 3/4	Miles	1/2	1 1/2	Stretch	Finish	1/2	3/4	Finish

Key to Symbols, Abbreviations in Past Performances

FOREIGN-BRED HORSES
An asterisk (*) preceding the name of the horse indicates foreign-bred. (No notation is made for horses bred in Canada and Cuba.)

MUD MARKS
*—Fair mud runner   X—Good mud runner
⊗—Superior mud runner

COLOR
B.—Bay   Blk.—Black   Br.—Brown   Ch.—Chestnut
Gr.—Gray   Ro.—Roan   Wh.—White
Dk. b. or br.—Dark bay or brown
(Lt. before color denotes Light)

SEX
c—colt   h—horse   g—gelding   rig—ridgling
f—filly   m—mare

PEDIGREE
Each horse's pedigree lists, in the order named, color, sex, year foaled, sire, dam and grandsire (sire of dam).

BREEDER
Abbreviation following breeder's name indicates the state, place of origin or foreign country in which the horse was foaled.

TODAY'S CLAIMING PRICE
Claiming prices for horses entered today appear in bold face type to right of trainer's name.

RECORD OF STARTS AND EARNINGS
The horse's racing record for his most recent two years of competition appears to the extreme right of the name of the breeder. This lists the year, number of starts, wins, seconds, thirds and earnings. The letter "M" in the win column of the upper line indicates the horse is a maiden. If the letter "M" is in the lower line only, it indicates the horse was a maiden at the end of that year.

DISTANCE
a—preceding distance (a6f) denotes "about" distance (about 6 furlongs in this instance.)

TURF COURSES
Ⓣ—before distance indicates turf (grass) course race.
Ⓣ—before distance indicates inner turf course.
Ⓓ—before distance indicates inner dirt course.

TRACK CONDITIONS
ft—fast   fr—frozen   gd—good   sl—slow
sy—sloppy   m—muddy   hy—heavy
Turf course races, including steeplechase and hurdles:
hd—hard   fm—firm   gd—good   yl—yielding   sf—soft
Note: SC in place of track condition indicates Synthetic Course in use at various tracks. The condition of this synthetic course is fast at all times.

CLOSING ODDS
2ᴬ—favorite   2e—entry   15f—mutuel field

APPRENTICE OR RIDER WEIGHT ALLOWANCES
Allowance (in pounds) indicated by superior figure following weight—117⁵.

ABBREVIATIONS USED IN POINTS OF CALL
no—nose   h—head   nk—neck

POST POSITION
Horse's post position appears after jockey's name—WilsonR4.

RACE CLASSIFICATIONS
10000—Claiming race (eligible to be claimed for $10,000). Note: The letter c preceding claiming price (c10000) indicates horse was claimed.
M10000—Maiden claiming race (non-winners—eligible to be claimed).
10000H—Claiming handicap (eligible to be claimed).
O10000—Optional claiming race (entered NOT to be claimed).
10000O—Optional claiming race (eligible to be claimed).
Mdn—Maiden race (non-winners).
AlwM—Maiden allowance race (for non-winners with special weight allowance for those having started in a claiming race).
Alw—Allowance race.
HcpO—Overnight handicap race.
SplW—Special weight race.
Wfa—Weight-for-age race.
Mtch—Match race.
A10000—Starter allowance race (horses who have started for claiming price shown, or less, as stipulated in the conditions).
H10000—Starter handicap (same restriction as above).
S10000—Starter special weight (restricted as above).
Note: Where no amount is specified in the conditions of the "starters" race dashes are substituted, as shown below:
A———   H———   S———

STEEPLECHASE AND HURDLE RACES
ⒸS—Steeplechase   ⒸH—Hurdle race

STAKES RACES
AlwS—Allowance stakes.
HcpS—Handicap stakes.
ScwS—Scale weight stakes.
SpwS—Special weight stakes.
WfaS—Weight-for-age stakes.
50000S—Claiming stakes (eligible to be claimed).

INVITATIONAL RACES
InvA—Invitational allowance.
InvH—Invitational handicap.
InvSc—Invitational scale weight.
InvSp—Invitational special weights.
InvW—Invitational weight-for-age.

RACES EXCLUSIVELY FOR FILLIES, MARES
Ⓕ—Immediately following the speed rating indicates races exclusively for fillies or fillies and mares.

SPEED RATINGS
This is a comparison of the horse's time with the track record established prior to the opening of the meeting. The track record is given a rating of 100 and one point is deducted for each one-fifth second slower than the record. When a horse breaks the track record one point is added to the par 100 for each one-fifth second faster than the record. One-fifth of a second is considered the equivalent of one length.

No ratings are given for hurdle or steeplechase events, for races less than three furlongs, for races where the horse's speed rating is less than 25.

Note: Speed ratings for new distances are computed and assigned when adequate time standards are established. At Caliente, Mexico, which operates throughout the year, rating changes are made whenever a track record is broken.

EACH HORSE'S MOST RECENT WORKOUTS APPEAR DIRECTLY UNDER THE PAST PERFORMANCES
For example, July 30 Bel 3f ft :38b indicates the horse worked on July 30 at Belmont Park. The distance of the trial was 3 furlongs over a fast track and the horse was timed in 38 seconds, breezing. The following abbreviations are used to describe how each horse worked:
b—breezing   d—driving   e—easily   g—worked from stall gate   h—handily   bo—bore out
trt following track abbreviation indicates horse worked on training track.   tc—turf course   TR—trial race
HC—Hillside Course

ABBREVIATIONS FOR NORTH AMERICAN TRACKS

Abbreviations below designate tracks in DAILY RACING FORM charts and past performances.

AC	— Agua Caliente, Mex.	Hag	—*Hagerstown, Md.	San	—*Sandown Park, Can.
Aks	— Ak-Sar-Ben, Neb.	Haw	— Hawthorne, Ill.	Sar	— Saratoga, N. Y.
Alb	— Albuquerque, N. Mex.	Hia	— Hialeah Park, Fla.	ScD	— Scarborough Downs, Me.
AP	— Arlington Park, Ill.	Hol	— Hollywood Park, Calif.	Sem	—*Seminole Downs, Fla.
Aqu	— Aqueduct, N. Y.	HP	—*Hazel Park, Mich.	SFe	— Santa Fe Downs, N. Mex.
AsD	—*Assiniboia Downs, Can.	JnD	—*Jefferson Downs, La.	ShD	— Shenandoah Downs,W.Va.
Atl	— Atlantic City, N. J.	Jua	— Juarez, Mex.	Sol	—*Solano, Calif.
Ato	—*Atokad Park, Neb.	Kee	— Keeneland, Ky.	Spt	—*Sportsman's Park, Ill.
BB	—*Blue Bonnets, Can.	Key	—*Keystone Race Track, Pa.	SR	—*Santa Rosa, Calif.
BD	—*Berkshire Downs, Mass.	LaD	— Louisiana Downs, La.	Stk	— Stockton, Calif.
Bel	— Belmont Park, N. Y.	LaM	—*La Mesa Park, N. Mex.	StP	—³*Stampede Park, Can.
Beu	— Beulah Park, Ohio	Lat	— Latonia, Ky.	Suf	— Suffolk Downs, Mass.
BF	—*Brockton Fair, Mass.	Lbg	—*Lethbridge, Can.	Sun	— Sunland Park, N. Mex.
Bil	—*Billings, Mont.	LD	—*Lincoln Downs, R. I.	Tdn	— Thistledown, Ohio
BM	— Bay Meadows, Calif.	Lga	— Longacres, Wash.	Tim	— Timonium, Md.
Bmf	— Bay Meadows Fair, Calif.	Lib	—*Liberty Bell Park, Pa.	TrP	— Tropical Park, Fla.
Boi	— Boise, Idaho	LnN	—*Lincoln State Fair, Neb.	TuP	— Turf Paradise, Ariz.
Bow	— Bowie, Md.	Lrl	— Laurel Race Course, Md.	Was	— Washington Park, Ill.
CD	— Churchill Downs, Ky.	Mad	—*Madison, Neb.	Wat	— Waterford Park, W.Va.
CdA	— Coeur d'Alene, Idaho	Mar	—*Marlboro, Md.	Wey	—*Weymouth Fair, Mass.
Ceg	—*Victoria Park, Can.	MD	—*Marquis Downs, Can.	Win	—*Windsor Raceway, Can.
Cen	— Centennial Race Track, Colo.	Mex	—*Mexico City, Mex.	WO	— Woodbine, Can.
Cka	—*Cahokia Downs, Ill.	MF	—*Marshfield Fair, Mass.	YM	— Yakima Meadows, Wash.
Cls	—*Columbus, Neb.	Mol	—*East Moline Downs, Ill.		
Com	—*Commodore Downs, Pa.	Mth	— Monmouth Park, N. J.		**HUNT MEETINGS**
Crc	— Calder Race Course, Fla.	Nar	— Narragansett Park, R. I.		
CT	—*Charles Town, W. Va.	Nmp	—*Northampton, Mass.	Aik	— Aiken, S. C.
Cwl	—¹*Commonwealth	NP	—*Northlands Park, Can.	Atl	— Atlanta, Ga.
	Race Course, Ky.	OP	— Oaklawn Park, Ark.	Cam	— Camden, S. C.
DeD	—*Delta Downs, La.	Pen	— Penn National, Pa.	Clm	— Clemmons, N. C.
Del	— Delaware Park, Del.	Pim	— Pimlico, Md.	DR	— Deep Run, Va.
Det	— Detroit Race Course, Mich.	Pit	—*Pitt Park, Pa.	Fai	— Fair Hill, Md.
Dmr	— Del Mar, Calif.	PJ	—*Park Jefferson, S. D.	Fax	— Fairfax, Va.
Dov	—*Dover Downs, Del.	Pla	—*Playfair, Wash.	FH	— Far Hills, N. J.
EIP	— James C. Ellis Park, Ky.	Pln	— Pleasanton, Calif.	Gln	— Glyndon, Md.
EP	—*Exhibition Park, Can.	PM	— Portland Meadows, Ore.	GN	— Grand National, Md.
EvD	—*Evangeline Downs, La.	Pmf	— Portland M'd'ws Fair, Ore.	Lex	— Lexington, Ky.
FD	—²Florida Downs, Fla.	Poc	—*Pocono Downs, Pa.	Lig	— Ligonier, Pa.
FE	— Fort Erie, Can.	Pom	—*Pomona, Calif.	Mal	— Malvern, Pa.
Fer	—*Ferndale, Calif.	PR	— Puerto Rico	Med	— Media, Pa.
FG	— Fair Grounds, La.	Pre	—*Prescott Downs, Ariz.	Mid	— Middleburg, Va.
FL	— Finger Lakes, N. Y.	RaP	—*Raceway Park, Ohio	Mon	— Monkton, Md.
Fno	— Fresno, Calif.	RD	— River Downs, Ohio	Mtp	— Montpelier, Va.
Fon	—*Fonner Park, Neb.	Reg	— Regina, Can.	Oxm	— Oxmoor, Ky.
FP	— Fairmount Park, Ill.	Ril	—*Rillito, Ariz.	Pur	— Purchase, N. Y.
GaD	—*Gator Downs, Fla.	Rkm	— Rockingham Park, N. H.	PW	— Percy Warner, Tenn.
GBF	—*Great Barrington, Mass.	Rul	—*Ruidoso Downs, N. Mex.	RB	— Red Bank, N. J.
GF	—*Great Falls, Mont.	SA	— Santa Anita Park, Calif.	SH	— Strawberry Hill, Va.
GG	— Golden Gate Fields, Calif.	Sac	— Sacramento, Calif.	SoP	— Southern Pines, N. C.
GM	—*Green Mountain, Vt.	Sal	—*Salem, Ore.	Try	— Tryon, N. C.
GP	— Gulfstream Park, Fla.			Uni	— Unionville, Pa.
Grd	—*Greenwood, Can.			War	— Warrenton, Va.
GS	— Garden State Park, N. J.			Wel	— Wellsville, Pa.

*Indicates tracks less than one mile in circumference.   ¹Formerly named Miles Park.
²Formerly named Sunshine Park.   ³Formerly named Victoria Park.

'Points of Call' in Thoroughbred Charts

Following is a tabulation listing the "points of call" for the various distances in charts of thoroughbred racing:

Distance	PP						Str	Fin
3 Furlongs	PP	Start					Str	Fin
3½ Furlongs	PP	Start	¼				Str	Fin
4 Furlongs	PP	Start	¼				Str	Fin
4½ Furlongs	PP	Start	¼				Str	Fin
5 Furlongs	PP	Start	3-16	⅜			Str	Fin
5½ Furlongs	PP	Start	¼	⅜			Str	Fin
6 Furlongs	PP	Start	¼	½			Str	Fin
6½ Furlongs	PP	Start	¼	½			Str	Fin
7 Furlongs	PP	Start	¼	½			Str	Fin
7½ Furlongs	PP	Start	¼	½			Str	Fin
1 Mile	PP	Start	¼	½	¾		Str	Fin
1 Mile, 30 Yards	PP	Start	¼	½	¾		Str	Fin
1 Mile, 70 Yards	PP	Start	¼	½	¾		Str	Fin
1 1/16 Miles	PP	Start	¼	½	¾		Str	Fin
1 1/8 Miles	PP	Start	¼	½	¾		Str	Fin
1 3/16 Miles	PP	Start	¼	½	¾		Str	Fin

Note: In races at 1 1/4 Miles to 1 11/16 Miles, the Start call is eliminated and the ¼ mile call is substituted (as shown below):

Distance	PP						Str	Fin
1 1/4 Miles	PP	¼	½	¾	1		Str	Fin
1 5/16 Miles	PP	¼	½	¾	1		Str	Fin
1 3/8 Miles	PP	¼	½	¾	1		Str	Fin
1 7/16 Miles	PP	¼	½	1	1¼		Str	Fin
1 1/2 Miles	PP	¼	½	1	1¼		Str	Fin
1 9/16 Miles	PP	¼	½	1	1¼		Str	Fin
1 5/8 Miles	PP	¼	½	1	1⅜		Str	Fin
1 11/16 Miles	PP	¼	½	1	1⅜		Str	Fin

In races at 1 3/4 Miles or more, the first call is at the ½ mile (as shown below):

Distance	PP						Str	Fin
1 3/4 Miles	PP	½	1	1¼	1½		Str	Fin
1 13/16 Miles	PP	½	1	1¼	1½		Str	Fin
1 7/8 Miles	PP	½	1	1⅜	1⅝		Str	Fin
1 15/16 Miles	PP	½	1	1⅜	1⅝		Str	Fin
2 Miles	PP	½	1	1½	1¾		Str	Fin
2 Miles, 70 Yards	PP	½	1	1½	1¾		Str	Fin
2 1/16 Miles	PP	½	1	1½	1¾		Str	Fin
2 1/8 Miles	PP	½	1	1½	1¾		Str	Fin
2 3/16 Miles	PP	½	1	1½	1¾		Str	Fin
2 1/4 Miles	PP	½	1	1½	2		Str	Fin
2 5/16 Miles	PP	½	1	1½	2		Str	Fin
2 3/8 Miles	PP	½	1	1½	2		Str	Fin
2 1/2 Miles	PP	½	1	1½	2		Str	Fin

THE PROPER WAY TO SET UP A POST POSITION SURVEY

For the period involved, note at each distance charted: (1) the number of races from each post position, (2) the number of wins per post, and (3) the win percentage per post. A separate category should be maintained for "outside post position" for all races. *Optional:* At the same time, record the number of wire-to-wire winners.

Several sample post position surveys appear below.

ROCKINGHAM

July 5 — Sept. 21, 1975 (67 days)

POST POSITION
SPRINTS (5 furlongs — 6 furlongs)

Post Position	Starters	Wins	Win Percentage
1	477	57	11.9
2	477	55	11.5
3	477	60	12.6
4	477	62	13.0
5	477	53	11.1
6	475	55	11.6
7	454	57	12.6
8	380	33	8.7
9	288	21	7.3
10	191	14	7.3
11	122	6	4.9
12	73	4	5.5
outside	477	40	8.4

Wire-to-wire winners — 27.3%

POST POSITION
ROUTES (1 mile 40 yds. — 1 ½ miles)

Post Position	Starters	Wins	Win Percentage
1	164	24	14.6
2	164	24	14.6
3	164	21	12.8
4	164	24	14.6
5	164	15	9.1
6	163	18	11.0
7	151	14	9.3
8	118	17	14.4
9	66	1	—
10	39	2	—
11	23	3	—
12	12	1	—
outside	164	13	7.9

Wire-to-wire winners — 15.2%

DETROIT RACE COURSE

April 1 — July 13, 1975 (90 days)

POST POSITION
Sprints (2 fur. — 6 fur., inclusive)

Post Position	Starts	Wins	Win Percentage
1	682	71	10.4
2	682	75	11.0
3	682	64	9.4
4	682	82	12.0
5	682	75	11.0
6	678	90	13.3
7	663	82	12.4
8	567	59	10.4
9	398	35	8.8
10	278	27	9.7
11	179	14	7.8
12	103	8	7.8
outside	682	84	12.3

Wire-to-wire winners — 24.8%

POST POSITION
Routes (1 mile and longer)

Post Position	Starts	Wins	Win Percentage
1	154	34	22.1
2	154	15	9.7
3	154	24	15.6
4	154	20	13.0
5	154	15	9.7
6	154	15	9.7
7	150	15	10.0
8	124	7	5.6
9	70	6	8.6
10	30	3	10.0
11	11	0	0.0
12	8	0	0.0
outside	154	10	6.5

Wire-to-wire winners — 14.9%

HOLLYWOOD PARK

April 11 - July 21, 1975 (76 days)

Post Position
Turf Course (all distances)

Post Position	Starters	Wins	Percentage
1	199	33	16.6
2	199	16	8.0
3	199	21	10.5
4	199	26	13.1
5	199	28	14.1
6	197	21	10.7
7	179	19	10.6
8	143	18	12.6
9	105	7	6.7
10	75	7	9.3
11	24	1	4.2
12	19	2	10.5
outside	199	20	10.1

Front-running winners — 8.5%

Post Position
Sprints (up to seven furlongs)

Post Position	Starters	Wins	Percentage
1	344	32	9.3
2	344	31	9.0
3	344	36	10.5
4	344	41	11.9
5	344	36	10.5
6	343	48	14.0
7	316	33	10.4
8	271	30	11.1
9	220	27	12.3
10	172	16	9.3
11	130	7	5.4
12	98	7	7.1
outside	344	35	10.2

Front-running winners — 25.3%

Post Position
Routes (one mile and over)

Post Position	Starters	Wins	Percentage
1	178	19	10.7
2	178	22	12.4
3	178	24	13.5
4	178	27	15.2
5	178	21	11.8
6	174	13	7.5
7	161	15	9.3
8	135	15	11.1
9	103	8	7.8
10	79	6	7.6
11	45	5	11.1
12	31	3	9.7
outside	178	18	10.1

Front-running winners — 15.2%

DEL MAR

July 23 — Sept. 10, 1975 (43 days)

POST POSITION
TURF RACES (all distances)

Post Position	Starters	Wins	Win Percentage
1	69	18	26.1
2	69	12	17.4
3	69	8	11.6
4	69	8	11.6
5	69	7	10.1
6	68	10	14.7
7	54	1	—
8	43	3	—
9	21	1	—
10	5	1	—
11	2	0	0.0
12	1	0	0.0
outside	69	4	5.8

Wire-to-wire winners — 20.3%

POST POSITION
SPRINTS (6 furlongs)

Post Position	Starters	Wins	Win Percentage
1	203	33	16.3
2	203	27	13.3
3	203	26	12.8
4	203	25	12.3
5	203	27	13.3
6	200	9	4.5
7	178	22	12.4
8	143	13	9.1
9	95	8	8.4
10	74	3	4.1
11	54	6	11.1
12	28	4	14.3
outside	203	18	8.9

Wire-to-wire winners — 30.5%

POST POSITION
ROUTES (1 mile — abt. 1¼ miles)

Post Position	Starters	Wins	Win Percentage
1	115	15	13.0
2	115	13	11.3
3	115	13	11.3
4	115	22	19.1
5	115	16	13.9
6	114	15	13.2
7	99	9	9.1
8	69	8	11.6
9	35	1	—
10	21	3	—
11	9	0	0.0
12	3	0	0.0
outside	115	12	10.4

Wire-to-wire winners — 26.1%

PERCENTAGE TABLE FOR COMPUTING
A MORNING LINE

The following table provides a reference for computing a morning line. The percentage totals for the field should equal 118 to 125 points. This allows for the pari-mutuel tax.

ODDS	PERCENTAGE POINTS	ODDS	PERCENTAGE POINTS
1 – 5	83	2 – 1	33
1 – 4	80	5 – 2	28
1 – 3	75	3 – 1	25
1 – 2	67	7 – 2	22
3 – 5	62	4 – 1	20
2 – 3	60	9 – 2	18
3 – 4	57	5 – 1	16
4 – 5	55	6 – 1	14
even	50	8 – 1	11
6 – 5	45	10 – 1	9
7 – 5	41	12 – 1	8
3 – 2	40	15 – 1	6
8 – 5	38	20 – 1	4
9 – 5	35	30 – 1	3

Below are two sample morning lines with percentage points.

HYPOTHETICAL RACE 1—1¼ MILES		
HORSE	ODDS	POINTS
Run Dusty Run	7 – 5	41
Royal Ski	2 – 1	33
Banquet Table	5 – 1	16
Sail to Rome	6 – 1	14
Sanhedrin	12 – 1	8
For the Moment	20 – 1	4
Ali Oop	20 – 1	4
		120 *total*

HYPOTHETICAL RACE 2—1¼ MILES

HORSE	ODDS	POINTS
Seattle Slew	3 – 5	62
Royal Ski	7 – 2	22
Banquet Table	6 – 1	14
Sail to Rome	10 – 1	9
Sanhedrin	20 – 1	4
Ali Oop	20 – 1	4
Bob's Dusty	20 – 1	4
Something Rotten	30 – 1	3
		122 *total*

COMPUTING APPROXIMATE PLACE AND SHOW PAYOFFS

Short of using the most sophisticated electronic equipment, no player can hope to generate all the possible place and show payoffs in a race. Place and show payoffs are determined by the order of finish itself, or more correctly, by the money bet in the place pool and the money bet in the show pool on each horse involved in the top two and three finishing positions. The player's best course is to compute the lowest possible place and show payoff—a single calculation—because the lowest possible payoff is statistically the most likely payoff. It is the one produced by the favorites in the race finishing in the money. The following example shows how this is done.

HORSE	PLACE POOL	SHOW POOL
Carry Back	$ 4,000	$ 2,500
Buckpasser	$ 8,500	$ 6,000
Count Fleet	$12,000	$ 7,000
Tom Fool	$ 9,000	$ 4,000
Native Dancer	$10,000	$ 5,000
Round Table	$ 5,500	$ 1,500
Swaps	$10,000	$ 8,000
Silky Sullivan	$ 1,000	$ 1,000
Totals	$60,000	$35,000

QUESTION : *How much will Native Dancer pay to place?*

ANSWER : Minimum payoff is computed in four steps.

STEP 1: Deduct 20 percent pari-mutuel takeout tax from place pool total (20 percent of $60,000 or $12,000). Net pool = $48,000.

STEP 2: Combine the amount of money bet on Native Dancer to place with the amount of money bet on the horse getting the most play in the race. In this case, Count Fleet with $12,000 is the favorite in the place pool; thus the combined total equals $22,000.

STEP 3: Subtract the $22,000 from the $48,000 net place pool to determine the amount of money available for profit. In this case, $48,000 − $22,000 = $26,000 profit.

STEP 4: Divide the $26,000 profit into two equal parts to determine the amount of profit available to Native Dancer place pool bettors. In this case

$$\frac{\$26,000}{2} = \$13,000$$

THUS: The odds on Native Dancer to place are $13,000 profit to $10,000 invested, or 13–10 ($1.30–$1.00). Native Dancer will pay a minimum place price of $4.60 (includes original $2 investment).

QUESTION : *How much will Tom Fool pay to show?*

ANSWER : Minimum show payoff is computed in four steps.

STEP 1: Deduct 20 percent pari-mutuel takeout tax from show pool total (20 percent of $35,000, or $7,000). Net pool = $28,000.

STEP 2: Combine the amount of money bet on Tom Fool to show ($4,000) with the amount of money bet on the two horses getting the most play in the race. In this case, Swaps is getting $8,000; Count Fleet,

$7,000. Thus the combined total for all three horses is $19,000.

STEP 3: Subtract $19,000 from the $28,000 net show pool to determine the money available for profit. In this case, $28,000 − $19,000 = $9,000 net profit.

STEP 4: Divide the net profit into three equal parts to determine Tom Fool's show pool profit. In this case

$$\frac{\$9,000}{3} = \$3,000$$

THUS: The odds on Tom Fool to show are $3,000 profit to $4,000 invested, or 3–4 ($.75–$1.00). Tom Fool will pay a minimum show price of $3.40 (includes breakage to nearest dime and original $2 investment).

With some practice, the place and show payoffs for any horse can be computed in this manner in a matter of seconds. *Hint:* Round off to convenient whole numbers.

The parallel time chart on page 204 includes a speed-rating system that is consistent with the value of one-fifth of a second at all rates of speed at all distances. The time values incorporated in the chart were developed mathematically through class-par research at New York racetracks. With some important exceptions, described in the following material, this parallel time chart is adaptable for use at any racetrack with a circumference of one mile or more. Because of the unique nature of smaller tracks (more turns, shorter straightaways), the time values for minor tracks can be generated only through class-par research.

CLASS PARS AND PARALLEL TIME CHARTS

The idea behind the Beyer-Kovitz speed-figure method is to compare the final times of main-track races run on a

PARALLEL TIME CHART

SPEED FIGURE	5½ FURLONGS	6 FURLONGS	7 FURLONGS	1 MILE	BELMONT (ONE TURN) 1⅛ MILES	AQUEDUCT (TWO TURNS) 1⅛ MILES
136	1:02⅘	1:09	1:21⅖	1:33⅘	1:46⅖	1:48⅕
132	1:03	1:09⅕	1:21⅗	1:34⅕	1:46⅘	1:48⅗
128	1:03⅕	1:09⅗	1:22	1:34⅗	1:47⅕	1:49
124	1:03⅗	1:09⅘	1:22⅖	1:35	1:47⅗	1:49⅖
120	1:03⅘	1:10⅕	1:22⅘	1:35⅖	1:48	1:49⅘
116	1:04	1:10⅖	1:23	1:35⅘	1:48⅖	1:50⅕
112	1:04⅖	1:10⅗	1:23⅖	1:36⅕	1:49	1:50⅘
108	1:04⅗	1:11	1:23⅘	1:36⅗	1:49⅖	1:51⅕
104	1:04⅘	1:11⅕	1:24⅕	1:37	1:50	1:51⅘
100	1:05⅕	1:11⅗	1:24⅗	1:37⅗	1:50⅗	1:52⅕
96	1:05⅖	1:11⅘	1:24⅘	1:37⅘	1:50⅘	1:52⅗
92	1:05⅗	1:12⅕	1:25⅕	1:38⅕	1:51⅕	1:53
88	1:06	1:12⅖	1:25⅗	1:38⅗	1:51⅗	1:53⅖
84	1:06⅕	1:12⅘	1:25⅘	1:39	1:52⅕	1:54
80	1:06⅖	1:13	1:26⅕	1:39⅖	1:52⅗	1:54⅖
76	1:06⅘	1:13⅕	1:26⅗	1:39⅘	1:53⅕	1:55
72	1:07	1:13⅗	1:27	1:40⅕	1:53⅗	1:55⅖
68	1:07⅕	1:13⅘	1:27⅕	1:40⅗	1:54	1:55⅘
64	1:07⅗	1:14⅕	1:27⅗	1:41	1:54⅖	1:56⅕
60	1:07⅘	1:14⅖	1:28	1:41⅖	1:55	1:56⅗

given day with a valid set of standards (par times). The parallel time chart above is an essential ingredient in that process. For absolute accuracy, such a chart might well be constructed by researching the average winning times for each class and distance run at the track in question. Fortunately, there are several mathematical relationships that can be relied upon to shorten the research effort.

ITEM: There is a natural, mathematical relationship between final times at various distances. For example, if a horse travels six furlongs in 1:13, it will have to travel the seven-furlong distance in 1:26⅕ to earn equal credit. This additional 13⅕ seconds for the extra furlong is based on considerable research, is mathematically sound, and incorporates the normal loss of speed we would expect for the added difficulty of a longer distance. Given a faster rate of speed, say 1:10 for six furlongs, the equivalent seven-furlong time would be 1:22⅗, or a difference of 12⅗ seconds. Given a slower rate of speed, say six furlongs in 1:14⅗, the equivalent seven-furlong time would be 1:28, or a difference of 13⅖ seconds.

ITEM: The above relationship assumes the presence of only one turn at each distance, and a similar mathematical relationship could be shown to exist for all other one-turn distances. For example, at Belmont Park, where a chute extends the track's ability to card one-turn races up to 1¼ miles, the following times are approximately equal to each other:

6 FURLONGS		7 FURLONGS		1 MILE		1⅛ MILES
1:14⅗	=	1:28	=	1:41⅖	=	1:55
1:13	=	1:26⅕	=	1:39⅖	=	1:52⅘
1:10	=	1:22⅗	=	1:35⅕	=	1:48

ITEM: The equivalent time for a race involving a half-furlong (i.e., 6½ furlongs or 1$\frac{1}{16}$ miles) can be interpolated from the above table. For instance, 1:39⅖ at one mile equals 1:46⅕ at 1$\frac{1}{16}$ miles.

ITEM: The presence of an extra turn destroys the mathematical relationship as represented by the table. Thus at Aqueduct, where 1⅛-mile races are contested around two turns, the only way to establish equivalent times is to conduct class-par research. To refresh your memory (Chapter 11), that means finding the average winning time (fast tracks only) for each class of race at each distance. What I am suggesting below is a shortcut.

STEP 1: For the most popular sprint distance (one turn), find the average winning time for every major race classification. At Belmont Park and Aqueduct, for instance, the class pars for older horses traveling six furlongs are as follows. The approximate speed-figure ratings can be obtained by consulting the parallel time chart.

CLAIMING RACES

$50,000+	1:10⅗	$11,000+	1:11⅗
$35,000+	1:10⅘	$ 8,000+	1:11⅘
$25,000+	1:11	$ 6,000+	1:12
$20,000+	1:11⅕	$ 5,000+	1:12⅕
$15,000+	1:11⅖		

MAIDEN CLAIMING		ALLOWANCE RACES	
$30,000+	1:12	$25,000 purse	1:10⅕
$20,000+	1:12⅖	$20,000 purse	1:10⅖
$12,000+	1:12⅘	$15,000 purse	1:10⅗
$ 8,000+	1:13	$12,000 purse	1:11
		$10,000 purse	1:11⅖

MAIDEN SPECIAL WEIGHT			
All ages	1:11⅘	Stakes races	1:10

STEP 2: Repeat the above class-par research for as many two-turn distances as you wish to include in the parallel time chart. Because the relationship between final time and class is an orderly one, someone handy with numbers may reduce the required research by skipping several class levels and filling in the missing time values through interpolation.

STEP 3: Using the following example as a guide, match the class pars for each distance so that each horizontal line represents an equivalent measure of speed. It is in this manner that the parallel time chart can be adjusted to reflect the true value of the extra turn.

AQUEDUCT—$25,000 CLAIMING

6 FURLONGS		1⅛ MILES
1:11	=	1:51⅕

AQUEDUCT—$15,000 CLAIMING

6 FURLONGS		1⅛ MILES
1:11⅖	=	1:52

SPEED FIGURES AND TRACK VARIANTS

Using class pars and the parallel time chart on page 204, we are now ready to compute a track variant.

PAR	ACTUAL SPEED FIGURE	VARIANT
88	91	−3
83	88	−5
90	92	−2
96	96	0
108	112	−4
turf	no figure	no variant
1½ miles	no figure	no variant
120	126	−6
108	109	−1
		Average variant = −3 (−21 for 7 races)

STEP 1: After today's races are run, compare the final times with the par time for the distance and class. At Belmont the par time for a $25,000 claiming race is 1:11 for six furlongs. On the parallel time chart that is worth 108 speed-figure points. If, however, the race was run in 1:10⅗, the winner has actually earned 112 speed-figure points. What we want to find out is whether the horse actually earned the high figure or whether he was helped to some extent by the speed conduciveness of the racetrack. For this we will need to compare all the speed figures and par times for main-track races run at Belmont Park that day.

STEP 2: At this point, deduct 3 speed-figure points from each horse's earned figure. It is obvious that the track contributed to the final times. When we enter the net speed figures in our permanent record, we will note the variant and the adjusted speed figures in the following manner:

		RACES								
DATE	VARIANT	1	2	3	4	5	6	7	8	9
6/11	−3	88	85	89	93	109	T	none	123	106

Of course, not every racing day is so easily compared. Sometimes the times will be much faster than par for the first few races and not as fast for the remainder of the card. Sometimes the one-turn races will be faster or slower than the two-turn races. It is for this reason that the player should set up the par time comparisons in the following manner (S = sprint, R = route).

PAR	ACTUAL SPEED FIGURE	VARIANT
90 – S	95	−5
84 – S	90	−6
100 – R	100	0
106 – S	112	−6
80 – R	77	+3
turf	no figure	no variant
94 – S	100	−6
120 – R	118	+2
88 – R	85	+3
	Sprints = −6 (−23 for 4 races)	
	Routes = +2 (+ 8 for 4 races)	

Deduct 6 speed-figure points from each sprint race speed figure. Add 2 speed-figure points to each route race speed figure. Enter the adjusted speed figures on the permanent record.

STEP 3: After a few weeks of compiling speed-figure ratings, you will be able to employ speed figures for handicapping purposes. To determine the speed figure of any horse, consult the permanent record and adjust the figure according to the beaten-lengths chart below.

STEP 4: (Optional) Andy Beyer's advanced speed-figure method eliminates the par times as a standard once the permanent record becomes functional. Instead of par times, Andy substitutes *projected* times based on the actual speed figures earned by the horses in prior races. In other words, if a race is run in 1:11 flat, instead of comparing the time to the expected par Andy compares the actual speed figure to the speed figure the horse's prior record indicates it should have run. Indeed, he projects speed figures for several horses in each race in order to get a valid standard. Obviously, this procedure is more accurate, but it is difficult to master. It should not be attempted until the player has complete familiarity with the class-par version of the method, which by itself provides an adequate *track* variant.

The interested handicapper should note these additional facts about speed figures:

1. Speed figures may be generated for turf races only at those racetracks where an electronic timing device is known to be accurate and in regular use.
2. The class pars for races carded exclusively for fillies are usually one-fifth of a second slower for each class at six furlongs.
3. The six-furlong class pars for three-year-olds are three-fifths of a second slower in January, two-fifths slower in June, and one-fifth slower in September.

BEATEN-LENGTHS CHART
(*Deduct Points from Winner's Rating*)

MARGIN	5 FUR-LONGS	6 FUR-LONGS	7 FUR-LONGS	1 MILE	1⅛ MILES
neck	1	1	1	0	0
½	1	1	1	1	1
¾	2	2	2	1	1
1	3	2	2	2	2
1¼	4	3	3	2	2
1½	4	4	3	3	3
1¾	5	4	4	3	3
2	6	5	4	4	3
2¼	7	6	5	4	4
2½	7	6	5	4	4
2¾	8	7	6	5	5
3	9	7	6	5	5
3¼	9	8	7	6	5
3½	10	9	7	6	6
3¾	11	9	8	7	6
4	12	10	8	7	7
4¼	12	10	9	8	7
4½	13	11	9	8	8
4¾	14	11	10	9	8
5	15	12	10	9	8
5½	16	13	11	10	9
6	18	15	12	11	10
6½	19	16	13	12	11
7	20	17	14	13	12
7½	22	18	15	13	13
8	23	20	17	14	13
8½	25	21	18	15	14
9	26	22	19	16	15
9½	28	23	19	17	16
10	29	24	20	18	17
11	32	27	23	20	18
12	35	29	25	21	20
13	38	32	27	23	22
14	41	34	29	25	23
15	44	37	31	27	25

4. Speed figures earned on severely biased racetracks should be regarded suspiciously for handicapping purposes.

RECOMMENDED READING LIST

STATISTICS AND GENERAL RACING INFORMATION

The American Racing Manual, published annually by the *Daily Racing Form.*

The Blood Horse's annual statistical review.

The Thoroughbred Record's annual statistical review.

Turf and Sport Digest (monthly magazine).

BREEDING AND TRAINING

The Blood Horse (weekly magazine).

Breeding the Racehorse, by Federico Tesio; tr. Marchese E. Spinola. British Book Center, 1973. $12.50.

The Thoroughbred Record (weekly magazine).

Training Thoroughbred Horses, by Preston M. Burch. The Blood Horse Library, 1953. $6.00.

Typology of the Racehorse, by Franco Varola. British Book Center, 1974. $37.50.

RACING HISTORY

Big Red of Meadow Stable: Secretariat, The Making of a Champion, by William Nack. Arthur Fields Books, 1975. $10.00.

The History of Thoroughbred Racing in America, by William H. Robertson. Bonanza Books, 1964. $25.00.

In the Winner's Circle, by Joseph A. Hirsh and Gene Plowden. Mason Charter, 1974. $7.95.

Run for the Roses: 100 Years of the Kentucky Derby, by Jim Bolus. Hawthorn Books, 1974, $12.95.

This Was Racing, by Joe H. Palmer. Henry Clay, 1973. $7.95.

HANDICAPPING

Ainslie's Complete Guide to Thoroughbred Racing, by Tom Ainslie. Simon and Schuster, 1968. $14.95.

Picking Winners, by Andrew Beyer. Houghton Mifflin, 1975. $7.95.